KEN SANCHEZ

Echoes of Destiny

Shadowguards Book One

This novel is entirely a work of fiction. The names, characters and incidents portrayed in it are the work of the author's imagination. Any resemblance to actual persons, living or dead, events or localities is entirely coincidental.

First edition

This book was professionally typeset on Reedsy.
Find out more at reedsy.com

Contents

Acknowledgement

To all of the people who believed in me. Thank you.

Prolouge

THE BATTLE FIELD QUAKED under the relentless assault of the Shadow Wraiths and the monstrous titan, Kronos. The clash of divine powers echoed like thunder, shattering the once serene landscape of Elysium. Hades stood at the forefront, his obsidian robes billowing in the chaotic winds, his eyes a fierce blaze of determination. He was the Lord of the Underworld, but now, he found himself fighting alongside his brethren, driven by a sense of duty to protect the mortal realm from this impending doom.

Apollo's golden aura illuminated the battlefield like a beacon of hope. His ethereal music weaved through the air, resonating with the hearts of the warriors and urging them to fight with renewed vigor. Yet, despite his radiant presence, Hades could see the strain etched on Apollo's face as he struggled to break the binding on Zeus. Every note he played seemed to carry the weight of the world, and it tore at Hades' soul to witness his beloved in such agony.

"Can't you feel it, Hades?" Persephone's voice cut through the chaos, her own radiant form standing beside him. "Apollo is pouring his very essence into this effort."

Hades nodded, his heart a tumultuous tempest of emotions. "I know, but I can't bear to see him risk himself like this."

Persephone placed a gentle hand on his arm, her gaze filled with understanding. "Sometimes, great sacrifices must be made to ensure the greater good. Apollo knows that, and so do you."

Hades wanted to argue, to find another solution, but he knew deep down that Persephone was right. Apollo had always been willing to give everything for the ones he loved, and this was no exception. It was both a source of pride and despair for Hades.

Amidst the tumultuous chaos of the ongoing battle, Hades stood entrenched, his gaze fixed upon the unfolding struggle before him. His heart, typically cloaked in a shroud of unyielding stoicism, now pulsed with a poignant mixture of worry and determination. The clash of titanic forces reverberated through the air, each clash of divine energy echoing like a thunderous symphony.

Apollo, a radiant figure amidst the maelstrom, drew Hades' focus like a gravitational force. His lithe form moved with both grace and urgency, a celestial warrior locked in a desperate struggle. With each meticulously aimed Divine Arrow, Apollo's brow furrowed in concentration, his ethereal eyes narrowing upon the formidable bindings that ensnared Zeus.

Hades could practically taste the tension in the air as each arrow soared forth, a streak of celestial light cutting through the turmoil. The Divine Arrows struck the bindings with a reverberating impact, each collision releasing a discordant shockwave that rippled through the battlefield. It was a visual and auditory spectacle, an intricate dance between powers that held the very fabric of Olympus in its balance.

Apollo's perseverance was both a beacon of hope and a testament to the sheer force of his godly nature. Hades admired the unwavering resolve etched upon Apollo's features, the lines of determination and exhaustion intersecting like a complex tapestry of emotions. In the face of this celestial conflict, Apollo's determination was a reminder that the gods were not merely embodiments of power; they were beings fueled by profound convictions.

With every arrow that left Apollo's bow, a fraction of his divine essence seemed to dissipate, carried away on the winds of fate. Hades' heart clenched with each expenditure of Apollo's energy, the weight of his feelings twisting like a knot within him. Apollo's commitment to the task at hand was both humbling and heartbreaking, a reminder of the sacrifices inherent in their immortal existence.

Hades longed to reach out, to lend his own strength to Apollo's cause, but he knew the intricacies of the battle demanded that each deity play their role. And so, he stood vigilant, a pillar of support and concern, his eyes fixed upon the enigmatic interplay of power and will that unfolded before him.

Then, as if fate itself was determined to test them further, Morvain, the traitor among them, made a treacherous move. In a blink of an eye, he lunged towards Apollo, seeking to disrupt his efforts. Time seemed to slow down as Hades reacted instinctively, intercepting Morvain just in time. Persephone and Dionysus swiftly joined the battle, their combined powers pushing back the traitor.

With Morvain momentarily neutralized, Apollo reached out to Hades, cupping his cheek with trembling hands.

"Please, Hades, trust me," he implored, his eyes a reflection of the love they shared.

"I do," Hades whispered, his voice choked with emotion. "But I can't bear to lose you."

Apollo's thumb brushed away a tear that escaped Hades' eye. "I'll come back to you," he promised, his voice steady despite the turmoil within.

Hades searched Apollo's eyes, seeking an answer that he couldn't comprehend. "How?"

Apollo's smile was tender, filled with a bittersweet mix of love and sorrow. "You'll know. Just take care of Persephone. She still loves you, despite everything."

"I promise," Hades vowed, his heart heavy with the weight of the sacrifice Apollo was about to make.

With a final gaze that conveyed all the love they shared, Apollo closed his eyes and began to sing. His voice rose like a blazing sun, and his golden aura intensified, bathing the battlefield in celestial radiance. Hades could only watch in awe as his beloved ascended to a level of brilliance that surpassed anything he had ever witnessed.

Tears blurred Hades' vision as Apollo's luminous presence expanded, engulfing everything around them. The world seemed to hold its breath, as if acknowledging the magnitude of this sacrifice. Then, with a breathtaking crescendo, Apollo's radiance erupted like a supernova, illuminating the entire realm.

Hades shielded his eyes, but he could still feel the overwhelming energy that surrounded them. He reached out, desperate to hold on to the fading essence of his love. Yet, as the light subsided, all that remained was darkness. A profound silence settled over the battlefield, leaving Hades and the others in a state of disbelief.

Grief threatened to consume Hades, but he knew that Apollo's sacrifice had not been in vain. It was now up to them to honor his memory, to stand together and fight for the world they held dear. The battle was far from over, and as the dust settled, Hades felt a newfound resolve rising within him. Apollo's love and sacrifice would forever guide them, and in the darkest moments, they would remember the brilliance of the sun and find strength to carry on.

1

Eryx

IN A PART OF NEW YORK CITY that most people didn't notice, there was a mysterious club, a hidden gem in the urban jungle. It was a place where the music pounded so loud that it shook your bones and pulsed through your veins.

For Eryx Ross, a musician in his mid-thirties with tousled blonde hair and piercing blue eyes, this felt like his sanctuary, a soothing elixir for his restless soul. Amidst the swirling, dancing crowd, he felt like he'd stumbled upon a secret haven where no one cared about who he was.

Eryx relished in the fact that he wasn't a big star here. It offered a respite from the relentless attention that sometimes followed him. He was known to a select few, but in this dimly lit haven, he could simply be Eryx.

On this particular Wednesday night, the club was unexpectedly packed, teeming with people who sought the same escape. Eryx had to navigate through the undulating sea of bodies, gently pushing his way toward the bar. The bar area was a refuge for those who needed a break from the dance floor's relentless energy. Even here, the crowd was formidable, and the three bartenders on duty were an eclectic mix of beings.

As Eryx approached the bar, he couldn't help but sense that two of the bartenders were different, not just ordinary humans. There was an elusive, almost magical aura about them—shifters, he suspected. The third bartender, on the other hand, exuded a typical human vibe, something that felt strangely familiar to Eryx.

Although he couldn't quite put his finger on it, Eryx had a gut feeling about these beings. But for now, his main focus was on quenching his thirst and taking a brief respite from the sensory overload. He was well aware of how things worked in this place—a club that welcomed all sorts of individuals, whether human or otherwise.

In a world where different beings coexisted, there were still pockets of prejudice that simmered beneath the surface. Eryx despised this division and the intolerance that sometimes reared its ugly head.

The shifter bartender flashed him a friendly smile, his features undeniably handsome, a natural allure that many supernaturals possessed. Eryx, however, was not here for any easy flings, tempting as they might be.

"I'll have a Gin and Tonic," Eryx replied, his voice cutting through the thumping bass of the music. The bartender moved with fluid grace, expertly crafting the drink as if it were a work of art.

"That'll be forty dollars," the bartender informed him, setting the finished drink on the bar with a soft clink.

Eryx reached into his pocket, retrieved a crisp fifty-dollar bill, and handed it over, gesturing for the bartender to keep the change. He wondered if what he was doing tonight made any sense at all. His presence at the club was an attempt to see if he could endure a night without resorting to the pills that had become his nightly companions, a habit Ari disapproved of but understood all too well.

The nightmares had haunted him since childhood, dark specters that tormented his sleep. They had defied explanation, stumping countless doctors his parents had taken him to. When his parents had passed away, the nightmares had intensified, as if fed by his grief and loss. That's when he'd taken matters into his own hands, purchasing over-the-counter pills that had worked like magic, casting a temporary reprieve over the malevolent visions that plagued his nights.

Eryx knew it wasn't a healthy solution, but all he wanted was a taste of normalcy, a chance to live without the constant specter of his nightmares haunting him.

As he took a sip of his drink and surveyed the club, Eryx couldn't help but be swept away by the atmosphere. The club had transformed since his arrival earlier in the evening. The initial subdued hum had evolved into a sensory overload of colors, lights, and beats that seemed to synchronize with the rhythm of his own heart.

The dance floor was a pulsating wave of bodies, each person lost in their own world, moving to the music's intoxicating spell. Strobes of neon light illuminated the dancers, casting surreal shadows that danced along with them.

He felt the music resonating deep within him, its pounding tempo creating a visceral connection. He knew that tonight, he was on a quest, an experiment to test the limits of his endurance without the pills. It was a battle he wasn't sure he could win, but he was determined to try.

As the night wore on, Eryx remained at the bar, his fingers tapping rhythmically against his glass. He watched the club's eclectic patrons, humans and supernaturals alike, coming together under the spell of the music. The unity in diversity was a sight that always warmed his heart, a testament to the power of music to bridge divides.

Eryx knew that tonight was about more than just escaping his nightmares; it was about embracing life and all its chaotic beauty.

Eryx decided that he needed to move and had danced the night away, losing himself in the throbbing heart of the club. The rhythm had possessed him, and he'd become one with the pulsating beats and the sea of moving bodies. It was as if the world outside the club had ceased to exist, and all that mattered was the music and the shared euphoria.

The club's atmosphere transformed into a steamy sanctuary. The collective body heat created a cozy sauna-like ambiance, beads of sweat glistening on foreheads and arms. Some revelers shed layers of clothing in response to the rising temperature, while others engaged in passionate embraces.

But, all good things must come to an end. As the music gradually tapered off, signaling the approaching dawn, Eryx felt the night slipping away like a dream. Disappointment and contentment mingled within him. He knew he couldn't dance forever, even though he wished he could.

With a sigh, he reluctantly stepped away from the dance floor. The restroom beckoned as a refuge, a place to gather his thoughts and let the adrenaline of the night settle. The moment he entered, the muffled sounds of the club outside were replaced by a hushed sanctuary.

Eryx moved to the sink, splashing his face with cool water.

The soft, diffused glow of the overhead lights created a cocoon of solitude within the bustling club. The world beyond seemed distant and inconsequential, allowing him to find peace in the quiet.

As he dried his hands, he heard the restroom door swing open. A man, clearly inebriated, entered with an eager look, ready to strike up a conversation. However, Eryx wasn't in the mood for small talk at this moment. He sensed the man's intentions but had no interest in that kind of interaction.

"You're quite the looker, huh?" the man slurred, pressing closer and grabbing Eryx's arm without permission.

Eryx's patience waned, and his temper flared. He seized the man's unwelcome grip on him and, despite the alcohol-induced haze, managed to forcefully push the intruder against the wall, taking control of the situation.

"Did I ever give you permission to touch me?" Eryx growled, his anger palpable.

"What the fuck, man? Let go!" Fear tinged the man's voice as Eryx's hand struck the wall next to his head, creating a hole and shattering the glass. The man scrambled away in a hurry, leaving behind the bewildering wreckage.

Eryx couldn't quite fathom the strength he'd just demonstrated. The surge of fury still coursed through him as he issued a final warning, "Don't let it happen again!"

After the confrontation, Eryx left the restroom, his emotions running high. The club, with its pulsing music and writhing bodies, felt different now. He was keenly aware of his newfound strength, and it unsettled him. He had never experienced anything like this before, and it raised questions about his past, about the unexplained nightmares that had plagued him.

Reentering the main area of the club, Eryx found the atmosphere had shifted once more. The music had evolved into a mellower groove, and the remaining dancers swayed more languidly, like leaves in a gentle breeze. Eryx couldn't help but feel a disconnect from this tranquil scene. His encounter in the restroom had left a mark, a crack in the facade of the club's carefree bliss.

Resolving to leave, Eryx hailed an Uber and rode back to his Upper East Side apartment in New York. The upscale neighborhood offered him the quietude he cherished. He reached into the fridge, grabbing a bottle of water to help clear his head from the lingering effects of alcohol.

Standing in his bedroom, he shed his club attire and stepped into the shower, the warm water washing away the scent of the night. As the water cascaded over him, Eryx's thoughts returned to the restroom confrontation. His newfound strength puzzled him, and he found himself revisiting his past, seeking answers to the nightmares that had driven him to the edge.

After he finished showering, he considered the comfort of his bed, contemplating the familiar solace of the pill that usually awaited him. But tonight, he decided to skip it. He needed to understand what had happened, to delve into the uncharted depths of his own abilities.

Drying off, he crawled into his bed, the room dark and quiet. He closed his eyes, hopeful that sleep would come without the aid of the pills, even though he knew he was diving into uncharted territory. The world of dreams remained elusive, a realm he hadn't visited in years.

As the night wore on, Eryx lay awake, contemplating the mysteries of the club, the confrontation in the restroom, and the newfound strength within him. Sleep finally embraced him, but it was dreamless, a realm of tranquility he had long yearned for but had yet to explore fully.

* * *

The morning light filtered through Eryx's bedroom window, rousing him from a restless slumber. His night had been devoid of dreams, a stark departure from the usual nightmares that plagued him. He felt both relieved and bewildered by the change, his newfound strength still lingering in his thoughts.

As he stretched and yawned, Eryx's phone chimed with a text message. It was from Ari, his best friend. The message read, "Rehearsal today! Don't be late, rockstar."

A smile crept onto Eryx's face as he recalled the upcoming rehearsal with his band. Ari was his steadfast supporter, always there to keep him grounded and motivated. Their friendship had weathered the storms of life, and Ari's snarky yet loving presence was a constant source of strength.

Eryx quickly got dressed in his usual rocker attire—a worn band tee and faded jeans. He grabbed his guitar case, adorned with stickers from gigs past, and headed out the door.

The rehearsal space was in a gritty but beloved music venue in the heart of Brooklyn. It was a place that held countless memories and had witnessed the birth of many songs. Today, Eryx's band was gathering for a final run-through before their upcoming show.

As Eryx entered the dimly lit venue, he spotted Ari perched on the edge of the stage, her legs swinging playfully as she checked her phone. She was the yin to his yang, with her wavy brown hair and a personality that was equal parts snark and sass. Her presence was a reassuring constant in his life.

He approached the stage, a grin spreading across his face. "Hey, rockstar," he greeted her, giving her a playful nudge.

Ari rolled her eyes but couldn't suppress a smirk. "Took you long enough, sleepyhead. I've been here for ages."

Eryx shrugged, feigning nonchalance. "Well, I had a wild night, you know."

Ari shot him a skeptical look. "You and your cryptic talk. Save it for your therapist."

Eryx chuckled as he began setting up his gear on the stage. The rest of the band members—Louis, the drummer with a perpetual grin, and Rion, the bassist with a knack for mischief—soon arrived. They exchanged greetings and started tuning their instruments.

As they launched into their first song, the rehearsal had turned into a hot mess real fast. Eryx's fingers fumbled over the guitar strings, and every note he played seemed to tangle up with the others like a bunch of drunken partygoers on a dance floor. The room oozed frustration; impatient glances and tight shoulders told the whole story. Sour notes hung in the air, making it a sonic trainwreck.

Eryx's heart sank lower than a submarine. He'd wanted to impress the band, show 'em he was more than just the guy who brought snacks to practice, but right now, he was causing more chaos than a bull in a china shop. The band's expectations weighed on him like a pile of bricks.

Finally, someone cried, "Break time!" The room collectively sighed in relief, like they'd all been holding their breath underwater. Eryx staggered over to a wall, chest heaving like a champ boxer after the final round. He stole a glance at his bandmates, and their faces echoed his exhaustion and frustration. The bond that used to be as tight as a zip tie now felt stretched, like it might snap any second. The music, once as smooth as a shot of whiskey, had turned into a tangled headphone cord.

During the break, the band members huddled up for a chat. Eryx strained his ears, but their words were as elusive as a squirrel on caffeine. Their body language, though, spoke volumes. They were gearing up for another round, like a team getting ready to storm the field. Eryx tightened his grip on his guitar, his knuckles going whiter than a ghost's bedsheet on Halloween night.

Ari stormed onto the stage. She grabbed him by the arm and pulled him away from the chaos like a superhero swooping in to save the day.

She shoved a cup of Starbucks coffee into his hands. "Drink this. It'll give you a little kick in the pants."

"When did you get this?"

"Oh, I slipped out after your fifth mess up and decided that you needed a pick me up."

Eryx took a sip and sighed in relief. "Do I ever tell you how awesome you are?"

Ari smirked. "Only when I bring Starbucks."

Eryx chuckled. "You got me there."

She leaned in and said, "Look at it this way, if we manage to salvage today, I'll treat you to Starbucks tomorrow."

Eryx raised his cup in a mock salute. "You're on."

As they returned to the rehearsal, things miraculously began to smooth out. Despite the rocky start, they found their groove and worked through the songs. The finish line was in sight, just one more run-through before they could call it a day. They gathered on the stage, ready for the final round.

But just when Eryx was thinking they might actually pull this off, a migraine hit him like a freight train. The timing couldn't have been worse. It was like a sledgehammer to the brain.

Eryx clenched his teeth, trying to power through the pain. The migraine was a cruel prankster, making every note he played sound like a banshee wailing in agony. But Eryx couldn't afford to mess up more than he already had.

He launched into the last part of the song, determination masking the agony in his head. He pushed himself harder. Yet, in the midst of his playing, something bizarre happened.

A weird sensation rippled through him, like a shiver running down his spine. It felt like his whole body was buzzing, like he'd accidentally touched an electric fence.

The ground beneath him wobbled, as if the earth itself had decided to join the chaos. Eryx's thoughts became a tangled mess.

Then, out of nowhere, he heard screams.

2

Alex

"THE SOUL OF YOUR BELOVED WILL BE REBORN IN A SOUL OF A HUMAN."

That was the last thing the Fates had said to him before he left the underworld. It had been thousands of years, and he was starting to lose hope.

After the war ended, he felt lost and confused. The sadness was almost too much to bear. Persephone asked Hypnos to change his memories. She thought it would help him, but he disagreed.

He didn't want to forget his memories of Apollo.

He changed how he acted. He became the tough ruler that everyone wanted him to be.

He took charge of punishing souls, using it as a way to deal with his anger and frustration. He treated those who deserved punishment harshly, finding a way to handle his own feelings by doing this. It was like a way to let out his emotions and feel like he had some control in a world that had hurt him deeply.

His title as King of the Underworld didn't mean much anymore. He had given that role to his son, Zagreus. Last he heard, Zagreus was doing well. As for Persephone, she had come to the human world with him to escape her overprotective mother, Demeter.

In this day and age, they went by the names Alex Knight and Lily Evans. The old stories about them had some truth. They were married, but things change over time. Their marriage had turned into a strong partnership they treasured. After being married for thousands of years, they decided to give each other a chance to love again.

Together, they founded Shadowguards, an organization dedicated to safeguarding both humans and supernaturals. Over time, their initiative evolved into something extraordinary.

The government had acknowledged them as a powerful ally. What had begun as a modest endeavor quickly expanded, eventually leading them to purchase an entire skyscraper in Manhattan that now stood as their towering headquarters.

To the ordinary humans, their true nature remained concealed. The inherent magic within their god souls granted them the ability to cloak their distinct magical identities. To any magical beings, they simply appeared to be regular humans.

Gods mingled with regular people, but they looked just like anyone else. These gods lived normal lives, using their magic quietly to help things along. Even though they were super powerful, they had feelings like regular folks and made friends. Most people didn't know they were gods, but some had a feeling. Stories and beliefs talked about them, but not everyone believed. The way gods and people mixed in the background affected history, keeping things in balance between the two worlds.

In the Shadowguards Training Facility, the air was thick with sweat and camaraderie. The clang of metal against metal and the whoosh of magical spells filled the room as the team of misfits pushed their limits, and the banter flowed as naturally as the magic that coursed through their veins.

Alex stood in the corner, arms crossed and a faint frown on his face. He watched his team with a mixture of exasperation and affection as they teased and challenged each other. His dark eyes followed each of his teammates in turn, taking in their unique abilities and personalities.

Gabriel, the team's strategist and witch, was deep in thought, his fingers tracing invisible patterns in the air as he planned their next move. His silver hair glinted in the dim light, and his intense green eyes rarely strayed from his calculations.

Emma, the team's enchanter, bustled around like a mother hen, fussing over everyone and making sure they were well-hydrated. Her auburn hair was pulled back in a messy bun, and her warm brown eyes twinkled with affection as she scolded Marcus for not stretching properly.

Marcus, the team's speedster and troublemaker, grinned as he dodged a fireball from Olivia, the arcane mage. He was a rare breed of magic user, and his ability to move at lightning speed made him both a formidable ally and a constant source of chaos. His brown hair was perpetually tousled, and his mischievous eyes danced with mischief.

Olivia, with her striking red hair and piercing blue eyes, reveled in the chaos. She loved nothing more than watching her team banter and spar, and she unleashed a barrage of arcane spells with a mischievous grin. She was there for the sheer joy of it, her magic a force to be reckoned with.

Lucas, the team's tech genius, had his nose buried in a holographic screen, furiously typing away as he monitored the team's vitals and progress. His dark hair fell into his eyes, and his cheeks were flushed with excitement as he watched the data stream in.

"Hey, Lucas, you still trying to impress Gabriel with your fancy gadgets?" Marcus called out, darting past Lucas in a blur of motion.

Lucas blushed furiously, his fingers stumbling over the keys. "N-No! I'm just…doing my job," he stammered, avoiding eye contact with Gabriel.

Gabriel, in response, merely raised an eyebrow and smirked. "Impressive as always, Lucas."

Emma chuckled as she handed Alex a bottle of water. "You know, Alex, you could join in once in a while. It won't hurt you to let loose a bit."

Alex took a long drink from the bottle and grunted in response. He had always been the serious one, the leader who held the team together with his unwavering determination.

"You're just upset because you can't keep up with us," Marcus taunted, dodging another fireball from Olivia.

Alex rolled his eyes and turned away, retreating to the punching bag in the corner. He began to throw punches with precision and power, his frustration evident in each strike.

"Stubborn as ever," Gabriel murmured, watching Alex with a hint of concern.

As the banter and laughter continued around him, Alex eventually finished his training regimen. He wiped the sweat from his brow with the back of his hand and announced, "I need to get back to my office."

His team paused for a moment, the teasing and spells coming to a temporary halt. Emma gave him a sympathetic smile, while Marcus and Olivia exchanged a knowing glance.

"Alright, boss," Lucas said, his fingers still tapping away on his holographic screen. "We'll catch up with you later."

Alex nodded, and without another word, he turned and left the training room, leaving behind a team that was as much a family as it was a group of warriors.

As the door closed behind him, he couldn't help but smile to himself. They were a ragtag bunch of misfits, each with their quirks and abilities, but together, they were unstoppable. And despite his stoic exterior, he wouldn't have it any other way.

Alex found himself engrossed in reading through a pile of reports when a sharp alert from his Shadow Holographic Device (SHD) captured his attention. Swiftly, he made his way to the briefing room, his footsteps echoing in the dimly lit corridor. Inside, his team was already immersed in dissecting the cause behind the alert. The room buzzed with a sense of urgency as they huddled around the holographic display.

"Alright, what do we have?" Alex's voice cut through the tension in the room as he took his place at the head of the table.

Gabe leaned over the holographic console. His fingers danced across the interface, pulling up data and images. He wore a focused demeanor, his brow furrowed in concentration. The others exchanged nervous glances, waiting for his revelation.

"Sir, I believe I've pinpointed the source of the alert,"

Gabriel stated, his voice steady but laced with a sense of urgency.

Alex leaned in closer, his eyes fixed on the holographic projection. "Show me."

The image shifted to reveal a map of Brooklyn, marked with a blinking red dot. It was a venue, and the blinking dot indicated its location.

Alex's jaw tightened as he studied the map. "What's at that location?"

Gabriel continued, his fingers deftly manipulating the holographic controls. "It's a music venue, sir. The alert indicates potential danger, and given our track record, we can't take this lightly."

Alex nodded in agreement, his mind already racing through the possibilities. Time was of the essence, and lives might be at stake.

Without wasting any time, he issued the order for his team to gear up. They moved with practiced efficiency, grabbing their specialized equipment and donning their gear. The room buzzed with tension as they prepared for the unknown.

Minutes later, they arrived at the location mentioned in the alert. Finding the venue was easy, all they had to do was follow the growing crowd. The sight outside the venue was surreal. A mixture of curiosity and anxiety had drawn a throng of people, their hushed whispers creating an eerie backdrop to the unfolding mystery.

They approached the venue, the exterior of the building still standing intact. It was an odd sight, considering the nature of the alerts they usually received. Typically, the buildings were in ruins by the time they arrived. This anomaly raised their suspicions.

Alex exchanged glances with his team as they stood before the entrance. Their unspoken question hung in the air: What had happened here?

As they stepped inside, they were met with a scene that defied logic. The interior of the venue resembled the aftermath of a tornado. Tables were upended, chairs lay strewn against walls, and lights dangled precariously from the ceiling. It was chaos incarnate.

Alex's eyes scanned the wreckage, his jaw set in a determined line. His stoic demeanor didn't waver, even as he took in the chaos that surrounded them. Gabe stood beside him, his brows furrowed in concentration.

"This doesn't make sense," Lucas muttered under his breath as he surveyed the scene. "The exterior's fine, but the interior… it's like a war zone."

Alex nodded in agreement, his mind already working to piece together the puzzle. "Stay alert, everyone. Something's not right here."

The team fanned out to conduct their reconnaissance. Emma checked for signs of magical tampering, her fingers trailing over scorched walls and shattered glass.

Marcus and his keen eyes was searching for any hidden threats. "I bet Olivia's arcane magic could've saved this place in a heartbeat."

Olivia shot Marcus an amused look as she examined the remnants of the venue. "Sometimes, Marcus, you need to appreciate the chaos before you can control it."

Lucas trailed behind the group. His infatuation with Gabriel was no secret, but the stubborn witch paid it little attention, focused on the task at hand.

As they ventured deeper into the venue, the suspense

thickened in the air like an impending storm.

Alex led the way, his instincts sharpened by years of experience. He couldn't help but wonder about the source of the alert and what could cause such a bizarre scenario. The deeper they delved, the more questions arose, and a sense of foreboding settled over him like a shroud.

Alex approached Gabriel, his voice low as he asked, "Gabe, get in touch with the Human Investigation Bureau. We need to find out what they know about this place and what could have caused this mess."

Gabriel nodded and pulled out his SHD. He tapped it and the device lit up with a faint blue glow. Moments later, a voice crackled through the communicator.

"HIB here. This is Agent Reilly. What's your situation?"

Gabriel, ever the eloquent one, replied, "This is Shadow-guard Team Alpha. We received an alert of unusual activity at the venue. Can you provide us with any information?"

Agent Reilly's voice held a hint of hesitation. "We don't have much, but we received reports of strange magical fluctuations in the area and that's more of you expertise than ours. Whatever you do, be cautious."

The tension among the team deepened as they heard the agent's words. They were in the dark, and the stakes had suddenly become much higher.

Alex's jaw tightened. "Keep your guard up, everyone."

With renewed determination, the team pressed on. The wreckage around them seemed to close in, the shadows growing darker and more foreboding with each step. Their banter had given way to silence, replaced by a shared sense of purpose and the gravity of the situation.

As they ventured further into the heart of the venue, the

unknown dangers lurking in the shadows became increasingly palpable. The team's bond, forged through countless missions and trials, was their greatest strength.

Alex saw someone rushing towards him. Alex stood frozen, her approach setting his senses on edge. He could feel it—faint, elusive, yet unmistakable. The presence of a deity. It rippled through the air like a whisper of divinity. His gaze locked onto her features, her striking beauty heightened by the divine aura that surrounded her.

"Artemis," he breathed, his voice tinged with a mix of awe and tension.

Artemis met his eyes, clearly taken aback by his recognition. "Hades?"

His urgency surged, and he moved her aside swiftly. "What are you doing here?"

Ari's imploring gaze met his. "I came to support my best friend, Eryx, during his performance when the earthquake struck. Please, you have to help him."

Alex clenched his jaw. "This isn't finished."

"And it is Ari, I haven't used that name for so long," she requested, and Alex nodded, acknowledging her wish.

"Where's your friend?" he inquired, determination etched on his face.

"He was on the stage, performing when everything happened," she replied, her worry evident.

Without hesitation, Alex sprang into action, striding purposefully toward the stage. The chaos that had gripped the venue had left it in disarray, but the stage itself remained untouched.

Once Alex reached the stage he sensed an impermeable barrier, formidable and unyielding, shrouding the area. It was unlike anything he'd ever encountered.

His eyes bore into the stage, focused on the unconscious figure of Eryx sprawled on the floor. Alex attempted to breach the barrier, but his efforts yielded no results. It resisted him, unwavering in its defiance.

Frustration and desperation gnawed at him, and he pivoted to survey his surroundings. His eyes closed as he tapped into the formidable power of the underworld coursing through his veins. With grim determination, he directed this potent energy toward dismantling the barrier.

Minutes felt like hours as he battled against the unyielding obstacle. The barrier's resistance began to crumble, inch by inch, yielding to his relentless assault. Finally, he achieved a breakthrough.

With mastery over his body restored, Alex hurried to Eryx's side. As he cradled him gently in his arms, an inexplicable sense of rightness washed over him. He shook off the feeling, focusing on the task at hand.

He assessed Eryx's vital signs, his heart pounding in his chest. Relief flooded him when he found stability. Retrieving a small vial from his pocket, he administered its contents into Eryx's mouth.

Tense minutes passed, the only sound the labored breathing of Eryx. Then, the vial's effects took hold, and Eryx's eyes fluttered open. The azure hue of his irises struck Alex like a bolt of lightning.

"What happened?" Eryx's voice held a deep resonance, a mixture of confusion and concern.

"You lost consciousness," Alex replied, his voice steady. "Your friend Ari mentioned there was an earthquake."

Eryx's brow furrowed with worry. "The rehearsal? Is

everyone alright?"

"As for the rehearsal, I'm not certain, but I can assure you that everyone has been accounted for," Alex reassured him.

Eryx attempted to stand but faltered. Alex steadied him, preventing a fall. "Stay here, Eryx. I'll call paramedics to make sure you're alright."

"No need... I'm alright. Just help me stand," Eryx insisted.

Alex supported Eryx as they navigated the disheveled surroundings, finally delivering him safely into Ari's care.

"Thank you," Ari's gratitude was palpable.

With a nod of acknowledgment, Alex suppressed his curiosity about Ari's presence. Duty took precedence, and he stepped away, rejoining his team as they gathered statements from the bewildered crowd.

The venue's atmosphere crackled with tension, and Alex couldn't shake the feeling that this unexpected encounter with a deity was only the beginning of something much larger and more perilous.

Alex's heart raced as he surveyed the chaotic aftermath. The scene was a mess, debris strewn across the area, and tension hung thick in the air. He had to act quickly, and Marcus, the team's agile operative, was his best chance.

"Marcus!" Alex's command sliced through the chaos, his voice heavy with urgency.

Marcus materialized before him in a blur, his eyes scanning the surroundings. "Yes, sir?" he replied, his tone calm but alert.

"I've got an assignment for you. You up for it?" Alex's eyes remained fixed on a man named Eryx, standing at the center of the turmoil.

Marcus gave a curt nod. "What do you need, sir?"

"I want you to keep a close watch on that man." Alex's finger pointed unswervingly at Eryx, his face revealing nothing. "His name's Eryx."

Marcus quirked an eyebrow, curiosity gleaming in his eyes. "Any particular reason, sir?"

Alex's jaw tightened for a moment, his thoughts racing. He needed to choose his words carefully. "Just follow through, Agent King. Consider it an order."

Without hesitation, Marcus acknowledged the directive with steely determination in his eyes. He vanished into the shadows, leaving Alex with one question nagging at his mind, who was this man?

As Marcus blended into the chaos, Alex couldn't help but wonder. Eryx had appeared out of nowhere, just when things had taken a turn for the worse. The mission was already a mess, but Eryx's presence added another layer of uncertainty. Alex knew he had to figure out who this guy was.

3

Eryx

A FEW DAYS HAD PASSED since the incident, and Eryx couldn't shake the sense of confusion that had settled within him. The chaos of that night had been overwhelming, yet they had somehow managed to go ahead with their performance. It was as if the universe had conspired to throw them off course, and Eryx felt like a ship lost at sea.

The aftermath was a blur of hurried clean-up and repairs. Thankfully, the equipment hadn't suffered extensive damage, but Eryx took responsibility for the remaining repairs at the venue. He couldn't help but feel a heavy weight of guilt for whatever had unfolded, even if he couldn't pinpoint exactly what that was.

Ari had tried to explain things, but Eryx found it difficult to make sense of it all. The details remained hazy, and there was an eerie sense that no one could determine where it had all begun. That night, he hadn't had any dreams, and strangely, he welcomed the change. The lack of dreams was a relief from the haunting images that usually plagued his sleep.

But as the days passed, a nagging feeling gnawed at him. It was as though the strange events at the bar and the venue were connected to his newfound absence of dreams. He couldn't shake the thought that there was a hidden link, a puzzle waiting to be solved. He wanted to dismiss it, to move on, but the curiosity and unease clawed at him from the inside.

Eryx stared at the ceiling, lost in thought. He knew he needed answers, and he needed them soon. Frustration welled up inside him, mingling with the anxiety that had taken root since that day.

"Why can't things just make sense for once?" he muttered to himself, his voice barely audible in the stillness of the room.

His phone buzzed with a message from Ari. She was checking in on him, concerned about how he was handling everything. Eryx appreciated her support, but he couldn't help feeling like a puzzle piece that didn't quite fit.

"Hey, Eryx. How are you holding up?" Ari's message read.

Eryx hesitated for a moment before typing out a reply. "I'm okay, I guess. Just trying to make sense of it all."

Ari's response was swift. "We all are. But we'll figure it out."

As he read her words, Eryx couldn't help but feel a glimmer of hope. Maybe, just maybe, they could unravel the mystery that seemed to have taken hold of their lives. He knew it wouldn't be easy, and the path ahead was uncertain, but he was determined to find the answers he so desperately sought.

Eryx couldn't shake the image of the stranger with kind brown eyes who had swooped in like a hero to save him. Gratitude, attraction, and uncertainty swirled within him, creating a maelstrom of feelings he couldn't quite comprehend.

His heart raced at the memory of those eyes, eyes that had locked onto his with an intensity that left an indelible mark. It wasn't just the rescue, it was the way the guy had looked at him, as if Eryx was the most important person in the world at that moment. It had made him feel safe, cherished, and wanted.

"Stop it," Eryx muttered to himself, rolling over in bed as if he could physically escape his thoughts. "He's probably straight, or worse, not interested in me at all."

But try as he might, he couldn't silence the relentless replay of that moment in his mind—the guy's strong arms lifting him effortlessly, the way their eyes had met, and the unspoken connection that had formed.

His body responded to the memories, a fluttering sensation in his chest, a rush of warmth that spread through him, and a tight knot in his stomach. Eryx groaned, burying his face in his hands. He had never felt this way before, and it was unsettling.

Images of the stranger's appearance began to surface in Eryx's mind. The guy had a rugged handsomeness, with tousled dark hair and a chiseled jawline. His shoulders were broad, and he moved with a confident grace that hinted at strength and capability. Eryx had noticed a faint scar on the guy's forearm, a testament to a past filled with challenges and resilience.

"Stop, stop, stop," Eryx scolded himself, his internal dialogue a relentless battle. "You don't even know his name. It means nothing."

But despite his efforts to push the thoughts aside, they persisted. Eryx's mind raced with questions about the stranger.

With a frustrated sigh, he threw off his covers and sat up, running a hand through his disheveled hair. He needed to get out of his head, to distract himself from the turmoil that threatened to consume him.

Sitting on his well-worn couch, Eryx took a sip of his morning coffee. The bitter warmth filled his mouth, a comforting contrast to the coolness of the room. He wasn't in the mood to talk to anyone, let alone answer his persistent ringing phone. But when he glanced at the screen and saw that the caller was his manager, Sam Mitchell, he knew he couldn't ignore it.

He sighed, resigning himself to the inevitable interruption, and swiped to answer. "Hey, Sam. What's up?" Eryx greeted, his voice a blend of reluctance and curiosity.

Sam's voice, always steady and compassionate, came through the phone. "Could you make it to the office today? We need to discuss some things."

Eryx's heart sank at the request, a heavy feeling settling in his chest. That didn't sound very promising. He shifted on the couch, the familiar texture of the worn fabric beneath his fingertips grounding him. "Sure, what time should I be there?"

"Just drop by whenever you can," Sam replied, his voice holding a hint of concern before ending the call.

Eryx stared at his phone, the prospect of this meeting left him both puzzled and concerned. He had come a long way in the music industry, a journey marked by highs and lows, but Sam had been the one constant figure who had believed in his talent from the beginning.

As he set down his coffee cup, the taste of its fading bitterness lingering on his tongue, Eryx couldn't help but reflect on the mentorship they'd shared. Sam had given him the chance to prove himself, and together, they had navigated the often tumultuous waters of the music world. It had been a partnership built on trust, and Eryx owed much of his success to the man on the other end of the phone.

The small living space around him offered few distractions from his thoughts. The sparse decor, a blend of minimalist design and personal mementos, spoke to his no-nonsense approach to life. The soft morning light filtered through the window, casting a gentle glow over the room, and the hum of the city outside was a constant reminder of the world beyond these walls.

The fear of disappointment gnawed at him, and the uncertainty of what lay ahead left him with a knot in his stomach.

He glanced at the clock and realized that time was slipping away. He had to get ready for this meeting, though he wasn't entirely sure what to prepare for. The anticipation of potential conflicts or challenges loomed over him, the unknown nature of the discussion creating a sense of unease.

Eryx set aside everything and stood up. He moved through his small living space, gathering the items he needed for the day. As he reached for his guitar case, his fingers brushed over the instrument's well-worn surface. It was a symbol of his passion and his craft, a source of solace in moments of doubt.

Eryx knew that whatever awaited him at the office, he would face it head-on. He had always been a stubborn soul.

As he left his apartment, locking the door behind him, Eryx couldn't help but reflect on his journey in the music industry. It had been a rollercoaster of emotions, with Sam as his guiding force. Theirs was a dynamic built on trust, respect, and a shared love for music.

The streets were bustling with the energy of a new day, people moving with purpose as they chased their own dreams.

Just before the lunchtime rush, Eryx arrived at Eternal Records. The building's exterior stood tall and imposing, with its sleek glass façade reflecting the morning sunlight. As he approached the entrance, a strange sensation washed over him. It was as if an invisible presence hung in the air, a feeling that prickled the fine hairs on his neck.

From the corner of his eye, he thought he glimpsed someone, a fleeting figure that vanished when he turned to look. Confused and mildly unsettled, he dismissed it as a trick of his imagination and pushed open the glass door.

Inside, Eternal Records was a sanctuary for artists, a place where creativity thrived, and dreams had the chance to take root. The modern interior seamlessly blended with a special ambiance, a blend of musical magic and urban energy. Vibrant posters of past artists adorned the walls, a testament to the label's history of nurturing talent.

As Eryx made his way through the building's polished halls, he noticed the warm lighting and comfortable seating areas that encouraged collaboration and inspiration. Artistic murals adorned the walls, and the faint strains of music drifted from nearby recording studios, adding to the building's unique charm.

Heading towards Sam's office, Eryx's eyes lingered on the nameplate. It read "Sam Mitchell - Artist Manager." The simple detail brought a smile to his face, a reminder of the supportive partnership he had with Sam over the years. He knocked on the door, hearing Sam's familiar voice inviting him inside.

"You wanted to see me?" Eryx asked as he entered, his tone a mixture of curiosity and anticipation.

Sam looked up from his paperwork, his expression professional yet welcoming. "Eryx, please take a seat. This won't take long."

Eryx complied, settling into a plush chair across from Sam's tidy desk. The room exuded an air of efficiency, with neatly stacked files and awards displayed on the shelves. A framed photograph caught Eryx's attention—a snapshot of the two of them at an album launch party, smiles wide and genuine.

As Sam began to speak, the strange sensation Eryx had experienced outside lingered in the back of his mind, a subtle undercurrent of unease. Sam's words only deepened his curiosity.

"I've been reviewing our upcoming projects, Eryx," Sam said, his tone measured. "And I've noticed that you've been… hesitant lately."

Eryx shifted uncomfortably in his chair, his confusion evident. "Hesitant? What do you mean?"

Sam leaned forward, steepling his fingers. "Your music, Eryx, it's your passion, your gift. But something has changed. I can sense it, and I believe your fans can too."

Eryx's brows furrowed as he grappled with Sam's words. He had always been stubborn, fiercely guarding his creative vision, but lately, a cloud of doubt had settled over him, like a shadow he couldn't dispel.

"Your last few performances," Sam continued, "they lacked the fire, the spark that made your music connect with people. It's not about selling records; it's about sharing your soul with the world."

Eryx's gaze dropped to his hands, fingers tracing invisible patterns on his jeans. Sam's words struck a chord deep within him, igniting a mix of emotions—confusion, frustration, and a hint of fear.

"Look, Eryx," Sam said, his voice softening, "I want the best for your career, for your artistry. But you need to find that fire again, that raw passion that sets your music apart. We can work together to rediscover it."

Eryx's shoulders sagged, and he nodded slowly, a reluctant acceptance settling over him. He had always been stubborn, but he trusted Sam's judgment more than anyone else's. Maybe it was time to let go of the uncertainty that had been holding him back.

"You're right, Sam," Eryx admitted, his voice tinged with vulnerability. "I've been lost lately, doubting myself. But I want to find that passion again, that connection with my music."A wave of worry passed through Eryx. He wondered if he was about to be let go from the label. "Am I being fired?" Eryx couldn't help but blurt out.

He shifted uncomfortably in the plush chair across from Sam's desk at Eternal Records, unable to meet his manager's eyes.

"Fired? Who said that? No, you're definitely not," Sam reassured him, leaning back in his leather chair. He paused, rifling through a stack of papers until he found the document he was looking for. Then, with a gentle smile, he handed Eryx a paper that looked suspiciously like a contract.

Eryx took it with trembling hands, his heart pounding as he skimmed the words. His brows knitted in confusion, his eyes widening in disbelief. This was way better than getting fired.

"As you can see," Sam announced, leaning forward, "I've managed to secure you a gig as the opening act for Richard Lane at Carnegie Hall."

Eryx's mouth fell open, his astonishment evident. He hadn't expected this at all, and the news was beyond his wildest dreams. Carnegie Hall, the very name sent shivers down his spine. It was a place he had always dreamed of performing, a symbol of success and recognition in the music industry.

"You did what?" Eryx finally exclaimed, his voice filled with disbelief as he stared at the contract.

Sam chuckled, clearly pleased with Eryx's reaction. "I know it's a big deal, but it's true. Carnegie Hall, in a week's time. Just sign the contract, and it's all set."

Eryx couldn't contain his excitement any longer. He leaped out of his seat, his heart bursting with joy, and enveloped his manager in a tight hug. "Thank you, Sam! This is incredible!"

Sam patted his back warmly, his expression reflecting pride and satisfaction. "I know how much you wanted to perform there, and I pulled some strings to make it happen. Now, go ahead and sign it."

Eryx released Sam and eagerly grabbed a pen from the desk. He scribbled his signature on the contract, his hand shaking with anticipation. As he handed it back to Sam, he couldn't help but feel a surge of relief and elation.

His manager took the signed contract and placed it carefully in a folder, his smile unwavering. "You deserve this, Eryx. Your talent and hard work have paid off."

Eryx nodded fervently, his eyes shining with gratitude. "I can't believe it's finally happening. Carnegie Hall, man! It's a dream come true."

Sam leaned back in his chair, folding his hands together.

"You've got the talent, Eryx. I've always believed in you. This is just the beginning."

Eryx sank back into his chair, his mind racing with the possibilities. Carnegie Hall was more than just a venue; it was a milestone, a validation of his artistry and dedication. He had poured his heart and soul into his music, and now, he was going to share it with an audience that had once seemed out of reach.

"I promise I won't let you down," Eryx vowed, his determination shining in his eyes. "I'll give it my all, Sam."

Sam's expression softened, his pride in Eryx evident. "I know you will, Eryx. You've got the talent, the drive, and now, the opportunity. Just remember to stay true to yourself and your music. That's what got you here in the first place."

Eryx nodded, his gratitude overwhelming. He had a lot of work to do in the coming week to prepare for the performance of a lifetime, but he was ready for the challenge. Carnegie Hall awaited, and he was determined to make it a night to remember.

As he left Sam's office, Eryx couldn't help but reflect on the journey that had led him here. It had been a rollercoaster ride of highs and lows, but this was the moment he had been working toward his entire life. Carnegie Hall was his stage, and he was ready to shine.

* * *

Ari's house stood out in the neighborhood like a burst of greenery amidst the concrete jungle of Brooklyn. It mirrored her personality—vibrant and lively, breaking the monotony of the mundane.

He knocked on her door, impatience etched on his face. Inside, the sounds of commotion reached his ears, and he couldn't help but wonder what Ari was up to today.

"The door's open!" Ari's voice called out, distracted.

Eryx pushed the door cautiously and entered. What greeted him was nothing short of peculiar. Ari was darting around the living room as if she was chasing an invisible ghost.

Eryx, intrigued yet bemused, couldn't help but inquire, "What's happening?"

Things seemed to get even more chaotic, but Ari didn't answer. So, Eryx, always one to take charge in peculiar situations, decided to investigate himself. With curiosity piqued, he followed the commotion, and it led him straight to her bedroom.

There, he witnessed Ari attempting to reach something hidden beneath her bed, her vibrant personality taking a backseat to determination. "Ari? Seriously, what are you doing?" Eryx chuckled.

"Hey, can you help me? Your arms are longer," Ari said, a bit out of breath, her lively spirit undeterred.

Eryx, still skeptical but always up for an adventure, inquired cautiously, "It's not something dangerous, right?"

"No, not at all. Just come here," Ari urged.

"Alright, but if something goes south, you're covering my hospital bill," Eryx teased as he approached her.

Sitting down beside Ari, he finally saw what was causing her trouble. His eyes widened in surprise. "Is… that a cat?" he exclaimed.

Ari sighed in relief. "Yes, he sneaked in last night, and I've been trying to catch him to take him to a rescue center."

Looking at the adorable cat, Eryx had an idea. "Do you still have that laser pointer from Dion's party?"

Ari retrieved the laser pointer and handed it to Eryx. He pointed it at the floor, and the cat, as if bewitched, immediately pounced towards the tiny red dot. Eryx seized the opportunity and effortlessly picked her up.

"Hello there, little one," he cooed to the cat, unable to resist her charm.

The cat, with its sleek orange coat and striking green eyes, responded with a contented purr, which brought a smile to Eryx's face. Ari observed, "Huh, he seems to like you."

"Of course, everyone likes me," Eryx playfully teased, earning a playful smack on the head from Ari. "Jealous much?" he asked with a grin.

With the cat securely in his arms, Eryx and Ari shared a laugh. The cat, having found its temporary savior, seemed to bask in the warmth of their camaraderie.

Eryx sat on the couch in Ari's cozy Brooklyn living room, sipping on a cup of tea. The afternoon sun streamed in through the window, casting a warm glow over the room. Opposite him, Ari perched on the armrest of the couch, a mischievous glint in her eyes.

Ari surprised him with a suggestion. "Would you prefer to have him?"

Eryx raised an eyebrow, his sassy nature coming to the forefront. "Him? Who are we talking about, Ari? Your latest crush or some mysterious stranger I should be worried about?"

Ari chuckled, her long, curly hair bouncing with mirth. "Oh, you wish, Eryx. I'm talking about this little fella." She leaned over and scooped up a small, fluffy cat that had been curled up beside her. The cat blinked sleepily as it was lifted into the air.

Eryx hesitated for a moment but eventually relented. "You know I can't keep pets around, Ari. Even though I adore them." He glanced at the cat, who was now giving him those irresistible pleading eyes. "Oh no, not those eyes, come on."

Ari grinned, knowing she was making progress. "Are you absolutely sure?" She raised an eyebrow skeptically, as if challenging his resolve.

Eryx let out a defeated sigh. "Okay, okay, fine. I can't resist that face."

The cat, apparently sensing victory, purred contentedly in Ari's arms.

"Well, my face is pretty irresistible," Ari chuckled.

Eryx smirked. "Not yours, the cat's! Yours is alright."

"You're impossible," she muttered.

"But you love me for it," he shot back with a wink.

Ari rolled her eyes playfully. "Yeah, yeah. Let's head to the living room, and I'll make some tea so we can talk about your gig."

As Ari placed the cat on the couch, it immediately stretched out, its tail flicking lazily. Eryx couldn't help but smile as he watched the furry creature make itself comfortable.

The living room was adorned with eclectic decorations, and the scent of freshly brewed tea filled the air as Ari worked her magic in the kitchenette. The sound of the kettle whistling and the clinking of teacups added to the cozy ambiance.

"So, spill the tea, Eryx," Ari said as she returned with a tray of tea, biscuits, and a pot of freshly brewed Earl Grey. She settled back into her spot on the armrest, and the cat promptly hopped onto her lap. "What's this gig at Carnegie

Hall all about? You've been keeping it under wraps like it's some top-secret mission."

Eryx's expression shifted from playful to contemplative. He took a sip of his tea, savoring the comforting warmth it offered. "Well, it's not just any gig, Ari. It's Carnegie Hall, you know? Sam gave me this incredible opportunity. It's a chance to perform in front of a prestigious audience, and it could really open doors for my career."

Ari leaned forward, her curiosity piqued. "Wow, Eryx, that's huge! How are you feeling about it? Excited? Nervous?"

Eryx's snarky façade cracked slightly, revealing a flicker of vulnerability. "A bit of both, to be honest. Excited because it's a dream come true, but nervous because the expectations are sky-high."

The cat on Ari's lap purred in response, as if offering its support.

Ari gave him an encouraging smile. "Eryx, you've got the talent, and you've worked your butt off for this. You're going to rock Carnegie Hall, and everyone will be talking about your performance for years to come."

Eryx felt a surge of warmth at Ari's words. Her unwavering belief in him was a source of strength. "Thanks, Ari. I needed to hear that."

As they continued their conversation, sipping tea and discussing Eryx's upcoming gig, the cat nestled comfortably between them. Its presence served as a reminder that sometimes, unexpected surprises could bring comfort and joy, even in the midst of life's challenges.

Ari smiled at him. "You two are going to get along just fine."

The cat, now contentedly nestled on his lap, purred and kneaded its paws in gratitude. "Needy cat," he chuckled.

"What did Sam tell you about the gig?" she asked, leaning forward, her body language animated.

Eryx's eyes twinkled with disbelief as he recounted the news. "I'm opening for Richard Lane. The Richard Lane." He emphasized the name, fully aware of the legendary status associated with the musician. Richard Lane was renowned for creating soul-stirring music that had the power to bring tears to anyone's eyes.

Ari muttered something under her breath, her lips quirking into a sly smile. Eryx strained to hear her, his curiosity piqued. "What was that?" he prodded, genuinely curious about her muttered comment.

Ari leaned closer, her voice slightly muffled as she repeated herself, "I said I'm genuinely happy for you."

Eryx's raised an eyebrow in mock skepticism, but he couldn't hide the glint of appreciation in his eyes. The cat, sensing his mixed emotions, snuggled up even closer, as if offering him comfort and reassurance.

"So, where do you want to go tonight? I'm pretty sure Dion is up for anything," Ari said, smoothly transitioning to a different topic.

She knew how to navigate Eryx's moods, and he was grateful for her ability to steer the conversation away from his momentary vulnerability.

Eryx pondered her question for a moment, his thoughts shifting from the upcoming gig to their plans for the evening.

"How about Aria?" he suggested with a playful grin.

Ari's eyes lit up, her enthusiasm palpable. "Ooh, yes, please!" She clapped her hands in excitement.

As they continued to chat about their evening plans, Eryx couldn't help but reflect on the significance of the gig.

Opening for Richard Lane was a dream come true for him. It meant recognition, exposure, and the chance to share his music with a wider audience. It was a step toward the career he had always envisioned.

But amidst the excitement, doubts and questions swirled in the back of his mind. Could he live up to the expectations of opening for a musical legend like Richard Lane? Would his own music resonate with the audience? The cat, seemingly attuned to his inner turmoil, nuzzled his hand, as if reassuring him that he had what it took.

Ari's exuberant personality provided a welcome distraction from his inner musings. She chattered on, her expressive gestures punctuating her words. Eryx couldn't help but be amused by her antics. She was the yin to his yang, the wild to his calm, and he wouldn't have it any other way.

Their banter flowed effortlessly, filled with playful jabs and affectionate teasing. It was moments like these that made their friendship so special. Eryx's sassy and snarky comments found their perfect foil in Ari's exuberance, creating a dynamic that brought out the best in both of them.

As they finalized their plans for the evening and the cat on his lap finally decided to grace Ari with its presence, Eryx couldn't help but feel a sense of anticipation building within him. The gig was a milestone in his career, and he was ready to embrace it

Eryx left Ari's cozy Brooklyn house with a newfound furry companion in tow. The sun cast a warm glow over the streets as he walked, the weight of the upcoming concert pressing on his mind. He looked down at the cat nestled in his arms and said, "I should give you a name, right? How about Mr. Whiskers?"

The cat responded with a satisfied meow, as if approving of the name choice. Eryx chuckled softly. "You like that, huh? Mr. Whiskers it is. Let's head home."

As Eryx strolled along, he couldn't shake the feeling that he had forgotten something important. It wasn't until he got back to his apartment and Mr. Whiskers began to meow in protest that it hit him. "Oops, forgot to buy cat food."

Mr. Whiskers gave him a stern, hungry look that seemed to say, "You better fix this, human."

Eryx sighed and shook his head, feeling a bit foolish. "Alright, Mr. Whiskers, we've got to fix this food situation pronto."

With Mr. Whiskers perched comfortably on his shoulder, Eryx hurried out to the nearest convenience store. He grabbed a bag of cat food, some toys, and a cozy little bed to make Mr. Whiskers feel at home. As he wandered the aisles, he couldn't help but notice the curious glances from other shoppers who seemed both surprised and amused by his feline companion.

Back in his apartment, Eryx set up a cozy corner for Mr. Whiskers. He placed a bowl of food and water, along with a soft bed for the cat to curl up on. Mr. Whiskers wasted no time and dove into his meal with gusto.

Eryx watched with a grin, his heart warming at the sight. "Looks like you're settling in just fine, buddy."

Mr. Whiskers finished eating and padded over to Eryx, purring contentedly. He nuzzled Eryx's hand, seeking attention and affection. Eryx obliged, scratching behind the cat's ears.

"Seems like you're quite the charmer, Mr. Whiskers," Eryx said, his doubts about the concert momentarily pushed aside.

He was starting to enjoy this unexpected companionship.

The sensation of Mr. Whiskers' soft fur beneath his fingertips was soothing, and Eryx couldn't help but reflect on the significance of this newfound responsibility. It felt like a small but important step in his life, a reminder that there were moments of warmth and connection to be found even in the midst of uncertainty.

As the afternoon sun bathed the apartment in a gentle golden light, Eryx settled into a routine with Mr. Whiskers. The cat became a constant presence, a furry friend who followed him around the apartment, curling up beside him while he worked on his music.

Eryx found solace in the simple moments: the soft purring as Mr. Whiskers dozed off in his lap, the playful antics when a toy mouse caught the cat's attention, and the warm companionship that filled the quiet spaces of his life.

The doubts about the concert still lingered in the back of Eryx's mind, but they felt less overwhelming now. He had Mr. Whiskers by his side, a reminder that sometimes, unexpected companions could bring comfort and joy in the most uncertain times.

As the day turned into evening, Eryx strummed his guitar, the music filling the apartment with a soothing melody. Mr. Whiskers curled up on the windowsill, his eyes half-closed in contentment.

Eryx glanced at his new friend and smiled. "You know, Mr. Whiskers, maybe this concert won't be so bad after all. With you around, I'm starting to believe that everything will turn out just fine."

And as the music flowed from his fingertips, Eryx felt a sense of peace settle over him. With Mr. Whiskers and his guitar by his side, he was ready to face whatever challenges the concert would bring, knowing that he had found a new source of inspiration and support in his life.

4

Alex

ALEX ENTERED THE DIMLY LIT BAR called Aria, the heavy wooden door creaking softly behind him. It was an unusual place, a puzzling mix of modern and old-fashioned aesthetics. The exterior had a classic charm, but once inside, it was a Victorian wonderland that unfolded before him.

He couldn't help but feel a bit out of place in his faded jeans and plain shirt. Marcus had conveniently forgotten to mention the bar's dress code. The mismatch between his attire and the bar's opulent interior was glaring.

The bar's decor was extravagant, with ornate chandeliers hanging from the ceiling, plush velvet curtains, and dark wood paneling. People sat at elegant wooden tables, engrossed in conversations that seemed to hum with an air of mystery.

Even the bartender, dressed in a tailored suit and tie, looked like he was attending a fancy gala rather than serving drinks. Alex couldn't help but think that he stuck out like a sore thumb in this sophisticated setting. However, he had already made the choice to come here, and there was no turning back now.

He found an empty stool at the ornate bar and took a seat. Alex observed discreetly, noting the mix of supernatural beings and humans who seemed to coexist in this unique establishment.

His attention turned to the menu, and he was not surprised to find an array of strong drinks meant for supernatural individuals who could handle their potency far better than humans. He had heard stories of the legendary concoctions served here, but he opted for something lighter.

The bartender, with a polite but somewhat aloof demeanor, approached him. "What can I get you, sir?" he asked in a tone that oozed professionalism.

"Vodka Lemonade," Alex replied, his voice steady and firm. It was a safe choice, a drink he could savor without losing his wits in this unfamiliar territory.

As he waited for his drink, Alex's gaze continued to wander. The bar's atmosphere was a fascinating blend of elegance and intrigue. Laughter and hushed conversations filled the air, mingling with the haunting strains of a piano in the corner.

The patrons, dressed in a wide array of styles and fashions, exuded an aura of mystery. There were vampires, their pale skin contrasting with the dark hues of their attire, and witches, their eyes sparkling with hidden knowledge. Humans sat beside creatures of the night, seemingly unfazed by the supernatural world that coexisted with their own.

Alex couldn't help but admire the way these beings carried themselves. They seemed at ease, comfortable in their own skin, and unapologetically true to their nature.

His Vodka Lemonade arrived, a crystal-clear glass filled

with ice and a slice of lemon. He took a slow sip, the cool liquid offering a momentary respite from the tension that had settled in his shoulders.

Alex's thoughts were interrupted as a group of patrons at the far end of the bar burst into laughter. Their joy was infectious, and for a brief moment, Alex allowed himself to relax.

He took another sip of his drink, the taste of vodka and lemonade blending on his tongue.

He wasn't exactly sure why he ended up in this place, but the idea of seeing Eryx again pushed him to come. Eryx had become a constant thought in his mind since that day at the venue. Alex's heart, usually as stoic as his demeanor, had an unfamiliar flutter to it.

The air thick with the mingling scents of perfume, whiskey, and the faintest hint of sweat. Soft jazz music played in the background, a soothing contrast to the vibrant life that pulsed through the place. Patrons laughed and whispered, their voices weaving a tapestry of secrets and desires.

It didn't take long for him to notice a man from across the bar. The man had been stealing glances at Alex since he sat down. He could tell the guy was just a regular human, and that didn't particularly interest him at the moment.

After a while, the man made his way over, a friendly smile on his face. "Hey there, how's it going?" he greeted, his voice warm.

Finally getting a good look at him, Alex saw that he was handsome in a classic sort of way, with chiseled features and a confident posture. However, he wasn't interested in small talk, especially when his thoughts were consumed by the anticipation of seeing Eryx.

"Sorry, not interested," Alex replied bluntly, getting straight to the point.

The man's smile faltered, replaced by a hint of irritation. "Wow, no need to be rude," he muttered before turning his attention to someone else who had caught his eye.

Alex rolled his eyes, a hint of frustration simmering beneath his stoic exterior. It was the same old story, and he had no patience for it tonight.

After nearly an hour of waiting, the soft swing of the door announced a new arrival, revealing Eryx. He was accompanied by Ari and another man whom Alex sensed was a god. As they got closer, he realized the third man was Dionysus, the Greek god of wine and revelry.

Alex couldn't help but wonder how Eryx managed to be friends with not one but two gods. His curiosity mingled with the emotions he had tried to suppress, and he tightened his auras to prevent them from sensing him.

Eryx looked as captivating, his tall frame clad in a finely tailored suit that hugged his body in all the right places. It made Alex feel strangely self-conscious in his casual jeans and shirt. He cleared his throat, berating himself for letting his emotions get the better of him.

Damn it, he thought, realizing he needed to regain control of his composure before he did something foolish. He took another sip of his whiskey, the smoky taste doing little to quell the turmoil within him.

As Eryx and his friends settled at a nearby table, Alex couldn't help but steal glances in their direction.

He watched as Eryx's eyes briefly met his, a flicker of recognition passing between them. Alex felt a jolt of electricity shoot through him at that moment, and he knew that there was no turning back. Eryx had a way of pulling him in, even when he least expected it.

To catch their conversation, Alex heightened his hearing. The bar's ambient noise faded into the background as he focused on Eryx and his friends at the adjacent table. They were engaged in a lighthearted conversation, the words flowing freely. While nothing they discussed seemed particularly important, one snippet caught Alex's attention, a tidbit that struck a chord.

"Hey, man," It was Dionysus who spoke up, "you ready for Carnegie Hall next week?"

Eryx, grinned back. "You know it, Dion. I've been rehearsing nonstop. It's a big deal for me."

Alex mentally noted the mention of Carnegie Hall, a prestigious venue. He filed the information away, thinking it might be useful later.

Alex found himself on his fifth drink, lost in the rhythm of Eryx and his friends. Eryx's laughter was infectious, and the camaraderie among the group was evident. It was clear that Eryx was cherished by those around him.

His god soul, a restless presence within him, seemed to be urging him to approach Eryx. It had been acting strangely lately, stirring up emotions and impulses that Alex wasn't accustomed to. Ignoring it might not be an option for much longer, and Alex was determined to give it a shot, even if he couldn't quite understand why.

The bar's ambiance began to shift as the lights dimmed, and a hush fell over the crowd. Alex's attention snapped to the stage as a figure emerged from the shadows.

"Hey, everyone!" the person on stage announced, their voice carrying through the silence. "We've got a special guest tonight."

The audience leaned forward in anticipation, their murmurs of curiosity filling the space. A spotlight moved across the room, finally settling on Eryx and his friends. Eryx's expression shifted from curiosity to confusion, his brows furrowing as he exchanged puzzled glances with his companions.

"Tonight," the person on stage continued, "we've got the talented Mr. Eryx Ross here."

Applause erupted throughout the bar as people recognized Eryx. The clapping and cheering grew in intensity, creating a warm wave of support and excitement.

Alex watched Eryx's emotions play across his face like a flickering candle. At first, there was confusion, uncertainty, and a hint of vulnerability as he stepped onto the stage, the weight of the unexpected moment settling on his shoulders. He adjusted the microphone stand, his fingers trembling ever so slightly.

But then something shifted. As he tapped the first chord of the piano on the stage, the initial uncertainty gave way to determination.

The atmosphere in the bar transformed. The hushed anticipation of the crowd was palpable, their eyes fixed on the stage. The soft glow of the spotlight created an intimate cocoon around Eryx, accentuating every note.

The tune that reached Alex's ears was one he hadn't heard in a long time—the Eternal Serenade. Its melancholic notes tugged at something deep within him, a memory long buried in the recesses of his mind. He couldn't fathom how Eryx knew this ancient piece, but he couldn't tear his gaze away.

As Eryx continued to play, Alex felt an inexplicable magic

enveloping him. The air seemed to shimmer with an other-worldly energy, though Eryx appeared to be nothing more than a regular human.

In that fleeting moment, as the haunting melody wrapped around him, Alex thought he sensed something familiar, a presence like that of Apollo. But it was gone in an instant, leaving him with a sense of intrigue and wonder.

Then, unexpectedly, Eryx began to sing. The original music didn't have any lyrics, but Eryx's voice wove seamlessly into the intricate composition. Alex hadn't anticipated vocals, but they added a layer of depth and emotion that resonated with his very soul.

Eryx's voice, a rich and resonant tenor, matched the melancholy of the Eternal Serenade perfectly. It was as if he breathed life into the music, infusing it with a raw, unspoken intensity. The audience, including Alex, was spellbound by the performance.

As Eryx sang, he glanced over at Alex, his eyes alight with excitement. Amidst the sea of faces in the dimly lit bar, their eyes met, and a connection sparked between them. Eryx's smile was like a secret shared, a moment of pure delight that transcended the music itself. Alex couldn't help but smile back, caught in the magic of the moment.

The music continued to weave its spell, each note carrying a weight of emotion that seemed to hang in the air. Alex's physical reactions were undeniable—he felt a shiver run down his spine, a lump forming in his throat, and his heart skipped a beat. It was as if the music had unlocked a hidden chamber of his heart, releasing emotions he had long kept buried.

In the dimness of the bar, the audience watched in rapt

silence, their attention wholly captured by the performance. Some closed their eyes, lost in the haunting melody, while others clutched their drinks, as if seeking solace in the potent combination of music and voice.

Alex felt a comforting hand on his shoulder, drawing his attention away from Eryx's mesmerizing performance. He turned around to find Ari standing there.

"Ari," he greeted her with a half-smile, grateful for her timely appearance.

"Hades. What brings you here?" Ari asked, her tone laced with playful curiosity.

Alex raised an eyebrow, his teasing grin surfacing. "Ah, come on, Ari. It's Alex," he replied, his voice holding a hint of humor. "Can't a guy enjoy a night out once in a while?"

Ari's perfectly arched brows shot up in mock surprise. "Well, well, aren't we a rare sight," she remarked, her eyes twinkling with mischief. "You, in a place like this."

Alex chuckled, appreciating Ari's playful banter. "I do have a life outside of work, you know. How did you know I was here?" he asked, genuinely curious about how Ari had tracked him down in the crowded venue.

Ari glanced over her shoulder, her gaze locking onto Eryx. "He's been looking at you for a while," she revealed with a knowing smirk.

Alex followed her gaze. "He's an amazing musician," he said softly, almost as if speaking to himself.

"He really is," Ari agreed, her tone softening for a moment. "So, why are you really here?"

"Apparently, your friend has taken up a permanent residence in my head these past couple of days."

"Do I need to ask him to start paying rent?"

Despite the humor, Alex knew it was time to address the matter at hand. He shifted the conversation to the real reason for his concern. "Why are you and Dionysus with him?"

Ari sighed, her expression growing more somber. "We were ordered to protect him."

"By who?" Alex's heart pounded with a sense of foreboding, a gut feeling that told him this was something far more significant than he had initially thought.

Ari hesitated for a moment, her eyes flickering with uncertainty before she finally revealed, "The Fates."

The revelation hit Alex like a lightning bolt, sending shockwaves of realization through him. Without wasting another moment, he grabbed his coat from the back of the chair and headed for the exit.

However, he was interrupted by Eryx's voice calling out, "Wait!"

Ignoring the plea, he stepped outside, needing air to process everything. The night air embraced him, its coolness providing a stark contrast to the warmth and chaos of the bar. He took a deep breath, attempting to shake off the weight of the newfound information.

Ari's touch on his elbow brought a sense of warmth, grounding him in the midst of turmoil. He turned, finding her beside him, her expression filled with a mixture of understanding and concern.

Alex's heart raced as he looked at Ari, his internal struggle mirrored in his physical reactions. His palms were moist, and his breathing had become irregular, a battle between attraction and the weight of the revelation threatening to overwhelm him.

He fought to regain his composure, his gaze shifting past

Ari to where Eryx stood. The musician's presence had been like a captivating spell, and Alex's thoughts had spiraled into a whirlwind of emotions.

Eryx approached them, his blue eyes filled with genuine concern. He was an enigma, a temptation that Alex had never anticipated. The man's presence was magnetic, and his smile seemed capable of melting even the darkest corners of the underworld.

"Hey, you're the guy from the venue," Eryx said, breaking the silence. "I never got the chance to personally thank you and your team for what you did."

Alex struggled to find his words, the awkwardness palpable. "It wasn't a problem at all," he managed to reply, his voice softer than usual. "You're an incredible musician."

Eryx's gratitude and charm cut through the tension, making it increasingly difficult for Alex to resist his charismatic presence. "Thank you," Eryx said sincerely.

Alex knew he needed to bring this interaction to a close before he lost control. "Listen, I have to go," he muttered, turning to leave.

Eryx's voice followed him. "I never got your name!"

Alex paused, looking back at Eryx. He found himself drawn to those kind blue eyes and that inviting smile. "It's Alex," he said softly, his heart echoing the sentiment.

As he walked away, grappling with a storm of emotions that the Fates themselves couldn't have predicted, he couldn't help but wonder if fate had something more in store for him than he had ever dared to imagine.

5

Eryx

HE WORLD AROUND HIM BLURRED, leaving only the image of the warmest brown eyes he had ever seen.

Eryx recognized those eyes. They had occupied his thoughts since they first met.

The haze lifted, revealing Alex before him. A smile adorned Alex's face, and his laughter echoed in the air.

But as swiftly as clarity came, it vanished.

Eryx woke up suddenly, his body drenched in sweat, and his cheeks wet with tears. His bed, too, bore the marks of his restless night. He groaned, trying to shake off the remnants of the dream that had haunted him. These recurring nightmares were a constant, unwelcome visitor in his sleep.

His dreams were usually a maddening mix of haunting scenes: a dense, shadowy forest where twisted trees whispered secrets, war-torn landscapes where desperate cries echoed, and his own voice, choked with sorrow. But this time, it was different. The dream had gripped him with a sense of deja vu, as if it was a memory he'd somehow forgotten.

He brushed a hand across his damp forehead, taking deep breaths to steady his racing heart.

Just as he started to regain his composure, the alarm clock on his nightstand went off with a jarring blare. Eryx's head snapped toward the clock, and he cursed under his breath. It was time for archery practice with Dion, and he was running late.

Mr. Whiskers took that moment to leap onto his bed, purring as if to remind him that breakfast couldn't wait. Eryx gave the cat a quick scratch behind the ears before reluctantly getting out of bed.

He fed Mr. Whiskers, his mind still swirling with the remnants of the dream. It clung to him like a shadow, casting doubt and confusion over his thoughts. He couldn't shake the feeling that there was more to these nightmares than met the eye.

After a speedy shower, Eryx dressed in record time, throwing on his usual ensemble of a black T-shirt and jeans. He slung his bow over his back, a constant companion, and headed for the door.

As he stepped outside, he was hit by the crisp morning air, a welcome shock to his senses.

The archery range was a familiar place, one that offered him solace and a sense of purpose. It was where he could leave behind the turmoil of his thoughts and focus on his skills. But today, even the comforting routine of the range felt disrupted.

He arrived at the range just in time to see Dion, his friend and archery partner. Dion's vibrant purple hair and warm brown eyes always managed to brighten Eryx's mood. He greeted Eryx with a smile that seemed to melt away some of the morning's darkness.

Dion had sported purple hair for as long as Eryx had known him. Eryx never really asked about it, assuming it was just a phase that would fade away. But the purple hair stuck around, and Eryx didn't mind.

"Late again, I see," Dion teased, his voice carrying a playful lilt.

Eryx smirked, though his eyes still held a trace of the earlier unease. "Blame it on Mr. Whiskers. He insisted on a royal breakfast."

Dion chuckled, his laughter a soothing melody in the quiet morning air. "Well, you can make it up with a perfect bullseye today."

"What brings you out here?" Eryx asked his friend as they stood outside the archery range.

Dion's smile faded a bit. "That fae is here again."

"You mean the instructor?" Eryx teased.

"Ugh, why does he have to show up every time?" Dion's annoyance was palpable.

Eryx couldn't help but chuckle. The dynamic between Dion and their archery instructor was a mix of love and hate. Honestly, Eryx suspected there was some unresolved tension between the two. The sexual energy between them was off the charts, and Eryx wondered why they were holding back.

"Well, he is supposed to teach us," Eryx pointed out.

"He could teach us from a distance, like, from a different zip code," Dion grumbled.

"Come on, he's not that terrible," Eryx tried to reassure his friend.

"Not that terrible? He called me a grape. A grape!" Dion was being his usual dramatic self.

"He kind of has a point there," Eryx admitted with a smirk.

"What's that even supposed to mean?"

"Nothing! Let's just get inside before we're late," Eryx said, grabbing Dion's arm and leading him indoors.

The two of them entered their respective shooting booths and set up their gear. Eryx wasted no time and began firing arrows at the target dummy. Glancing over at Dion's booth, he couldn't help but chuckle at his friend's struggles. Dion's actions were always a source of entertainment.

Their instructor, whose name was far too elaborate to remember, was making his way toward Dion. Eryx paused in his shooting to observe the unfolding scene. He was curious if this interaction would be more dramatic than a soap opera.

Actually, scratch that. This was pure Oscar-worthy material. Eryx watched as Dion swatted at the fae instructor, who seemed determined to intervene. The fae even attempted to take Dion's bow to demonstrate the proper technique. The growing crowd around Eryx seemed equally captivated, like spectators at a sporting event.

It wasn't long before the swatting escalated into a full-blown showdown. Eryx realized he had to step in before things got too out of hand. "Alright, you two drama queens, simmer down. People are watching, and they were ready to place bets on the winner," Eryx playfully teased, motioning to the amused onlookers.

The fae instructor straightened his attire and left, much to the crowd's disappointment.

"What was that all about?" Eryx asked his friend.

"He was trying to demonstrate, and then he asked me out," Dion replied, clearly irritated.

"Seriously?" Eryx was taken aback.

"Yes! That insufferable jerk."

"And what did you say?"

"Obviously, I said yes!" Dion exclaimed.

"So, what was the fight about?"

"We couldn't agree on where to go," Dion grumbled.

Eryx couldn't believe what he was hearing.

"Alright, let's get out of here. I need to get ready."

They exited their booths and left the archery range, leaving behind the spectacle they had caused. The sun was setting, casting a warm glow over their surroundings. As they walked away, Eryx couldn't help but shake his head in amusement. Dion and his dramatic love life were always good for a laugh.

Eryx strolled through the grocery store, his thoughts divided between mundane concerns and the unsettling feeling that he was being watched. He hadn't planned on a shopping trip today, but the need for proper cat food for Mr. Whiskers had nagged at him like a catchy tune he couldn't forget.

Inside the store, the fluorescent lights buzzed overhead, and the air was thick with the mingling scents of fresh produce, bakery goods, and cleaning supplies. Eryx made a beeline for the pet aisle, grabbing a bag of cat food without much thought.

A few steps away, he paused, contemplating the ingredients for a dish he wanted to cook. Cooking had always been one of his hidden talents, something only a few close friends knew about. He picked up a bundle of fresh herbs, a pack of pasta, and some tomatoes, a faint smile tugging at the corner of his lips. If he weren't a musician, he might have pursued a career as a chef.

As he added the items to his shopping cart, the nagging sense of being followed intensified. He scanned the crowded store. Shoppers bustled about, oblivious to his unease. Something felt off, and he couldn't shake the prickling sensation at the back of his neck.

Hastening through the checkout process, Eryx felt an unsettling presence nearby. It was as though the shadows themselves were closing in on him.

Outside, the streetlights cast eerie pools of light on the pavement. Close to his house, in the cloak of darkness, he noticed a pair of crimson eyes gleaming. He froze, heart pounding in his chest.

The figure drew nearer, and Eryx's breath caught in his throat. The creature was unmistakably a wolf, its powerful form and glistening fur illuminated by the dim light. But it wasn't just any wolf; it was a shifter. The crimson eyes marked it as an alpha, a dominant and potentially dangerous being.

Eryx felt a cold shiver crawl down his spine. He sensed other wolves lurking in the shadows behind him, their presence a silent threat. But his focus remained on the alpha before him.

What struck him most were those eyes—the eyes that seemed to pierce his soul. They were soulless, devoid of any warmth, and they held a darkness that sent a chill through his bones.

Stepping back cautiously, Eryx dropped his bags on the pavement. He was armed with his bow, a weapon he hadn't thought he'd need for a simple shopping trip. His fingers found the familiar grip of the bow, and he notched an arrow, his body tense and ready.

The alpha wolf advanced slowly, its movements calculated and deliberate. Eryx's hand tightened on the bowstring, his gaze locked onto the creature. The tension in the air was palpable, like the prelude to a thunderstorm about to break.

The moment the alpha wolf lunged at him, Eryx reacted with instinct honed through years of surviving in the supernatural world. He released the arrow, and it sailed through the air, striking the wolf above the heart. A strangled yelp escaped the creature as it crumpled to the ground, paralyzed but not dead.

Amidst the chaos of snarling wolves and snapping jaws, Eryx spun around to confront the other potential threats. But what he saw next stopped him in his tracks. The wolves lay defeated, their furry forms sprawled on the ground, and standing amidst them was a figure he recognized all too well.

Standing behind him was Alex and he couldn't quite comprehend why he was here. But a wave of relief swept over him at the sight of his familiar face, a reassuring anchor in the midst of chaos.

Alex turned to face him, his normally stoic expression etched with genuine concern. "Are you alright?" he asked, his voice cutting through the lingering tension in the air.

Eryx, still trying to catch his breath and slow his racing heart, managed to stammer out a response. "Y-Yeah. Thank you." His words were barely coherent as he moved on sheer instinct, closing the distance between them in an impulsive rush.

Without another thought, Eryx enveloped Alex in a tight hug, the physical sensations overwhelming him for a moment. He felt the solidity of Alex's body, the warmth that radiated from him, and the reassuring strength in his embrace. It was a stark contrast to the cold and ferocious battle that had just taken place. Holding Alex close brought an inexplicable sense of comfort and safety.

As Eryx clung to Alex, he couldn't help but let out a shaky breath, his trembling gradually subsiding. It was as if the storm inside him had found a calm center, a respite from the turmoil of the world outside.

Alex's reaction was a mix of surprise and understanding. He didn't hesitate to return the hug, his arms encircling Eryx with a protective assurance. For a moment, their unspoken connection transcended words, conveying more than mere conversation ever could.

Eryx finally pulled back, his cheeks flushed with a mixture of embarrassment and gratitude. "I didn't expect to see you here," he admitted.

Alex offered a small, genuine smile. "You seem to have a knack for finding trouble."

Eryx chuckled, a shaky but genuine sound. "I guess I do." He glanced around at the defeated wolves, his skepticism returning. "But this was a bit more than I bargained for."

Alex's expression grew serious as he surveyed the scene. "We'll need to figure out what brought them here."

They exchanged a few more words, sharing their concern and their relief at finding each other amidst the unexpected chaos. The scent of blood and the echoes of the battle lingering in the air. But their reunion offered a brief respite, a moment of connection amidst the danger.

6

Alex

ALEX STRODE THROUGH THE STREETS of Manhattan, his steps purposeful as he made his way toward the headquarters. The city's morning rush was in full swing, with people rushing to their destinations, lost in the rhythm of daily life. Tall buildings loomed overhead, casting long shadows on the pavement.

His SHD buzzed with an incoming call. He fished the device from his pocket and glanced at the screen.

"Gabe." Alex answered the call, his voice steady and calm amidst the city's chaos.

"Sir, we've got a situation," Gabe's voice was urgent, and Alex's senses immediately went on high alert.

"What's going on?" Alex asked, his footsteps slowing as he listened intently.

"The HIB just got in touch. They want us at the scene," Gabe explained, the gravity of the situation evident in his tone.

Alex halted in his tracks, his eyes narrowing. The HIB, or Human Investigation Bureau, was responsible for dealing with cases involving human crimes. Their involvement signaled that this was no ordinary situation.

"Why? What's going on?" Alex's voice was low and focused, his mind racing through possible scenarios.

"They found a body in a house near Broadway," Gabe replied, his words hanging in the air like an ominous cloud.

The news hit Alex like a lightning bolt. A body. The mere mention raised a red flag, as the cases that required their intervention were typically far from mundane.

"Could it be connected to The Order?" Alex asked, his mind immediately jumping to a troublesome organization they had encountered before.

"We're not sure, sir," Gabe's voice carried uncertainty, a rare sight from the usually composed strategist.

Alex's jaw tightened. The Order, an enigmatic and sinister organization, had caused chaos in the human world for as long as he could remember. Their motives were shrouded in mystery, but one thing was clear: they needed to be stopped.

"We need more details," Alex stated with unwavering determination. "Send me the address, and I'll head over."

"Will do, sir," Gabe affirmed before ending the call.

As the call disconnected, Alex's mind raced with thoughts and concerns. The backdrop of Manhattan seemed to blur as his focus narrowed on the looming investigation.

The Order, a name that sent shivers down the spine of anyone who had encountered them. They were a clandestine organization with a dark history, responsible for numerous incidents that threatened the balance between the human world and the supernatural.

Alex had crossed paths with The Order on more than one occasion, each encounter leaving a mark, both physical and psychological. Their relentless pursuit of power and their willingness to employ any means necessary to achieve their goals made them a formidable adversary.

The thought of a body found near Broadway, potentially connected to The Order, sent a surge of adrenaline coursing through Alex's veins. He couldn't afford to underestimate the situation or the threat it posed to the fragile peace between humans and the supernatural.

His resolve solidified, and he quickened his pace, heading in the direction of the headquarters. The city's chaos served as a stark reminder that danger lurked in the most unexpected places, and it was his duty to confront it head-on.

Upon reaching the headquarters, he wasted no time in gathering the essentials for the upcoming investigation. There was no room for hesitation in the face of a potential threat from The Order.

As he prepared to leave, his SHD buzzed once more. Gabe's message, with the address of the crime scene, flashed on the screen.

He set out toward the scene, ready to confront whatever darkness awaited him and to protect the human world from the malevolent forces that sought to disrupt its fragile peace.

The old, decrepit building stood like a forgotten relic amidst the backdrop of the modern city. Its weathered façade, with paint peeling and windows boarded up, was a stark contrast to the sleek glass skyscrapers that loomed nearby. Alex parked his car and approached the scene, his boots echoing on the cracked pavement.

Officer Cruz, a young and somewhat nervous presence, greeted him at the entrance. Alex, recognizing the officer's unease, tried to soften his usual imposing demeanor. "Officer, what's the situation here?" he asked, his voice low and steady.

"I'll take you to Detective Collins. He can explain everything," the officer replied, gesturing for Alex to follow.

Inside the house, the air was thick with an eerie stillness that contrasted sharply with the bustling city outside. Detective Collins, a disheveled man with salt-and-pepper hair, was bent over the gruesome sight before him.

"Detective," Alex acknowledged as he approached. The detective glanced up, weariness etched into his features. "I'm from Shadowguards. Officer Cruz mentioned you could brief me on the situation."

Alex's expression didn't betray the unease that churned within him as he surveyed the scene. The once clean and beautiful house now reeked of blood, the scent hanging heavy in the air. He took in the gruesome tableau before him—the body mutilated, yet the chest and head eerily intact. It was the work of someone who seemed devoid of humanity.

The detective's voice pulled him back into the grim reality of the crime scene. "She was discovered by her roommate, who called it in. We found her like this."

Alex observed in silence, his thoughts growing darker. He had seen his fair share of horrors, but this scene was a stark reminder of the darkness that lurked in the shadows.

"What else did the roommate mention?" Alex asked, his voice low and measured. "Do we know the victim's name?"

The detective replied, his tone tired but professional. "The roommate said she was dating someone that the roommate didn't approve of. And yes, her name is Rina Lane, twenty-seven years old, a local from Brooklyn."

Alex nodded, his mind already racing with questions. "Have her parents been informed?"

The detective shook his head. "Not yet."

"Is there anything else?" Alex inquired, his gaze sweeping the room. He reached out instinctively to sense magical traces but found an unexpected barrier blocking his abilities. It was as if an invisible wall had been erected, keeping him from accessing his magic.

The detective, sensing Alex's frustration, called over someone who had arrived at the scene—a necromancer, their presence unmistakable.

Alex couldn't help but tense at the sight of the necromancer. In his line of work, he had encountered beings of all kinds, but the presence of a necromancer always stirred a unique unease within him. Their abilities to communicate with the dead often led to unsettling revelations.

Introductions were made with Leo Rodriguez, the Medical Examiner. Alex followed him as they approached the lifeless body, lying cold and motionless on a sterile examination table. The morning light filtered through the blinds, casting long shadows over the scene.

"What can you tell me?" Alex inquired, his voice steady, but his eyes betraying a hint of unease.

Leo adjusted his glasses and leaned in for a closer look at the body. His fingers moved with practiced precision as he examined the pale skin and the curious mark upon it.

Leo revealed a circular symbol on the woman's chest, as if it had been branded deliberately. "The symbol was marked on her, quite intentionally."

As Alex studied the symbol, his heart sank. He recognized it, the Mark of Kronos. A sinister emblem, an embodiment of darkness. It was etched into his memory from past encounters, a mark that signaled a terrifying presence, hinting at the malevolent influence of Kronos and his followers.

The Mark of Kronos, a circle with intricate, intertwining lines, represented an ancient and malevolent force. Its history was steeped in darkness, a symbol of power wielded for sinister purposes. Alex knew that its presence in any situation was a grave cause for concern.

Standing up, Alex approached the detective with a grave expression. "Inform Director Hernandez that Shadowguards will take over this case."

"What? Why? This is our jurisdiction," the detective protested, his brows furrowing in confusion and concern.

"Remember, you requested our assistance. We're here to help," Alex replied, his tone carrying a hint of frustration. He was aware of the delicate balance between local law enforcement and the Shadowguards, but this symbol raised a level of threat that couldn't be ignored.

Curiosity growing, the detective asked, "What did you find?"

Alex hesitated for a moment, deliberating how much information to reveal. He couldn't disclose everything, not yet. "It's not something you need to worry about right now. Please relay my message to Director Hernandez," he stated before turning and making his way towards the exit.

The tension in the room lingered, the unspoken questions weighing heavily on Leo's mind. Alex's departure left a sense of foreboding, a silent promise that the shadows of the past were creeping closer, and that a storm was brewing on the horizon.

Alex couldn't shake the feeling of unease that had settled over him. The Mark of Kronos was a symbol of darkness that he had hoped never to encounter again. It represented a threat that transcended the ordinary, a force that required the unwavering dedication of the Shadowguards to confront.

Inwardly, he wrestled with the decision to involve his team in this dangerous game. But this case, with its ominous mark, had awakened old fears and uncertainties.

He made his way to his car, the morning sun casting long shadows across the pavement, he knew that there was no turning back. The Mark of Kronos had resurfaced, and it was a threat that could not be ignored.

At the Shadowguards Headquarters, the air was tense. Alex wasted no time in calling for a meeting.

Gathered around the long, polished table, Alex laid out all the information he had gathered. His stern expression mirrored the gravity of the situation. "This Mark of Kronos – how can we be sure it's connected to the Order?" Gabe, the team's strategist and witch, inquired, his sharp eyes fixed on the documents spread before him.

"That's what I need you guys to find out," Alex directed.

"But this mark hasn't been seen in their previous activities. Something's changed," Emma pointed out, her brow furrowed with concern.

Alex echoed her thoughts with a deep frown. If the Order was indeed using this symbol now, it indicated a concerning shift in their tactics – a dangerous escalation. "We need to understand why they've adopted this symbol and what it means for their objectives."

Lucas leaned back in his chair, his fingers tapping rhythmically on the table. "I can set up surveillance, track any unusual online chatter or communication that might give us a clue."

Alex nodded in approval. "Good. Keep a close watch on their movements, Lucas."

"I'll reach out to Ms. Lane's parents and inform them about the situation. They deserve to know." Emma said.

"Marcus," Alex turned to Marcus. "Monitor the roommate. We need to know if he's involved or just an unwitting pawn."

Marcus grinned. "You got it, boss."

Olivia leaned forward, her red hair cascading over her shoulders. "I'll dig into the boyfriend's identity. See if there's any connection there."

The Order's newfound tactics were a worrying sign. They had faced this enemy countless times, but this shift hinted at something darker, something more sinister than they had ever encountered before.

The room itself had an air of sophistication, with its high-tech screens displaying maps and data, but it couldn't conceal the tension that filled the space.

Gabe, always the strategist, looked lost in thought as he analyzed the information before him. Lucas, with his tech expertise, was already mentally mapping out the surveillance plan. Emma's concern for the victim's family weighed heavily on her, a burden she carried willingly.

Alex couldn't shake the feeling that they were on the brink of something dangerous. The Mark of Kronos was a dark omen, a symbol that hinted at a sinister agenda.

* * *

After his eventful day, all Alex could think about was seeing the person who had turned his world upside down.

He found himself staking out near Eryx's house. Thanks to Marcus' impressive information-gathering skills, he had managed to locate Eryx's residence. The setting sun bathed the neighborhood in a soft, dusky light as Alex watched from a discreet vantage point.

Alex scanned the area for any unusual magical signatures, his senses attuned to the supernatural currents that flowed through the world. But nothing caught his attention. Still, he remained cautious. The protective spells surrounding the house were potent, radiating a sense of ancient magic that even gods would struggle to breach.

Admittedly, he felt a bit like a stalker, but he couldn't bring himself to care. His focus was solely on Eryx. Eryx had stirred something within him, something he couldn't quite explain.

Finally, after what felt like an eternity, he spotted Eryx walking down the quiet street toward his house. Carrying bags of groceries in one hand and a sleek bow slung over his shoulder, Eryx had an air of nonchalance about him, as if the world were merely a stage for his own amusement.

Just as Eryx was approaching his house, something strange happened. Eryx froze in his tracks, his body tensing as if caught in an invisible web. Alex's heart raced, and he cursed inwardly. His supernatural senses strained to detect anything amiss, but he found nothing, no magical interference, no hidden threats.

Eryx stood there, bags of groceries suspended mid-air, his features etched with a mixture of surprise and confusion. It was a scene that defied explanation, and it sent a chill down Alex's spine. The atmosphere had shifted from one of quiet anticipation to a tense and eerie stillness.

Alex watched, hidden in the shadows, his mind and heart racing.

As seconds stretched into minutes, Eryx's bewilderment

deepened, and he attempted to move again, but it was as if an invisible force held him in place.

Suddenly, a wolf emerged from the darkness, its predatory instincts keen. Adrenaline surged through Alex's veins as he watched in astonishment, puzzled at how he hadn't sensed the wolf's presence until now. His heart raced, and he instinctively reached for the hidden well of magic within him.

Alex's breath caught in his throat as Eryx sprang into action. Eryx drew his bow with an almost fluid grace, his movements a testament to his combat skills honed through countless trials. In a split second, an arrow was nocked, aimed, and released, flying true and striking the wolf square in the chest.

The wolf yelped, its fur bristling with pain, but it wasn't alone. Others of its pack closed in on Eryx, teeth bared and eyes gleaming with feral hunger. The wind seemed to rush past them, carrying the wild scent of the approaching pack.

Alex extended his hands, and tendrils of dark energy erupted from his palms. The magical tendrils coiled around the remaining three wolves, their movements swift and precise, weaving a complex pattern in the air. These tendrils, dark as the midnight sky, glimmered with an eerie light.

As the wolves lunged, the magical tendrils ensnared them in a web of pulsating energy. They thrashed and struggled, but the tendrils held them fast. Alex's eyes blazed with an intensity that matched the dangerous situation they were in.

Alex channeled a surge of magic through the tendrils. The energy flowed into the wolves, not with the intent to harm, but to lull them into a deep, sleep-like state. The wolves' struggles grew weaker with each passing second, their eyelids drooping until they collapsed, unconscious and immobilized.

After the immediate danger was dealt with, Eryx turned to look at Alex, surprise evident in his expressive eyes. Alex couldn't help but admire the way Eryx had handled the situation with quick thinking and precision.

"Are you alright?" Alex's concern was genuine, his voice softening as he took in Eryx's still-rapid breaths and the lingering tremor in his hands.

Eryx managed to stammer out a response, his relief palpable. "Y-Yeah. Thank you."

Alex didn't expect the hug that Eryx gave him, but he welcomed it, the physical contact a reassurance that they were both unharmed. They separated, their gazes locking for a moment, an unspoken understanding passing between them.

"Come on," Alex said, taking the lead, "let's get you inside." He helped Eryx carry his bags, their steps synchronized as they moved with a newfound camaraderie.

They entered Eryx's cozy house, and the tension from the encounter outside slowly ebbed away. The living room was warm and inviting, a stark contrast to the chilling encounter they had just faced. Eryx disappeared into his room to stow away his bow.

Alex took the opportunity to call Marcus and Gabe, relaying the situation. "Bring in the four shifters," he instructed them, his voice steady but laced with a sense of caution.

Once he ended the call, he returned to the kitchen where Eryx was waiting. The bags were placed neatly by the door, a silent reminder of the events that had transpired.

Eryx leaned against the kitchen counter, his expression a mix of gratitude and curiosity. "I didn't know you had those kinds of powers," he admitted, his tone tinged with awe.

Alex shrugged. "It's not something I talk about much."

"You saved me again." Eryx said softly.

Alex smiled at Eryx fondly.

The evening had taken an unexpected turn, their bond growing stronger through the shared danger and relief.

Alex felt a slight tug on his jeans and glanced down to find an orange cat playfully scratching his leg. Without hesitation, he scooped up the furry troublemaker, and it rewarded him with an affectionate lick on the cheek.

"What's your name, you cute troublemaker?" Alex grinned, addressing the feline in his arms.

"That's Mr. Whiskers. My friend Ari gave her to me yesterday after he got in her apartment."

Setting Mr. Whiskers down gently, Eryx grabbed a fresh bag of cat food and poured a generous portion into a waiting bowl.

Alex couldn't help but feel a swell of fondness for Eryx as he watched him care for the cat.

"Are you really okay?" Alex asked.

Eryx ran a hand through his unruly hair, and Alex had to fight the urge to step closer and help him tame the wild locks. His heart raced at the mere thought, and he couldn't deny the attraction he felt for Eryx. It was a dangerous territory, one he had been tiptoeing around for too long.

Eryx's smirk faded, revealing a vulnerability that Alex rarely saw. "Yeah, I'm fine. Just life being a pain in the ass, you know?"

Alex nodded, understanding all too well the struggles that came with life's ups and downs. He wished he could be the one to ease Eryx's burdens, but their complicated history made it challenging to bridge the gap between them.

As Eryx continued to feed Mr. Whiskers, Alex couldn't help but admire the way his fingers moved with gentle care. It was a side of Eryx that few had the privilege to witness, and Alex cherished the moments when he could see it.

He had been drawn to Eryx from the moment they met, his stoic exterior melting away in the face of Eryx's snarky charm.

Eryx glanced up, meeting Alex's gaze with an intensity that sent shivers down his spine. "You know, Alex, you've got this way of making even the most mundane moments interesting."

Alex chuckled, a hint of color tinging his cheeks. "It's a talent, I suppose."

Eryx set the now-empty cat food bag aside and leaned in closer, their proximity sending a jolt of electricity through the air. "You should come by more often. Mr. Whiskers seems to like you."

Alex's heart skipped a beat at the invitation. He knew there was more to Eryx's words than met the eye.

"I'd like that," Alex replied, his voice low and filled with sincerity. "And who knows, maybe Mr. Whiskers will teach me a thing or two about causing trouble."

Eryx's laughter rang through the kitchen, a sound that warmed Alex's heart. It was moments like these that made him believe there was something worth exploring between them.

Eryx leaned against the kitchen counter, his fingers idly tapping on the marble surface as he sighed. "Man, my week hasn't been going well," he muttered, his voice tinged with bitterness.

Alex, standing nearby, turned his attention toward Eryx, concern etched across his usually stoic face. "What's bothering you?"

Eryx shook his head, his vibrant blue eyes clouded with worry. "It's been a strange week for me. First, the club situation, then the venue, and now this?" He couldn't help but shake his head in disbelief.

Alex's expression turned serious as he stepped closer. "What happened at the club?" His voice was low and steady, a soothing presence amidst the chaos that seemed to surround Eryx.

Eryx looked up at him, his gaze almost pleading. "Can we just forget I mentioned that?" He wanted to put it all behind him, to move on and not dwell on the unsettling memories.

Alex, however, wasn't willing to let it go. His voice remained gentle but firm. "I can't do that, Eryx. Please, go on."

Eryx sighed, a mixture of reluctance and resignation in his eyes. "Why would you even care? We don't even know each other."

"Just tell me," Alex insisted, his determination unwavering.

"Okay, fine," Eryx exhaled, his voice tinged with hesitation. "I don't know why I'm saying this, but here goes. I was in the restroom, and out of nowhere, this guy grabbed me without my permission. I managed to fight him off, and weirdly enough, I was strong enough to smash the bathroom wall and mirror."

Alex's frustration simmered beneath his calm exterior as he processed the information. "Did you recognize that man?"

Eryx shook his head, his expression a mix of frustration and confusion. "No, he was a complete stranger."

The weight of the situation hung in the air, the silence heavy with unspoken questions. Alex couldn't help but pry further. "Why were you even at the club?"

Eryx's response was distant as he walked to a nearby drawer, retrieving a bottle of pills. "Does it really matter?"

Alex watched him closely, his concern deepening. "What's that for?"

Eryx hesitated for a moment before answering. "I take them to help me sleep better." Alex decided not to push further on this topic. "By the way, what brings you here?"

"I was nearby," Alex replied, attempting to keep things light. "Your archery skills were quite impressive, by the way. Have you been practicing for long?"

Eryx's eyes brightened, and he leaned against the counter, a playful grin tugging at his lips. "No, just a few months. My instructor insists I have a knack for it."

Alex found himself smiling in return, the tension of the previous conversation momentarily forgotten. "You were fantastic. I haven't seen someone handle a bow that skillfully in a while."

Eryx's gaze held a hint of mystery, and he couldn't resist dropping a teasing hint. "There's a bit of a backstory there."

"There was." Alex said as he thought of Apollo.

Their gazes locked, a connection forming between them that transcended the ordinary. In that moment, as their smiles lingered, a spark of something unspoken passed between them, a shared understanding of the complexities that life could throw their way.

The ring of his SHD broke the moment, jolting Alex from his cozy cocoon of emotions. He checked the message quickly, confirming that the shifters were now in custody. Duty beckoned, and he reluctantly withdrew from Eryx's comforting presence.

"I have to go," he said to Eryx, his voice tinged with regret.

Eryx's sassy smile danced on his lips. "Okay."

Eryx led him to the door, their footsteps echoing softly in the corridor. Before he could step out, Alex turned back, his heart pounding with a mix of longing and vulnerability. He gently held Eryx's cheeks, their faces inches apart, and gazed into his beautiful eyes, like pools of endless depth.

"Would you like to have dinner with me tomorrow?" Alex's longing was clear in his earnest tone.

Eryx's smile, warm and inviting, crept back onto his face. "Are you asking me out?"

Alex felt a touch of embarrassment color his cheeks. "If not, that's perfectly fine."

Eryx's laughter, a soft melody in the evening air, brushed against Alex's skin. "You're quite the silly man. Of course, I'd love to."

He leaned in, and their lips met in a gentle kiss on Alex's cheek. The softness of Eryx's skin against his, the warmth of their breath mingling, sent a shiver down Alex's spine. It was a simple gesture, but it held the promise of something more.

"Goodnight," Eryx whispered, their noses brushing against each other.

Finally, Alex felt a sense of relief wash over him. "Goodnight."

He left Eryx's house with a smile on his face, his heart lighter than it had been in a long time. The night seemed brighter, the stars above winking conspiratorially as if celebrating this small but meaningful step in his life.

As he drove away, his thoughts swirled with anticipation for their dinner date. He couldn't help but wonder what the evening would bring, what new conversations and emotions would bloom between them. Alex was no stranger to danger and intrigue, but this felt like a different kind of adventure, one that stirred his heart in a way he hadn't expected.

7

Eryx

ERYX LOUNGED IN THE COZY CORNER of his sunlit kitchen, his fingers wrapped around a steaming mug of coffee. The soft hum of morning traffic filtered through the open window, mixing with the scent of freshly brewed java that enveloped him like a warm embrace. It was his favorite time of the day, a moment of solace before the world woke up.

"Hey, Sam, what's up?" he answered Sam's call, taking a sip from his coffee with a relaxed sigh.

"Richard Lane was asking for you," Sam's voice cut through the tranquil morning, instantly jolting Eryx from his caffeine-induced reverie. He nearly spluttered his coffee across the table but managed to set the mug down with grace.

"Why does he want to see me?" Eryx questioned, eyebrows raised in curiosity as he leaned forward, his interest piqued.

"He didn't say, just mentioned he wanted you to visit his studio in the city."

Eryx considered this for a moment, his mind whirling with possibilities. Richard Lane, a name he hadn't heard in a while, was a renowned artist with a reputation for eccentricity. Whatever this meeting was about, it promised to be anything but ordinary.

"Alright, send me the address," Eryx requested, a hint of anticipation in his voice. He was always up for an intriguing twist in his routine.

The message with the address came through, and Eryx glanced at it on his phone's screen. "Thanks, Sam. Take care."

"You too," Sam replied before they hung up.

As Eryx leaned back in his chair, he couldn't help but smile. The day had taken an unexpected turn, and he relished the thought of the adventure that lay ahead. With a decisive nod, he got up, leaving his half-empty coffee mug behind, and began the process of getting ready for the trip to Richard Lane's studio.

With each step, the excitement built within him. He wondered what could have prompted the artist to reach out to him after all these years.

His morning routine was a whirlwind of activity, a mixture of selecting the right outfit to make a statement without appearing too eager, and practicing his nonchalant expression in front of the mirror. As he tied his shoelaces, he couldn't help but think about the possibilities that awaited him at Richard Lane's studio.

Eryx took a few extra moments to ensure that everything was well-arranged in his house. He meticulously checked each window, making sure they were all firmly closed to prevent Mr. Whiskers from escaping. The fluffy feline was currently perched on a sunlit windowsill, his tail swaying like a playful metronome as he pawed at a dangling string.

Eryx had heard of Richard's music, and it had left an

impression on him. The melodies seemed to carry emotions he couldn't quite put into words, resonating with something deep within him. He had often found himself lost in the hauntingly beautiful tunes, wondering about the person behind the music.

Standing in his living room, he stole a glance at the clock and realized it was time to head out. After giving Mr. Whiskers a final pat on the head, Eryx left the house. The anticipation of meeting Richard Lane stirred a mixture of excitement and nervousness within him. He hadn't spoken to Richard yet, but there was something about this meeting that felt significant, like the beginning of an unexpected journey.

Eryx kept glancing at the address on his phone, ensuring he was heading in the right direction. The city's bustle and the cacophony of street sounds seemed to match the rapid rhythm of his heart. It was moments like these that made life interesting, and Eryx was determined to embrace whatever awaited him with open arms.

Finally, he arrived at the studio, an unassuming building nestled among the hustle and bustle of the city.

Eryx stepped into Richard Lane's studio, feeling a strange mix of excitement and nerves. He was greeted by a woman who seemed to exude a sense of calm and professionalism, a sharp contrast to the whirlwind of emotions inside him.

"Hi, I'm here for Richard Lane," Eryx announced, his voice carrying a hint of uncertainty.

The woman smiled warmly. "Oh, you must be Mr. Eryx Ross. Yes, come this way."

Following her through the maze of corridors and sound-proof doors, Eryx arrived at a recording booth. The woman gestured toward the entrance and then left, leaving him alone in the room.

Eryx took a moment to absorb his surroundings. The studio was a musician's dream, equipped with an array of instruments, a mixing console that looked like it belonged on a spaceship, and soundproofing that could probably withstand a hurricane. It was a wonderland for someone like him, but also a little overwhelming.

After a deep breath, he knocked on the door that led to the control room, where Richard was presumably waiting. It swung open smoothly, revealing the man himself, Richard Lane. Eryx couldn't help but be captivated by the sight of him. Richard had wavy brown hair that looked like it had a mind of its own, and his dark eyes held a comforting warmth that put anyone at ease.

"Eryx?" Richard's voice pulled Eryx from his thoughts.

"Mr. Lane," Eryx replied formally, his nervousness showing through.

"Please, call me Richard. Mr. Lane is my dad," Richard teased, motioning for Eryx to come in. "Come on in."

Eryx stepped inside, his curiosity piqued. "So, why did you want to see me, Richard?"

Richard's gaze lingered on Eryx for a moment, a thoughtful expression crossing his features before he finally spoke. "Hmm, interesting."

Eryx furrowed his brow, puzzled. "What's interesting?"

"Your aura," Richard said cryptically, leaving Eryx feeling like he'd missed something important. "My mom was skilled in reading auras; it seems I inherited that from her."

Eryx didn't quite grasp the concept. "I'm not sure I understand."

"Sorry if I read you without permission," Richard apologized, his tone genuinely contrite. "I didn't mean to invade your space."

Eryx shook his head, his nerves starting to ease. "No problem, I just wasn't prepared for it."

Richard grinned. "I guess I left you speechless, huh?"

Eryx chuckled, finding himself drawn to Richard's easygoing demeanor. "Are you always like this?"

"Pretty much. What you see is what you get," Richard replied with a shrug. "Now, let's get to the reason I called you here. Grab a guitar, and let's record."

Eryx was taken aback. "Wait, you want me to record a song?"

"Yes, and if it's good, I'll feature it in my next album. Are you up for the challenge?" Richard's eyes sparkled with anticipation.

Eryx felt a mix of surprise and nervousness. "Um, sure."

Richard's grin widened. "Great, let's see what you've got then."

Eryx took a moment to gather his thoughts and emotions. This meeting with Richard Lane was turning out to be quite different from what he had expected. As he picked up a guitar and began to strum a few chords.

"What song should I sing?" Eryx asked, his voice tinged with a hint of nervousness as he sat in the recording studio.

Richard leaned back in his chair. "Sing whatever you feel like. Actually, why not make up a song on the spot?" he suggested, a playful glint in his eyes.

Eryx arched an eyebrow, his snarky side surfacing. "Is this some kind of test?" he inquired, a touch of uncertainty in his voice.

Richard shook his head. "No, I'm just curious to hear your

voice."

With a sigh, Eryx conceded, "Alright." He closed his eyes, taking a moment to gather himself. He started singing, creating a song on the spot, but as he went on, he sensed something wasn't quite right with what he was producing. Doubt crept in like an unwelcome guest at a party.

After a few attempts, self-doubt began to creep in. "I don't think I can do this, Richard," Eryx confessed.

Richard, ever patient and composed, leaned forward, his expression reassuring. "Okay, if you're open to it, I can offer some help."

"Yeah, sure. Can't hurt," Eryx replied, feeling the weight of the opportunity before him. He wanted to make the most of it and not mess things up.

"Close your eyes and take a deep breath," Richard instructed, his voice as smooth as silk.

Eryx followed his guidance, closing his eyes and inhaling deeply. The room, filled with the soft hum of recording equipment, carried the scent of polished wood and old records. The play of light and shadow danced around him.

"Good. Now, feel the music within you. Focus on the vibrations in your body," Richard continued, his words a soothing melody.

Eryx wasn't sure how this approach would help, but he gave it a try. And then, unexpectedly, he felt it – a gentle touch, as if someone had clasped his hand reassuringly. It was like a secret connection to the music he had never experienced before.

"Now, sing, Eryx," Richard's voice encouraged, his words as warm as the morning sun.

Eryx began to sing, allowing the newfound connection he

felt to guide his voice. The melody flowed naturally, like a river finding its course, and the lyrics tumbled from his lips effortlessly. It was as if the song had been waiting within him, begging to be set free.

"Open your eyes," Richard directed, his eyes sparkling with genuine excitement.

Eryx obeyed, looking at Richard with a mix of hope and uncertainty. "Did I do it?"

Richard's smile was warm, like a fond memory. "More than did it. You were incredible. Your aura wasn't wrong. I'm really looking forward to performing with you."

"Thank you," Eryx's gratitude was evident in his voice, and he couldn't help but feel a surge of pride at the accomplishment.

They recorded a few more times, fine-tuning the song, before bidding their farewells. As Eryx left the recording studio, he couldn't help but reflect on the unexpected break-through. The touch he had felt, the connection to the music, was a revelation. It was a reminder that sometimes, the best performances came from within, guided by the heart and soul.

He had a newfound confidence, a belief in his own abilities, and a mentor in Richard Lane who saw potential in him. As he stepped out into the morning sun, he couldn't wait to see where this musical journey would take him next.

* * *

Eryx had plans to meet up with Ari, and the excitement was bubbling inside him. The fact that he had actually recorded with Richard still felt surreal. He couldn't believe his luck.

He knew Ari would be over the moon when she found out.

They had arranged to meet at a shopping center near Ari's place in Brooklyn. Eryx stood outside, checking his phone and occasionally glancing up. He eventually spotted Ari's familiar figure. When she finally darted toward him, her excitement evident, he couldn't help but break into a grin. He welcomed her with a warm hug, and their laughter filled the air.

Ari playfully pushed him away and quirked an eyebrow. "So, what's the big emergency?"

Eryx scratched the back of his neck nervously. "I kinda have a date tonight."

Ari's joyful expression intensified, her eyes sparkling with delight. "Finally! Who's the lucky guy?"

Eryx couldn't help but chuckle at her enthusiasm. "You remember the guy from the venue? The really handsome one who came to my rescue?"

Ari nodded, her curiosity piqued. "Yeah?"

"It's him," Eryx confirmed with a hint of excitement in his voice. "His name's Alex."

Ari's smile widened, but there was a trace of caution in her eyes. "Are you absolutely certain?"

Eryx raised an eyebrow. "Yeah, I'm sure. Why? Do you know something about him?"

Ari paused for a moment, choosing her words carefully. "Sort of, but it's a long story."

Eryx's concern showed as he furrowed his brows. "Should I be worried about something?"

Ari chuckled, shaking her head. "No, it's not like that. Just… I'm genuinely happy for you. He's a really good guy."

Eryx sensed an underlying hesitation and couldn't resist

prodding further. "I sense a 'but' in there."

Ari playfully rolled her eyes, a signature move. "Oh, come on. Let's find you some new clothes."

With that, Ari pulled Eryx inside the shopping center. The atmosphere was a bustling blend of colors and sounds, an eclectic mix of styles and personalities. The crowd swirled around them, each person lost in their own world of fashion and shopping.

Ari led the way, her confident stride guiding Eryx through the maze of clothing racks. She couldn't help but tease him as she browsed through a rack of button-down shirts. "So, Alex, huh? Guess it's time for a wardrobe upgrade."

Eryx smirked and retorted, "Oh, please. Like I'd let a hot guy like him see me in this old junk."

Ari chuckled and plucked a shirt from the rack, holding it up to him. "How about this one? It's a classic, and it'll make your eyes pop."

Eryx examined the shirt, a deep blue that seemed to match the color of his eyes. "Not bad, Ari. You might have some fashion sense after all."

Ari feigned offense, placing a hand over her heart. "Why, Eryx, you wound me."

As they continued shopping, Ari shared more about her knowledge of Alex. "So, Alex is actually a pretty decent guy. He's got this stoic thing going on, but deep down, he's a softie. He's loyal to a fault and takes his responsibilities seriously."

Eryx raised an eyebrow, intrigued by her insights. "Sounds like you know him better than you let on."

Ari winked and said, "Well, you know me, I know everyone."

Eryx's heart warmed at her words. "Thanks, Ari. You're the best."

They moved on to select various clothing items that Ari thought would suit him. The shopping montage was a whirlwind of colors, fabrics, and styles. Eryx tried on outfits he wouldn't have considered before, and Ari's laughter and playful commentary made the experience enjoyable.

Ari held up a leather jacket for him to inspect. "How about this? You'll look like a rockstar."

Eryx smirked as he tried it on. "I can get used to this."

Their camaraderie was evident as they continued their shopping spree. Eryx couldn't help but feel grateful for Ari's support and guidance. The upcoming date with Alex was a significant step for him, and he knew he wouldn't have made it this far without his sassy, snarky, and caring friend by his side.

As they shopped, Eryx couldn't help but wonder about Ari's connection to Alex. However, he pushed those thoughts aside for now.

As they left the shopping center with bags filled with new clothes, Eryx couldn't contain his excitement. The date with Alex was just around the corner, and with Ari's help, he felt more ready than ever to take on whatever the night had in store for him.

Evening descended upon Eryx's cozy house, and a flutter of excitement mixed with nervousness danced in his chest. He had no idea what Alex had in store for their date, and it left him feeling a tad anxious. He'd picked out an outfit earlier in the day, and now, standing before the mirror, he took a moment to appreciate his own reflection.

Eryx had taken extra care in choosing his attire, wanting to strike the perfect balance between making a good impression and feeling comfortable. He slid into a deep blue shirt that complemented his olive complexion. Each button he fastened felt like a tiny victory, and he decided to leave a couple undone, aiming for a blend of casual and enticing.

The sleeves of his shirt were rolled up neatly, showing a glimpse of his wrists and adding a hint of nonchalant charm. A pair of well-fitted jeans clung to his legs, the denim a comforting choice that paired harmoniously with his blue shirt, creating a pleasing contrast.

As he ran his fingers through his hair, he contemplated whether to apply some styling product for that "effortlessly cool" look. Eventually, he settled on a slightly tousled appearance, exuding an air of easygoing confidence. Mr. Whiskers meowed as if giving his approval. Eryx grinned and scooped the cat into his arms.

"Do I look okay, Mr. Whiskers? Ready for a night out?" he asked playfully. Mr. Whiskers responded with another meow, and Eryx chuckled. "I'll take that as a yes. You be good while I'm out, alright?"

Mr. Whiskers affectionately licked Eryx's cheek before he gently set the cat down and headed toward the door. Just as he was about to reach for the handle, a knock sounded on the other side.

As Eryx swung open the door to his home, his eyes widened at the sight of Alex standing before him. A rush of emotions swept through him, a mixture of surprise and warmth. Alex's snug sweatshirt clung to his frame, highlighting muscles that Eryx hadn't seen in quite this way before. In his hand, Alex held a bunch of vibrant flowers, a sweet and thoughtful gesture that tugged at Eryx's heart.

A smile curved Eryx's lips as he took in the unexpected sight. He felt a connection forming, a simple yet impactful moment that made his heart race a bit faster. He couldn't help but be captivated by Alex's appearance and the flowers. It was a delightful combination.

"Hey," Eryx greeted with a warm smile, stepping aside to let Alex enter.

"Hi, Eryx. You look amazing," Alex replied, his eyes filled with sincerity.

Eryx couldn't help but blush a little at the compliment. "Thanks, come on in."

Alex stepped inside, his presence filling Eryx's home with a sense of warmth. Eryx couldn't ignore the flowers any longer and couldn't stop himself from asking, "Are those for me?"

Alex grinned, a twinkle in his eye, as he extended the bouquet toward Eryx. "Yeah, they're for you. Hope they're okay."

Eryx took the flowers gently, appreciating the vibrant colors and the delicate fragrance that enveloped them. "They're beautiful, thanks."

With care, he placed the flowers in a vase filled with water, making sure they would stay fresh. It was a simple act, but it felt meaningful and cherished.

"Ready to go?" Alex asked, his voice tinged with excitement.

Eryx turned to face Alex, his curiosity piqued. "Where are we headed?"

A grin played on Alex's lips as he revealed their destination. "I reserved a table at an Italian restaurant in Manhattan."

Eryx's smile widened at the thought of Italian cuisine. "Sounds good. Let's not wait then. Ready?"

Before they left, Eryx slipped into leather jacket that hung conveniently by the door. The jacket was a statement piece, black and stylish, adding a hint of edge to his ensemble. Its snug fit accentuated his frame, and he felt a surge of self-assuredness as he zipped it up.

As they prepared to depart, Eryx took Alex's hand in his own. It was a simple gesture, but it conveyed a connection, a spark of something meaningful. Alex's eyes met his, and they shared a moment of understanding and anticipation.

With the warmth of the flowers filling the room and the excitement of the evening ahead, Eryx and Alex headed to Alex's car, ready for an evening that promised new memories and the potential for something more. The city awaited them, and as they embarked on this date.

8

Alex

ALEX COULDN'T HELP BUT FEEL a mix of anticipation and nervousness as he stood in front of Eryx's door. It had been a while since he'd been on a date, and he wasn't entirely sure he remembered how it worked.

His responsibilities as the king of the underworld had kept him occupied, but tonight was different. He was going on a date with Eryx, and that alone was enough to make him slightly jittery.

When the door swung open, revealing Eryx in all his glory, Alex's nerves seemed to dissipate. Eryx looked fantastic, and for a moment, Alex entertained the thought of skipping the restaurant and going straight to dessert. But he quickly reigned in his impulses. Politeness came first.

The car ride to the restaurant was surprisingly calm. Both men seemed a bit nervous, and the air in the car was thick with the anticipation of the date. Alex stole glances at Eryx, who appeared a tad more self-assured than he felt. It was as if Eryx's presence had temporarily suspended his usual responsibilities, allowing him to just be Alex.

"So, Eryx," Alex began, trying to ease the tension with conversation, "what have you been up to lately? Anything interesting?"

Eryx flashed a mischievous grin. "Oh, you know, the usual. Stirring up trouble, causing mayhem, and charming my way out of it."

Alex chuckled. Eryx's nonchalant demeanor was a stark contrast to his own seriousness. "I can imagine you're quite skilled at charming your way out of things."

Eryx raised an eyebrow. "Are you saying I'm a trouble-maker?"

The question hung in the air for a moment, and then they both burst into laughter. It was a good sign, a shared moment of humor that helped ease their nerves.

As they neared the restaurant, the excitement in Alex's chest grew. The night felt like an adventure, a chance to explore something new and unexpected. They arrived at the restaurant right on schedule, greeted by a friendly waitress who exuded a sense of warmth and familiarity. Alex sensed that she was a wolf shifter, another reminder of the supernatural world they inhabited.

"Welcome to Le Lune," the waitress said with a warm smile. "My name is Luna. I'll be taking care of you tonight. Follow me."

They were guided to an outdoor table with a fantastic view of the New York City skyline.

The city lights turned the night into a starry tapestry woven into the urban fabric. Skyscrapers reached for the sky, lit windows creating a sparkling mosaic against the dark backdrop. Every building pulsed with life, reflecting the city's ceaseless energy and the dreams it held. Streetlights cast a warm, amber glow on the bustling streets, offering a comforting ambiance below.

From their high vantage point, the flow of traffic resembled a river of light, an ever-playing visual symphony. A gentle breeze carried the city's sounds – distant laughter, occasional sirens, and the steady rhythm of footsteps and conversations. It was an urban symphony, a blend of diverse experiences converging in this vibrant hub.

Alex sat across from Eryx , a soft smile playing on his lips as he watched Eryx's eyes light up with delight.

"Alex, this is incredible! Thank you!" Eryx beamed after a while, his enthusiasm contagious.

"This happens to be my favorite Italian spot in the city. I thought you'd like it too," Alex responded, his heart warming at the sight of Eryx's smile.

Eryx leaned back in his chair, his gaze fixed on the city lights twinkling in the distance. "The view is absolutely breathtaking."

"Yes, it is," Alex agreed, but his eyes remained fixed on Eryx. He couldn't help but feel a warmth spreading through him, a connection that went beyond the stunning cityscape.

Eryx turned to him, and Alex noticed a faint blush coloring his cheeks. It was endearing, and it made Alex's heart skip a beat.

Taking a deep breath, Alex gently reached for Eryx's hand, their fingers naturally intertwining. The emotions that surged within him were overwhelming; this man had a way of stirring feelings he hadn't experienced in a while.

Eryx's voice shifted the focus, providing a welcome distraction from Alex's increasingly tight pants. "So, what do you do?"

"I work for the Shadowguards," Alex answered.

"What's that?" Eryx inquired with curiosity, his eyes never leaving Alex's.

Alex couldn't help but feel a sense of relief at Eryx's genuine interest. "We're an organization that keeps both humans and supernaturals safe from rogues."

"Hmm, what's your role in it?"

"I co-own it with my partner Lily. She's currently in Washington, working on expanding Shadowguards and building alliances."

Alex and Lily thought that expanding their organization was crucial to ensure broader safety and protection. The increasing threats from supernatural forces demanded a stronger presence, and reaching out to potential allies could provide more resources and manpower. Lily's efforts in Washington aimed to forge alliances with other organizations that shared similar goals, enhancing their collective ability to combat supernatural threats effectively. This expansion would create a network of support, enabling them to tackle challenges that might be beyond their individual capacities.

"That sounds incredibly demanding. I struggle with daily tasks, and you're out there saving the world," Eryx confessed, his eyes sparkling with admiration.

Alex chuckled, unable to resist the charm in Eryx's words. "Just wait until you have a team of your own driving you up the wall with their antics."

Eryx's smile was infectious. "I'd love to meet them someday. They sound like a lively bunch."

With a tender squeeze, Alex reassured Eryx. "Really? You'd be okay with that?"

"Sure, it'd be nice to get to know your friends. Is that moving too fast, though? I sometimes struggle with how quickly things should progress," Eryx admitted, his uncertainty palpable.

"Of course not. In fact, why don't you drop by our headquarters tomorrow at lunch? I can introduce you," Alex suggested, his heart fluttering with hope.

"Seriously? That sounds great. I've been wanting to thank them for what they did at the venue. They cleaned everything up so quickly."

As they continued to talk and share their thoughts and dreams, Alex couldn't help but feel a sense of wonder. The man before him had a magnetic pull that was hard to resist. Alex couldn't help but think that Eryx might just be the best thing that had happened to him in a long time.

After a while, the waitress returned to take their orders. They both chose pasta and steaks, the menu offering a mix of flavors that seemed just right for the evening.

"How about you? What do you do?" Alex asked once they were alone again, his gaze gentle and inviting.

Eryx leaned back in his chair, a playful glint in his eyes. "As you already know, I'm a musician. You might have heard some of my songs, or maybe not. Either way, no judgment." He spoke with a hint of sass, as if daring Alex to admit he was a fan.

Alex couldn't help but smile. He had indeed heard and loved every one of Eryx's songs. "And, um, I also knit and sell my creations online."

"Wait, what? You knit?" Alex repeated, genuine surprise in his voice. Eryx's cheeks flushed, and he fidgeted with his napkin.

"Yeah, I know it might sound a bit uncool, but I enjoy it," Eryx shrugged, his tone carrying a hint of self-deprecation.

Alex quickly reassured him, his eyes warm. "I didn't mean it that way. I just find it really charming."

Eryx chuckled, the tension in his shoulders easing. "Yeah, sure."

Changing the subject, Alex asked, "So, how about your parents? If it's too much to talk about, you don't have to."

Eryx paused, his gaze momentarily distant as if lost in thought. "It's alright. They passed away shortly after I turned twenty-one."

Alex mentally scolded himself for bringing up such a sensitive topic, but he couldn't help but be curious about Eryx's past. "I'm sorry," he quickly apologized. "I didn't mean to bring up painful memories."

Eryx gave Alex's hand a gentle squeeze, managing a soft smile. "It's been almost ten years. I should be okay."

Curious, Alex leaned in a little closer. "Did you know what happened?"

Eryx took a deep breath, his eyes reflecting the gravity of his words. "Yeah. A drunk driver fell asleep at the wheel and crashed into them. They were on their way back from watching a gig I was performing at."

Alex's heart ached for Eryx. He wished he could somehow take away his pain. "They must have loved you so much," he said softly.

Eryx nodded, his eyes shimmering with a mix of sadness and fondness. "They did. I still miss them sometimes."

Alex offered a small comfort, his voice gentle. "The best way to honor them is to live a life that makes them proud, no matter where they are."

"Thank you," Eryx said, his smile returning. Alex hoped he hadn't said anything to make things worse.

As their conversation continued, the restaurant's cozy ambiance wrapped around them like a warm embrace. The dim lighting created an intimate setting, softening their features and allowing them to connect on a deeper level.

Eryx's music became a topic of discussion, and he leaned in, his eyes sparkling with mischief, and shared stories about his songwriting process. "You know, there's this one song," he began, "called 'Midnight Whispers.' It was inspired by a night I spent in Paris, wandering the cobblestone streets under a full moon."

Alex was drawn in immediately, his usually stoic expression replaced by rapt attention. "Tell me more," he encouraged, his voice gentle.

Eryx grinned, his lips curling into that sassy smile that Alex couldn't resist. "Well, it was a night filled with secrets, you see. The city was alive with whispers and mysteries. I sat on a bench by the Seine River, and the melody just came to me. It's about love, longing, and the magic of the night."

As Eryx spoke, Alex could almost hear the soft strains of the melody in his mind, a haunting and beautiful tune that painted a vivid picture of that Parisian night. It was as if he had been transported there, feeling the cool breeze on his skin and the weight of the world's secrets in the air.

Eryx's storytelling continued, each song carrying its own unique tale. He spoke of a song inspired by a childhood memory of chasing fireflies in the summer twilight, another born from the pain of a heartbreak that had left him shattered but stronger.

With each story, Eryx's passion for his craft shone through, his voice a melodic journey through his experiences and emotions. He described the sensation of standing on stage, the lights washing over him, and the electric connection with the audience.

"When I'm up there," he confessed, "it's like I can feel every heartbeat in the room. The energy is palpable, and for those few minutes, we're all connected through music."

Alex couldn't help but be captivated, not just by Eryx's words but by the depth of emotion in his eyes. It was clear that music was more than a career for him; it was his soul laid bare for the world to see.

As Eryx continued to share, Alex felt a growing connection between them. Eryx's openness and vulnerability drew him in, and he found himself sharing his own thoughts and experiences in return. It was as though they were forging a deeper connection, one that went beyond mere attraction.

Their conversation flowed effortlessly, punctuated by shared laughter and subtle flirting. Eryx's snarky humor blended seamlessly with Alex's more reserved nature, creating a harmonious dynamic between them.

"I can't believe you've shared so much with me," Alex admitted, his tone soft and genuine. "Your music and your stories… they're a window into your soul."

Eryx's gaze softened, his usual sass momentarily replaced by a heartfelt sincerity. "I've never met someone who listens the way you do, Alex."

Their eyes locked, and for a moment, the world faded away, leaving only the two of them in their intimate bubble of connection. It was a sweet and tender moment, a glimpse into the potential for something beautiful between them.

Eryx's stories continued, each one a piece of his heart that he willingly shared with Alex. They talked about music, dreams, and the winding paths that had brought them to this moment.

They also discovered a shared interest in travel, both of them recounting their favorite destinations and dream adventures. With each exchange, their connection deepened, like two puzzle pieces slowly finding their perfect fit.

As the evening wore on, they found themselves laughing, sharing stories, and enjoying the simple pleasure of each other's company.

Soon, their food arrived, providing a welcome distraction from further questioning. Alex was relieved, as he didn't want to accidentally bring up more painful memories.

As they neared the end of their meal, Alex suddenly sensed a change in the air, a distinct scent that reminded him of burning ozone. It was an ominous sign, a scent from the depths of hell itself. He glanced around, trying to pinpoint the source, and his gaze landed on a man in a suit sitting at the bar. Dread crept over him – Thanatos.

Alex's snarky demeanor dissolved into a tense stoicism as Thanatos stood up and made his way towards the restroom.

Alex's mind raced. He had to find out why Thanatos was here. With his heart pounding, Alex knew he couldn't let this opportunity slip away.

"Do you mind if I use the restroom?" Alex asked Eryx.

"Sure, I'll be here," Eryx replied, and Alex headed towards the restroom.

Once inside, he spotted Thanatos standing there, and he heard the door lock behind him.

"Thanatos, why are you here?" Alex questioned the enigmatic figure.

The room seemed to close in, and the air grew heavy with tension. Thanatos, his countenance unyielding, turned to face Alex. His obsidian eyes bore into Alex's, revealing nothing.

"I've been sent by the Fates," Thanatos answered.

Hearing that made Alex tense.

"Why?" Alex asked.

"They wanted me to give you a warning," Thanatos said.

Alex couldn't help but feel on edge. "Why couldn't they come here and tell me themselves?" He growled.

"You know the Fates. I'm their messenger since Persephone is on here," Alex knew this, but it didn't ease his unease about the situation. The Fates always seemed to keep their distance from him for a reason.

"What's the warning?" Alex's tone was stern.

"To ensure Eryx doesn't fall into the wrong hands," Thanatos's words sent a shiver down his spine.

"Why? What's the connection between Eryx and them?"

"They didn't reveal that to me. You're the one who can uncover it in due time, Hades," Thanatos offered a cryptic response.

"Fine. What else did they foresee?"

"They attempted to see, but the future is uncertain now that you're involved," Thanatos explained.

"Is that all?"

"Yes, until we meet again." Thanatos opened a portal to the underworld. "Remember, protect Eryx from them."

"Who are 'them'?" Alex's frustration grew with the elusive answers.

"You already know who they are," Thanatos replied before vanishing.

Alex turned and left the restroom after a moment, his mind racing with questions and concerns.

The unexpected encounter with Thanatos had left him with more questions than answers, and he couldn't shake the feeling that Eryx's safety was hanging by a fragile thread.

The sense of unease that had washed over him upon sensing Thanatos's presence lingered. It was as if the very air around him had grown heavier, burdened with the weight of impending danger. Alex couldn't help but wonder about the cryptic messages from the Fates and the ominous warning to protect Eryx.

As he rejoined Eryx at the bar, he offered no explanation for his sudden disappearance. The mysterious encounter with Thanatos had left him with a lot to digest, and he couldn't risk revealing too much to Eryx, not yet.

Their evening had taken an unexpected turn, and as they continued their conversation, Alex's thoughts remained clouded with uncertainty. The unknown dangers that lurked in the shadows and the enigmatic connection between Eryx and the ominous "them" weighed heavily on his mind.

The atmosphere had shifted, the once-casual evening now tinged with an undercurrent of suspense. Alex knew that he needed to tread carefully, to protect not only himself but also the enigmatic Eryx from whatever threats lay ahead.

The scent of burning ozone, a harbinger of the supernatural, still lingered in the air, a reminder of the world he inhabited—a world where secrets, danger, and the unyielding presence of beings like Thanatos were a part of his daily existence.

Returning to the table, Alex found Eryx gazing out at the city's twinkling lights. His heart skipped a beat at the sight of the man he had grown so fond of, but thoughts of Thanatos' cryptic warning still lingered in the back of his mind. He couldn't shake off the feeling that something was amiss.

A warm smile graced Alex's lips as he took a seat and greeted Eryx. "Hey."

Eryx turned to face him, those mischievous eyes locking onto Alex's. "Hey there. Everything alright? You were gone for a while."

Alex nodded, careful not to let the worry show. "Yeah, I'm fine." He knew Eryx was curious, but he didn't want to burden him with the details of his unsettling encounter with Thanatos. "Hey, how about we leave this place?"

Eryx's hand moved to his wallet, ready to split the bill as he always insisted, but Alex stopped him with a gentle touch on his wrist.

"I'll take care of it this time," Alex insisted.

Eryx raised an eyebrow, a playful glint in his eyes. "But..."

"You can get the next one," Alex interrupted with a wink.

Eryx rolled his eyes in mock exasperation, a hint of a smile playing at the corners of his lips. "You're pretty confident that there will be a next time."

Alex arched an eyebrow, the playful banter coming naturally to them. "And you're saying there won't be?"

Eryx's smirk was positively infectious. "Of course there will be, you goof!"

Alex couldn't help but laugh. Eryx's sassy attitude was something he had grown to appreciate more and more. It was a refreshing change from his usual stoicism.

With the bill settled, Alex stood up and moved to help Eryx with his jacket. Their fingers brushed, and Alex felt a familiar warmth spreading through him.

"Do you mind if I hold your hand?" Eryx asked, his voice soft and vulnerable, revealing a side of him that he didn't often show.

"I'd actually be disappointed if you didn't," Alex replied with a chuckle. He cherished every moment they spent together.

Eryx's face lit up with a smile that could rival the city lights outside. He reached out, and their fingers entwined. Alex's hand felt warm in Eryx's, and it sent a rush of anticipation coursing through him.

"Alright then, let's get out of here," Eryx said, his voice filled with excitement, and they left the restaurant together, hand in hand.

As they stepped out into the cool evening air, the city's sounds and scents enveloped them. The soft hum of distant traffic and the faint scent of street food vendors filled their senses. It was as if the world had slowed down just for them.

They strolled down the bustling sidewalk, their fingers still intertwined, their steps in sync. The playful banter continued, Eryx's snarky remarks drawing laughter from Alex.

The evening was alive with possibility, and for a moment, all the worries and doubts faded into the background. Alex couldn't help but feel grateful for this unexpected connection, for the way Eryx had brightened his world.

As they walked, Eryx leaned in closer, his shoulder brushing against Alex's. It was a small gesture, but it held a world of meaning. Alex glanced at Eryx, their eyes locking for a heartbeat, and in that moment, they both knew that this was just the beginning of something beautiful.

Thanatos' warning still loomed in the back of Alex's mind, a shadow that he couldn't ignore. But for now, he chose to focus on the warmth of Eryx's hand in his, the shared laughter, and the promise of a future filled with moments like this.

They eventually ended up in Central Park. They walked together along the paths. It was getting darker, and the streetlights were starting to turn on.

They found a bench near a small pond, and they sat down. Eryx rested his head on Alex's shoulder, and they looked at the water reflecting the moonlight.

They realized it was getting late. They looked at each other and smiled. They got up from the bench, ready to leave. The city lights were on now, making everything look cozy.

They walked together to Alex's car and drove off.

Driving Eryx back home, the silence between them was comfortable.

Alex could sense Eryx's contentment, and that was all that mattered to him.

When they reached Eryx's place, Alex walked him to his door, their fingers intertwined.

"Alex, tonight was amazing. I had so much fun," Eryx said sincerely.

Alex gently cupped Eryx's cheeks. "Can I kiss you?"

Eryx hesitated for a moment, then nodded. Alex closed the gap between them, their lips meeting in a tender kiss. Eryx's taste was exquisite, and Alex wanted to deepen the kiss, but he restrained himself. He broke the kiss, his thumb softly caressing Eryx's cheek.

"See you tomorrow?" Alex asked.

"Definitely. See you tomorrow," Eryx nodded with a smile.

Alex made his way to his car, hearing the sound of Eryx closing his door behind him. However, before driving off, Alex knelt down and pressed his hand to the ground, allowing a bit of his power to create a protective ward around the area.

This way, he'd be alerted if Eryx ever found himself in trouble. Feeling the subtle hum of the protective ward, Alex rose to his feet and left with a sense of reassurance.

9

Eryx

ERYX WAS FEELING A BIT FRANTIC. Okay, maybe more than a bit. His kitchen had turned into a battlefield of ingredients, and his mind was a whirlwind of doubts. He had no idea what to prepare for Alex and his teammates. It wasn't every day that Eryx got the chance to cook for a group of people.

With a sigh, he decided to call Ari, for some much-needed advice.

The voice on the other end sounded groggy and annoyed. "Eryx, seriously? It's way too early for phone calls."

"I know, Ari, I'm sorry. But I really need your help!"

Ari let out an exaggerated groan. "Alright, what's the emergency this time?"

"I don't know what to prepare! Alex invited me to their headquarters, and I wanted to make something for them."

Ari chuckled, her voice gradually losing its sleep-induced irritation. "Is that all? Eryx, honey, Alex will be thrilled with whatever you bring. How about baking your famous cookies? They're a hit."

Eryx's anxiety started to ease at the suggestion. "Oh right, I forgot you've met Alex."

Ari laughed. "So relax, bake your cookies, and you'll be golden."

"Thank you, Ari. I owe you a latte."

"You better remember that. Now go on, I need sleep," Ari replied, and the call ended.

Eryx let out a relieved sigh and turned his attention back to the chaos in his kitchen. He began gathering the ingredients for his famous chocolate chip cookies. The scent of vanilla extract and the feel of flour between his fingers started to calm his nerves.

As he measured out the ingredients and began mixing the dough, he couldn't help but think about the upcoming visit. He hoped that his cookies would be a hit with Alex and the team. It wasn't just about impressing them; it was about showing his appreciation for their work and forming a connection beyond their usual encounters.

With the cookie dough ready, Eryx preheated the oven and started scooping out generous portions onto a baking sheet. The anticipation of the sweet, warm treats filling the air only added to his excitement.

As the cookies began to bake, he took a moment to glance around his kitchen. It was a cozy space, filled with the warm colors of home. The aroma of baking cookies combined with the morning sunlight filtering through the curtains created an inviting atmosphere.

With a sense of accomplishment, Eryx checked the time. He still had a few hours before he had to go. He decided to use that time to clean up the kitchen and make sure everything was perfect.

Ari's words of encouragement echoed in his mind as he worked. He felt grateful for her unwavering support and friendship. It was moments like these that reminded him of the importance of having someone who believed in him, even when he doubted himself.

Finally, as the last batch of cookies came out of the oven, Eryx couldn't help but smile. The kitchen was spotless, and the air was filled with the irresistible scent of freshly baked cookies. He had done his best, and that was all he could ask for.

As the clock ticked closer to the appointed time, Eryx carefully arranged the cookies on a plate, ready to share them with Alex and his team. He couldn't wait to see their reactions.

Earlier that day, Alex had texted him the address, although Eryx couldn't quite remember when he'd given Alex his number. Pushing aside the thought, he found himself walking to the Shadowguards headquarters, holding a basket of cookies like a modern-day Red Riding Hood, just before lunchtime.

Once inside, Eryx was taken aback by the surprisingly intricate modern design of the place. It felt like a blend of cool modernity and practicality. The glass walls allowed sunlight to stream in, giving a glimpse of the outside world. It seemed to promise transparency and a readiness to tackle any challenges that came their way.

Eryx found himself standing nervously, fidgeting with the basket of freshly baked cookies he had brought for Alex's team. He had heard so much about them, and the anticipation mixed with anxiety left him both excited and apprehensive.

Before he could get lost in his thoughts, a man with wavy

brown hair approached him, his warm smile immediately putting Eryx at ease. He couldn't help but smile back in response.

"Hey! You must be Eryx. I'm Marcus. The Boss wanted me to fetch you," Marcus greeted, his enthusiasm practically radiating.

Eryx extended a hand. "Hey, Marcus. It's nice to meet you too."

Marcus, ever the curious one, sniffed the air, his interest suddenly piqued. "Do I smell cookies?"

Eryx chuckled. "Yeah, I made cookies for the whole team."

A spark of excitement lit up Marcus's eyes. "Oh! What kind are they?"

Eryx liked Marcus already. "Why don't you take me to Alex first, and then we can unveil the cookie mystery, shall we?"

"Sure thing. Can I hold your basket?" Marcus looked almost hungry for the cookies.

Eryx raised an eyebrow playfully. "If I let you hold it, can you promise not to sneak a peek?"

"Huh? Yeah, sure, I promise," Marcus agreed, though his mischievous grin made Eryx a bit skeptical. Nevertheless, he handed over the basket.

Marcus took it with a childlike eagerness and then extended his hand to Eryx. Confused, Eryx asked, "Why?"

"It'll be quicker this way," Marcus winked, and before Eryx could process it all, everything blurred, and they arrived somewhere in seconds.

Eryx's stomach lurched as he stumbled upon arrival, feeling disoriented and queasy. "What was that?!"

Marcus chuckled, seemingly unaffected. "I'm a fast runner."

Eryx couldn't help but groan, trying to regain his composure. "Next time, give a guy a heads-up."

Amidst his heavy breaths, Eryx heard a deep, gravelly voice that he was starting to enjoy hearing.

"Marcus, what did you do? I said pick him up, not traumatize him," Alex's voice carried a hint of amusement but with an underlying edge.

"Sorry, sir. I just wanted to check out the cookies he brought for the team," Marcus apologized.

With Alex's help, Eryx managed to stand up, his gaze meeting Alex's stunning eyes. "Are you okay?" Alex's concern was evident.

Caught in that mesmerizing gaze, Eryx couldn't help but smile. "Yeah, I'm fine. Just caught me off guard."

Alex's lips quirked up into a half-smile. "Do you want Marcus to be on office duty for the foreseeable future?"

Eryx quickly interjected, not wanting Marcus to get into trouble. "Ease up, he was just excited about the cookies."

With the basket still in hand, Alex turned his attention to Eryx. "You didn't have to do this," he said, accepting the basket.

Eryx couldn't help but blush as he confessed, "I wanted to do something nice for you and your team, and yes, I baked them."

Alex's eyes softened, and he leaned in to kiss Eryx's cheek. "Thank you." Eryx's heart skipped a beat at the unexpected gesture.

"Now," Alex continued, "shall we introduce you to the team?"

Eryx's nervousness resurfaced, but he managed a determined smile. "Sure, let's get this over with."

With Alex leading the way and Marcus trailing behind

them, Eryx felt a mixture of excitement and trepidation as they headed deeper into the Shadowguards headquarters. He couldn't help but wonder what kind of adventures and camaraderie awaited him in this world of supernatural beings.

Eryx followed Alex into the Shadowguards Headquarters, his heart racing with a mix of excitement and anxiety. He was just here to visit and deliver cookies, not to join a team of magic-wielders. Magic had always fascinated him, and being in the heart of it all made him feel like a kid in a candy store.

They walked into what appeared to be a briefing room, where four individuals were engrossed in various tasks. Eryx couldn't help but be intrigued by their presence, their auras practically buzzing with magical energy. He wondered about the kind of magic each of them wielded, eager to learn more.

Alex cleared his throat, capturing everyone's attention. "Alright, Agents, this here is Eryx. Eryx, meet the team," Alex introduced, his voice warm and protective. He pointed to a silver haired man with striking green eyes. "This is Gabe, our resident witch and one of our top strategists."

Gabe offered a friendly nod, his gaze thoughtful. "Nice to meet you, Eryx."

Alex then indicated a dark-haired man with an air of sophistication. "This is Lucas, our sorcerer and hacker."

Lucas gave Eryx a sly grin and extended a hand. "Pleasure to make your acquaintance. Hope you brought some of those cookies with you."

Lastly, Alex pointed to the two women on the team. "The red-haired woman is Olivia, our Arcane specialist."

Olivia smiled warmly at Eryx, her blue eyes twinkling with curiosity. "Cookies are always welcome here."

"And lastly," Alex continued, "we have Emma, our enchanter."

Emma's eyes sparkled with warmth as she approached Eryx. She extended her arms for a welcoming hug, which he gladly accepted. "We've heard so much about you, Eryx. It's a pleasure to finally meet you."

Eryx's thoughts were a whirlwind of curiosity as he considered the possibilities. He was excited about the prospect of getting to know these people.

The briefing room itself was a cozy and well-lit space, with a large wooden table at the center adorned with various magical artifacts. A crystal ball shimmered with an inner light, and symbols of protection were etched into the table's surface. The room had an air of both tradition and modernity, a reflection of the team's blend of magic and technology.

Eryx's excitement bubbled up as he looked around, taking in the mystical atmosphere.

As the team settled back into their tasks, Eryx couldn't help but feel a sense of belonging, even if it was just for this moment. He knew he was in the right place, among friends who were not just skilled magic-wielders but also kind-hearted individuals.

"Alright, I baked some cookies for you all. Hopefully, they survived the speedy journey here thanks to Marcus," Eryx said with a mixture of excitement and anxiety. He watched as Alex carefully placed the cookies on the briefing room table. The tantalizing aroma of freshly baked treats filled the room.

The team eagerly gathered around, their eyes lighting up as they took in the sight of the cookies. Alex's team had heard about Eryx but hadn't met him in person yet, and they were just as curious about him as he was about them.

"Oh my gods, these are amazing. Are these white chocolate chip?" Emma inquired as she picked up a cookie.

Eryx nodded, his nerves slowly easing as he saw their positive reactions. "Yes, I didn't have much time to bake different flavors, unfortunately."

"Don't worry, they're fantastic," Lucas assured, taking a bite and giving Eryx a warm smile.

As the team enjoyed the cookies, Eryx noticed Alex smiling at him throughout. The team's friendly chatter and laughter made him feel welcome, as if he had always been a part of their group.

Alex leaned in closer to Eryx and whispered, "See? I told you they'd love your cookies."

Lunch continued with animated conversations flowing seamlessly. Alex's team shared anecdotes from their missions, peppered with laughter and camaraderie. They asked Eryx about his music career, showing genuine interest in his passion.

The cookies disappeared quickly, and soon, they moved on to the sandwiches and salads that had been provided. Eryx couldn't help but be amazed by how effortlessly Alex's team worked together. They were a well-oiled machine, each member complementing the others, and it was clear that their bond ran deep.

As the team shared stories, Eryx's admiration for them grew. He marveled at their skills and dedication, and a part of him wished he could be a part of their world, even just for a day.

Lunch had been delightful, and Eryx spent the rest of the afternoon absorbed in observing Alex and his team at work. The briefing room buzzed with activity as they discussed plans and strategies for their next mission. Eryx couldn't help but be impressed by their professionalism and the trust they placed in each other.

Alex kindly offered to drive Eryx home. Gratitude welled up within Eryx, but he declined with a polite smile. He needed to attend a rehearsal for the upcoming concert, and he didn't want to impose on more of Alex's time.

"Make sure to give me a call once you're back home, alright?" Alex's request held a touch of concern, and it warmed Eryx's heart.

"Absolutely," Eryx agreed, feeling a sense of longing as he looked into Alex's eyes. Just before he left, Alex planted a kiss on him that felt like a promise of more to come. It left Eryx with a lingering feeling of warmth and happiness.

Eryx stepped away from the Shadowguards Headquarters and headed off to his rehearsal, the echoes of laughter and camaraderie from his lunch with Alex's team still fresh in his mind.

* * *

Eryx had been informed that the rehearsal would take place at Richard's house, and so he made his way there. Luckily, it wasn't too far from his own place.

As he arrived, he couldn't help but be taken aback by the sheer size of Richard's house. It stood tall and imposing, a mansion that seemed to dwarf his own home threefold. His eyes widened as he took in the architectural details—the ornate columns that reached for the sky, the intricate carvings that adorned the façade, and the stained glass windows that sparkled like jewels in the sunlight.

"Wow," Eryx muttered to himself as he approached the grand entrance. His humble abode suddenly seemed like a cozy cottage compared to this mansion.

The exterior exuded an air of grandeur, with its meticulously crafted architecture and sprawling design. The house was surrounded by lush, manicured gardens that seemed to frame the building like a natural tapestry. Vibrant flowers added splashes of color, their sweet scent filling the air as they danced in the gentle breeze. Eryx couldn't help but take a deep breath, savoring the fragrant aroma that enveloped him.

Well-trimmed hedges and stone pathways created an inviting atmosphere, beckoning him further into the enchanting world that was Richard's home. The garden was a paradise of greenery, where every blade of grass seemed to have a purpose, and every bloom held its own secret. It was like stepping into a fairy tale.

Eryx's footsteps on the cobblestone path were the only sound, the distant laughter from within the house a gentle hum in the background. The sun was high in the sky, casting a warm and inviting glow over the scene. It was a sunny morning, the perfect backdrop for the grandeur that surrounded him.

He couldn't help but wonder about the significance of this place to Richard. It had to hold some special meaning, or perhaps it was just a testament to the musician's success. Whatever the reason, Eryx felt honored to be here, to witness a piece of Richard's world.

As he approached the front door, he noticed a central focal point in the garden—a majestic fountain adorned with intricate sculptures of mythical creatures. Water cascaded down in a mesmerizing dance, creating ripples in the pool below. Eryx couldn't resist pausing to take in the sight, the play of sunlight on the water creating a magical spectacle.

Eryx reached for the doorbell. He didn't know what to expect, but he was eager to meet Richard and the rest of the band.

As the door swung open, Richard greeted him with a warm smile and an enthusiastic embrace. "Hey! The band's out back, getting ready to start," he said, his eyes alive with excitement.

Eryx couldn't help but feel a rush of gratitude. "Did I come too late?" he asked, his nerves bubbling beneath the surface.

"Nope, right on time. Let's go," Richard replied, leading the way into another room that doubled as a studio. The walls were adorned with framed posters of various concerts and musical legends. The studio had a cozy, dimly lit ambiance, with soft overhead lights casting a warm glow.

Richard gestured around the room. "I sometimes do online streams from here."

Eryx took in the sight, his eyes widening with awe. "This place is incredible."

The band was already there, a motley crew of musicians tuning their instruments and checking the sound. Richard introduced Eryx to everyone, and each member welcomed him with genuine warmth.

"This is Eryx, our guest for today," Richard announced, and the band members exchanged knowing glances.

The drummer, a vivacious man with fiery red hair, extended his hand with a grin. "I'm Joey. Nice to meet you, Eryx. You've got quite the reputation."

Eryx shook his hand, feeling a surge of excitement.

"Thanks, Joey. I hope I can keep up."

The bassist, a laid-back guy with a perpetual grin, introduced himself as Jake. "Don't worry, man. We're all about having a good time here."

Next was the keyboardist, Sarah, a soft-spoken woman with an air of elegance. "It's a pleasure to meet you, Eryx. We've heard great things."

Eryx nodded, feeling a growing sense of camaraderie. "Likewise, Sarah."

Finally, the guitarist, a quiet but intensely focused man named Chris, nodded in greeting. His fingers danced over the strings as he continued to fine-tune his instrument.

Richard clapped Eryx on the back. "Let's grab your guitar and join the party."

Eryx retrieved his guitar from its case, his fingers caressing the familiar strings. The air in the studio was filled with the heady scent of polished wood and the soft hum of anticipation. He couldn't help but feel a mixture of excitement and nervousness as he plugged in and joined the band.

The band members huddled together, discussing their setlist and the songs they wanted to play. Eryx listened intently, his heart pounding in time with the rhythm of their conversation. It was clear that this group shared a deep connection, their interactions filled with laughter and easy camaraderie.

As they began to play, the studio came alive with the rich sound of music. The instruments melded together seamlessly, creating a harmony that resonated through the room. Eryx's fingers danced over the frets, his heart swelling with the joy of making music with such talented musicians.

The music flowed freely, each member adding their unique

flair to the performance. Richard's voice soared, a powerful instrument in its own right. Eryx couldn't help but be captivated by the raw passion and energy of the band.

During a brief pause in the music, Richard turned to Eryx with a grin. "Your turn, Eryx. Show us what you've got."

Eryx felt a surge of adrenaline as he launched into a soulful guitar solo. His fingers moved with precision, pouring his emotions into the music. The band members watched in awe, their expressions a mix of admiration and excitement.

The jam session continued, each member taking their turn to shine. The room was filled with laughter, shared glances, and the unspoken language of musicians who understood each other without the need for words.

As the session drew to a close, the band members exchanged satisfied smiles. Richard clapped Eryx on the back once again. "You've got some serious talent, my friend. We should do this more often."

Eryx, his heart still racing from the exhilarating experience, grinned from ear to ear. "I'd love that, Richard. This has been incredible."

The band members echoed their agreement, their laughter filling the room. It was a night filled with music, camaraderie, and the shared joy of creating something beautiful together.

As Eryx packed up his guitar and said his goodbyes, he couldn't help but feel a profound sense of gratitude. This rehearsal session had been more than just a musical experience. It had been a glimpse into a world where passion, talent, and friendship converged, and he couldn't wait to be a part of it again

Eryx arrived home after a perfect day, the warm, fuzzy feeling still lingering within him as he settled into his cozy bed. He didn't want the day to end, but there was one thing he needed to do before drifting into slumber. He reached for the small pill bottle on his nightstand, a daily ritual he couldn't ignore.

After swallowing the pill, he felt the soothing embrace of the medication, and any worries that had clung to him throughout the day began to melt away. The room around him was a comforting sanctuary, a place filled with memories of moments he treasured.

With a contented sigh, he picked up his phone, the screen bathing his face in a soft, bluish glow. His heart skipped a beat when he saw Alex's name on the screen, and he answered after just one ring. Alex's deep voice, a constant source of fascination for Eryx, washed over him.

"Hey, did you make it home okay?" Alex's voice held a warmth that settled deep in Eryx's chest.

"Hey, yeah, I had a fantastic day. And you? Did you all manage to finish the cookies?" Eryx asked, his mind drifting back to their shared laughter and playful cookie-making earlier.

"Ah, I'm glad to hear that. The cookies fell victim to Marcus," Alex chuckled softly, his voice like a soothing melody. "My day was exhausting, just work stuff. On the bright side, we tracked down the pack related to the wolves that attacked you the other day."

Eryx couldn't hide his surprise and curiosity. "Really? Can you give me the details?"

"Perhaps. Mind if I come over? I already miss you," Alex's voice carried a hint of weariness, but there was an underlying desire in his words that sent a shiver down Eryx's spine.

"Of course, what time should I expect you?" Eryx asked,

just as he heard a knock on his door, interrupting their conversation. "Hang on a sec, someone's at the door."

Eryx placed his phone on the nightstand and rose from his bed, his heart beating a little faster. He wasn't expecting anyone, and the knock had taken him by surprise. As he approached the door, he couldn't help but wonder who it could be at this hour.

Opening the door, he found Alex standing there. Alex entered and immediately took charge, locking their lips in a relentless kiss.

"Was that alright?" Alex questioned, and Eryx managed to nod. Thinking coherently became challenging after that.

Alex continued the intense kiss, his hunger apparent. Eryx's body went into overdrive, and a rush of heat engulfed him. He could feel Alex's cock pressing against him.

Without breaking the kiss, Alex lifted Eryx and carried him to his bedroom.

"Please Alex…" Eryx moaned.

"Please what, baby?"

"Fuck me! Please." He pleaded.

Without hesitation, Alex swiftly turned him over, their clothes discarded in a rush of urgency. As they joined, a wave of heat and longing enveloped them. Alex's hungry mouth explored him with a fervor that sent shivers down his spine.

The sensation of Alex's stubble against his skin set off sparks of pleasure, making his body tremble. Each touch, each kiss, spoke volumes about their connection, a connection that pulsed with desire and intimacy..

"Are you ready for my cock, baby?"

"Alex, please. Stop teasing and fuck me already" Eryx moaned.

And Alex did exactly that. Eryx felt the impressive thickness of Alex as he entered, and he tried his best not to come right there and then. The feeling of Alex's cock sliding deep inside him sparked waves of pleasure, each movement creating a powerful sensation that left him feeling overwhelmed and breathless.

After some time, the intensity grew between them, and they could tell they were both getting closer. Finally, in a rush of sensation, Alex reached his peak and came inside of him , and Eryx also let go, spilling onto the sheets.

Eryx and Alex lay side by side in the cozy bedroom, the soft glow of a bedside lamp casting warm shadows across the room. Their bodies bore the marks of a night of intense passion, and the air was thick with a sense of intimacy and vulnerability.

They eventually got up and cleaned themselves, then headed back into the bedroom. Still naked, Eryx chuckled as he noticed the state of his bed sheets. Deciding to take care of it, he put them in the wash, only to find that Alex had already changed them when he returned.

"You didn't have to do that," Eryx told Alex, a soft smile playing on his lips.

Alex kissed his nose, making Eryx blush. "It's the least I could do for showing up here so late and, you know, messing up your sheets."

Sitting down on the bed, Eryx rested his head on Alex's shoulder. His heart swelled with affection for the man beside him. "Will you tell me about those wolves now?"

Alex let out a sigh, his fingers gently tracing circles on Eryx's back. "I was hoping you'd forget about that after everything."

Eryx shifted closer, the warmth of Alex's skin against his own making him feel safe and loved. "Come on, spill it," he urged, his voice a soft plea.

"They belong to the Hansen pack," Alex revealed, his tone serious and tinged with a hint of concern.

Eryx knew the Hansen pack was highly regarded in New York City, but that was the extent of his knowledge. He furrowed his brow, his curiosity piqued. "What's your plan?"

Alex's fingers brushed through Eryx's hair as he spoke, his voice low and soothing. "We want to talk to them, but they are still unconscious."

Eryx couldn't help but worry. "Did we hurt them that badly?" he asked, his eyes searching Alex's for reassurance.

Alex turned to him, his expression soft and filled with tenderness. He gently held Eryx's cheeks, his thumbs stroking his skin. "No, I don't think so." He leaned in, pressing a sweet kiss to Eryx's lips. "Come on, let's go to sleep."

Eryx nodded, a sense of trust and contentment settling over him. With a kiss on the tip of his nose, Alex settled down beside him, their bodies fitting together like two pieces of a puzzle. The weight of the night's events hung in the air, but in each other's arms, they found solace and comfort.

As they cuddled, their breathing synchronized, and the room seemed to shrink until it was just the two of them, sharing a moment of quiet intimacy. Eryx closed his eyes, feeling the rise and fall of Alex's chest against his own.

In the silence, their thoughts began to drift. Eryx couldn't help but reflect on the man beside him, on the way Alex had opened up to him in ways he had never expected. He wanted to share everything with Alex, to let him into the deepest corners of his heart.

10

Alex

"DR. SLOANE, WHAT HAVE YOU FOUND?" Alex asked as he answered.

Early in the morning, Alex had reluctantly left Eryx's house while Eryx was still sleeping. He left a note for Eryx on the bedside table, a simple message stating he would call later and encouraging Eryx to message anytime.

Now seated in his office, the somber ambiance mirrored his own conflicted state. His thoughts revolved around the inexplicable connection he felt with Eryx, and why he had allowed himself to be swept away by it the night before. It was a vulnerability he rarely exposed.

His SHD alerting him to an incoming call from Dr. Sloane snapped him back to the present. Dr. Finn Sloane, the team's medic and healer with precise magic skills, was a crucial member of their group. His ability to sense souls was rare and invaluable, making him one of the few privy to Alex's true identity.

"You need to come to where the wolves are. I have something to show you," Dr. Sloane's voice came urgently through the call, laden with an unspoken urgency.

Alex felt a knot of unease tighten in his chest as he acknowledged the message. He pushed himself away from his cluttered desk and rose to his feet.

"I'm here. What's going on?" Alex's concern was palpable as he approached the medical bay, a room bathed in sterile white light and filled with the faint hum of equipment. The wolves, their forms restrained in secure cages, watched him with wary eyes.

Dr. Sloane, his normally composed demeanor marred by the gravity of the situation, gestured toward the alpha wolf that had attacked Eryx. The creature's eyes held a glimmer of something Alex couldn't quite place.

"Can you sense anything?" Dr. Sloane's voice was steady, but his eyes betrayed his unease.

Alex closed his eyes briefly, attempting to tap into his unique ability. His connection to souls had always been a part of him, an intrinsic facet of his existence. But now, as he sought to sense the soul of the alpha wolf, he encountered an unsettling void.

"No, I can't sense anything," Alex admitted, his voice edged with frustration and confusion.

"That's the problem. I couldn't sense anything either," Dr. Sloane sighed as he explained, his shoulders slumping slightly under the weight of the revelation.

"What does that mean?" Alex pressed, his concern deepening.

"It means their souls have been stolen," Dr. Sloane's words hung heavily in the air, casting a pall over the room.

The gravity of the situation settled upon Alex like a suffocating shroud. Stolen souls were a grave matter, a sinister act that resonated with his deepest fears. He couldn't shake the feeling that this was merely the beginning of a dark and treacherous path, one that would demand everything from him and his team.

"I thought maybe you, being the king of the underworld, could try to retrieve their souls," Dr. Sloane suggested, his voice carrying a hint of desperation.

Alex's brow furrowed as he considered the doctor's words. The morning sunlight filtered through the medical bay's windows, casting long shadows across the sterile room. His gaze settled on the two unconscious individuals lying on the examination tables before him, their bodies bearing the telltale signs of a supernatural struggle.

"I can only guide souls to their rightful place," Alex replied, his tone heavy with the weight of the situation. "Recovering stolen souls is a different matter."

The concept troubled him deeply. Souls were sacred, a fundamental aspect of existence, and only those who had truly departed could be guided to their intended rest. Stolen souls disrupted the natural balance between life and death, potentially causing great harm.

His mind raced with the implications of the doctor's request. Tracking stolen souls was an intricate task, involving the challenge of locating the individual responsible for their theft. However, in this particular instance, the identity of the culprit remained veiled in mystery.

Alex pondered an alternative approach. He could tap into the unique abilities of a Soul Tracker, though they had long been gone and never heard from again. The mention of such rare individuals sent shivers down his spine. They possessed an uncanny knack for navigating the intricate web of the supernatural world, a gift he didn't share.

"Keep them here for now, and ensure their safety," Alex instructed, his voice firm but laced with concern. "Today, we'll contact the Hansen pack about this."

Dr. Sloane nodded, understanding the gravity of the situation. The Hansen pack was known for their expertise in dealing with supernatural matters, especially those involving rogue entities and the theft of souls.

He had always been a staunch guardian of the supernatural world, ensuring that the balance between life and death remained undisturbed. The stolen souls presented a threat not only to the individuals affected but also to the fragile equilibrium of the supernatural realm.

He grappled with reservations and doubts about his ability to handle this situation. The recovery of stolen souls was uncharted territory for him, a challenge that tested the limits of his powers. He couldn't help but wonder if he was truly equipped to face this perilous journey.

As he walked through the shadowed corridors of the Shadowguards' headquarters, he found himself reflecting on the history of Soul Trackers. They were a rare breed, elusive figures who had mastered the art of navigating the supernatural realm. Their abilities were legendary, but their disappearance from the world had left a void that was nearly impossible to fill.

The Hansen pack, on the other hand, had a reputation that preceded them. They were known for their unwavering commitment to maintaining order within the supernatural community. They possessed a unique understanding of the intricate politics and power struggles that often played out in the shadows.

The tension and suspense surrounding the mystery of the stolen souls hung over him like a shroud. He knew that the investigation that would follow would be fraught with danger and uncertainty. The culprits behind the theft were shrouded in darkness, their motives unclear, and their actions unpredictable.

Alex's unique abilities as the king of the underworld granted him authority and capabilities that set him apart. He could navigate the supernatural world with ease, and his ability to guide souls to their rightful place was a solemn responsibility he carried with unwavering dedication.

Alex, accompanied by Gabe and Emma, made their way toward the Hansen pack's territory, the morning sun casting a golden hue over the dense woods that surrounded them.

"Gabe, any progress on tracking the Order's movements?" Alex asked, his gaze fixed on the winding road ahead. Gabe, his attention locked onto his SHD device, shook his head slightly.

"Unfortunately, no progress, sir. The Order has been oddly quiet for the past few days," Gabe responded, his voice tense with frustration.

Alex frowned. "Do you think they might be planning something significant?"

Gabe sighed, his brow furrowing. "It's a possibility, sir. Their intentions are often hard to predict."

Turning to Emma, Alex inquired, "Have you informed the parents about Ms. Lane?"

Emma's expression was troubled as she nodded. "Yes, sir. But there's something strange about how they reacted."

"What do you mean, Emma?" Alex asked, concern evident in his eyes.

"It's like they were distant, almost emotionless when I delivered the news of their daughter's passing," Emma explained, her voice tinged with unease.

Without hesitation, Alex gave a firm order. "Emma, call Marcus. Ask him to accompany Dr. Sloane and visit the Lane residence for a welfare check."

Emma's brow furrowed in confusion. "Why? What's going on?"

Alex's gaze never wavered from the road, but his voice held a grim certainty. "The wolves we have in custody are missing their souls. If my suspicions are right, the same fate might have befallen the Lane family."

A heavy silence descended upon the car as Emma reached for her phone to make the call. The weight of the situation settled over them like a suffocating blanket, and the tension inside the vehicle was palpable.

Gabe's fingers tapped nervously against his SHD device as he glanced out the window. "This silence from the Order is unnerving. It's as if they're preparing for something big, something we can't foresee."

Alex nodded in agreement, his knuckles white as he gripped the steering wheel. "We need to stay vigilant. The Hansen pack might hold answers, and if there's any connection to the Order, we must find it."

The journey continued in silence, the dense woods giving way to the Hansen pack's territory. The atmosphere in the car was thick with uncertainty and a shared sense of urgency. The trio knew that they were walking into a situation fraught with danger, and the looming mystery of the Order's silence only added to their unease.

As they approached their destination, Alex's mind raced

with questions. What could the Hansen pack reveal about the Order's plans? Could they uncover any clues that might lead them to the missing souls of the werewolves in their custody? The weight of their mission pressed down on him, and he couldn't help but wonder if they were truly prepared for what lay ahead.

Gabe's fingers danced over the SHD device, his determination evident in the way he furrowed his brows. "We'll need to approach the Alpha with caution. We don't know how much they're aware of or if they're connected to the Order in any way."

Emma nodded, her gaze focused on her phone as she continued to communicate with Marcus and Dr. Sloane. "I've arranged for Marcus and Dr. Sloane to meet us there. They'll be discreet in their investigation."

The car came to a stop at the edge of the Hansen pack's territory, and Alex turned off the engine. He took a deep breath, steeling himself for what lay ahead. The sun had risen higher in the sky, casting dappled shadows through the trees.

The team stepped out of the car, and the forest seemed to close in around them. It was a stark reminder of the wild, unpredictable world they navigated, where danger lurked in the shadows and answers were often elusive.

As they began to approach the Hansen pack's dwelling, the tension in the air grew thicker. The weight of their mission hung over them like a storm cloud, and they knew that the answers they sought might come at a steep price.

Inside the pack's territory, the atmosphere was charged with a sense of both reverence and caution. They were entering the domain of powerful creatures, and the gravity of their mission was not lost on any of them.

Led by a Beta named Jake, they found themselves standing before Alpha Jared Hansen in the heart of his territory. Seated in his imposing chair, Jared looked every bit the man who had carried the weight of several centuries on his shoulders. His age was evident in the lines etched across his weathered face, and his broad shoulders spoke of strength built over a lifetime.

Unlike humans, shifters like Jared enjoyed longer lifespans, and this longevity was evident in the gravitas that surrounded him. His presence held an air of authority, a living testament to the experiences and challenges that had shaped him over time. Alex couldn't help but feel the weight of history as his gaze met Jared's, the depth of centuries lingering in the Alpha's piercing eyes.

Jared's face was adorned with a few days' growth of beard, a rugged detail that hinted at some hidden struggle he might be facing. It was a stark contrast to the polished facade Alex had expected from an Alpha.

"Alpha Hansen. We're here from the Shadowguards," Alex spoke firmly, introducing himself and his team in this tense moment.

"Leave us, Jake," the Alpha instructed his Beta, who obediently retreated, leaving them alone with Jared.

"What can I do for you?" the Alpha inquired, his voice carrying an undertone of both curiosity and suspicion.

Alex wasted no time, getting straight to the point. "Have you lost a couple of your pack members recently?"

The Alpha's silence was thick, the weight of the unspoken answer hanging in the air. Finally, he nodded. "Yes, my mate Henry and three other wolves."

Alex signaled to Gabe, who produced pictures of the

missing wolves they had in custody. He placed the images on the table before the Alpha, each photograph representing a missing piece of Jared's pack.

"Are these the missing wolves?" Alex's voice held a firm edge as he awaited the Alpha's response.

The Alpha's reaction was a low growl, his anger and concern merging into a formidable force. "What did you do to them?" His voice rumbled with a hint of the animal within.

Emma and Gabe, attuned to the rising tension, subtly prepared their magic, ready for any conflict that might arise. Alex's voice remained steady, determined. "We didn't do anything to them, so calm down before things get worse."

But the Alpha persisted, his growl underscoring his worry. "Then what happened to them?" He took one of the pictures into his large, rough hands, his fingers trembling slightly. "This is my mate," he said, his voice catching with a mixture of anger and deep sorrow.

Empathy surged within Alex as he observed the Alpha's grief. They had to navigate this delicate situation carefully. "Your mate and the others attacked someone in the Upper East Side a couple of days ago. We took them into custody before they could cause more harm."

"Attack? Impossible. My wolves, especially my mate, know that attacking humans is forbidden. Something must have gone terribly wrong."

Alex acknowledged this with a nod. "You're right. I learned this morning that their souls are missing."

The Alpha's reaction was immediate, another low growl escaping his lips. "What?" His eyes blazed with a mixture of disbelief and rage.

"Yes," Alex confirmed. "Their souls are gone. But we're determined to get them back."

The Alpha's desperation was palpable, his authority momentarily eclipsed by his grief and concern. "How? I've heard stories. Even if you retrieve stolen souls, the person won't come back the same."

Alex knew the stories well. When a person's soul was stolen, they underwent a profound metamorphosis—a shift at the very essence of their being. Memories, emotions, and even personality could be twisted and altered beyond recognition.

"It's true," Alex admitted. "But we'll do everything we can. We promise to bring your mate and the others back."

The Alpha's shoulders slumped, a mixture of desperation and resignation. "If you need anything, let me know. I'll gather my pack to help."

Alex nodded, appreciating the Alpha's willingness to cooperate. They exchanged a few more words, outlining their plan to retrieve the stolen souls. As they prepared to leave the Alpha's presence, the gravity of the situation hung heavily in the air.

This encounter with Alpha Jared Hansen had shown Alex the complexities of their world, the weight of responsibility he carried as a Shadowguard. It was a world filled with both darkness and moments of profound connection, where the boundaries between humans and shifters blurred, and where they were bound by the shared struggle to protect their kind.

As they departed, the Alpha's gaze lingered on the photographs of his missing pack members, a silent plea for their safe return. And Alex, with a heart heavy with the weight of responsibility, vowed to do everything in his power to fulfill that promise.

As they walked to their car, a sense of urgency hung heavy in the air. Alex's SHD emitted a sharp alert, a digital jolt that sliced through the morning calm like a blade. He wasted no time in answering the incoming call, Marcus's voice coming through with an edge of urgency.

"Marcus, give me an update," Alex instructed, his voice taut with anticipation.

"Sir. We've found two bodies inside the house. All signs point to them being the parents," Marcus reported, his tone grim and unyielding.

A heavy feeling settled in Alex's chest like a lead weight, his jaw clenching in frustration and concern. His team was at the Hansen Pack territory, and this development spelled trouble.

"Have you contacted the HIB to handle the bodies?" Alex inquired, his mind already moving to the necessary protocols.

"Yes, sir. They're en route," Marcus confirmed, his words curt and to the point.

"Good. Wait for me there," Alex concluded, determination coursing through his veins.

Closing the call, he turned to his companions, Gabe and Emma, who had been silently absorbing the information. Their expressions mirrored the gravity of the situation, each reacting in their own distinct ways.

Alex's thoughts raced. He couldn't help but worry about the potential implications of this discovery. The urgency of the matter weighed heavily on him.

"What do you want us to do sir?" Gabe asked.

"Both of you," he began, his voice authoritative but laced with concern, "head back to the office. Inform Lucas and Olivia about the situation. Also, see if you can trace the whereabouts of those four missing wolves before they vanished."

Gabe nodded, his gaze unwavering as he took in Alex's orders. "We'll handle it, sir. You take care of things there."

Emma's voice, though shaken, held determination. "You can count on us."

With a final nod, Gabe and Emma departed, leaving Alex to confront the grim reality that awaited him in the Lane residence.

Arriving at the Lane residence in Brooklyn, Alex managed to intercept the arrival of the HIB's team, his grim determination propelling him forward. He approached Dr. Sloane, who was already examining the scene.

"Dr. Sloane, have the souls been examined?" Alex's voice held an urgency that mirrored the weight of the situation.

Dr. Sloane met Alex's gaze with a grave expression. "The souls have been inspected, and as you might have anticipated, they have indeed been stolen."

A knot tightened in Alex's chest. The theft of souls was an ominous sign, a dark and dangerous act that threatened to unravel the very fabric of their supernatural world. Seeking more information, he turned to Marcus, his trusted colleague.

"What else have we found?" Alex's tone was serious, his eyes locked onto Marcus's.

"Both victims, Mr. and Mrs. Lane, were marked," Marcus stated, his voice carrying the weight of the revelation.

Alex's understanding deepened. These assailants weren't content with merely taking the souls of their victims; they also left the Mark of Kronos as a sinister signature, a chilling reminder of their presence.

As the HIB team arrived, led by Detective Collins, Alex

acknowledged the detective with a nod. Detective Collins' face reflected a mix of concern and curiosity as he assessed the situation.

"Director Knight, what's the situation here?" Detective Collins inquired, his tone edged with urgency.

Taking a moment to gather his thoughts, Alex began to brief the detective. He provided a concise account of the physical evidence and observable aspects of the crime scene, careful to withhold the information about the stolen souls. It was a delicate balance between revealing enough to cooperate and protecting the secrecy of their world.

The investigation continued, the team working diligently for the next hour. They collaborated with HIB personnel to extract the bodies from the residence, each movement deliberate and precise to preserve any potential evidence. The atmosphere remained heavy with tension and unease.

Leo, the medical examiner, approached Alex as they prepared to leave the scene. "Director Knight, we'll have the autopsy results and forensic analysis soon. Expect a call from me regarding the findings."

Alex acknowledged Leo's statement with a curt nod, his mind already racing with the possibilities of what they might uncover. The weight of the case pressed down on him, the knowledge that they were dealing with a malevolent force that could unravel their world. The stakes were higher than ever, and he couldn't afford to fail.

As they left the Lane residence, Detective Collins walked beside Alex, his brow furrowed in deep thought. The emotional impact of the gruesome scene was etched on his face, the weight of responsibility evident in his eyes.

"Director Knight," Detective Collins began, his voice laced

with concern, "this case… it feels different, doesn't it? More sinister."

Alex's jaw tightened, the gravity of the situation settling heavily on his shoulders. "Yes, Detective. It's unlike anything we've encountered before. We need to find those responsible and put an end to this darkness."

11

Eryx

ERYX WOKE UP THAT MORNING to an empty bed, the warmth of the morning sun streaming through the window, casting a gentle glow over his room. He stretched, feeling the sheets cool against his skin where Alex had once been. He wished Alex could have stayed longer.

Mr. Whiskers padded over to the bed, meowing in greeting. Eryx smiled and reached out to scratch the cat behind the ears. Mr. Whiskers purred in response, a soothing sound that brought a sense of calm to the room.

Glancing at his phone, Eryx realized it was almost lunchtime. He hadn't slept this late in a while, but he welcomed the rest. His life as a musician often kept him up late into the night, and the mornings were a precious time to unwind.

With a yawn, Eryx swung his legs out of bed and made his way to the bathroom. The sound of the shower filled the room, a comforting backdrop to his morning routine. He let the warm water cascade over him, washing away the remnants of sleep.

Eryx made his way to the kitchen, Mr. Whiskers following closely behind. In the kitchen, the aroma of coffee brewing greeted him, a familiar and comforting scent that never failed to put a smile on his face.

He poured himself a cup of coffee, black with just a hint of sweetness, and took a moment to savor the rich flavor. It was a simple pleasure, but one that he cherished.

As he sipped his coffee, Eryx noticed a note that Alex had left on the counter. His heart skipped a beat, and he felt a rush of both anticipation and longing. He picked up the note, fingers trembling slightly with excitement.

Eryx,

Hey there, sleepyhead. I had to head out early for a meeting, but I didn't want to wake you. Call me if you need me.

—Alex

Eryx's lips curled into a gentle smile as he read the note on the kitchen counter. It was a reminder of a meeting with an old friend later that day. He placed it back carefully, sparing a glance at Mr. Whiskers, who purred contentedly nearby.

Pouring cat food into Mr. Whiskers' bowl, Eryx's day seemed off to a tranquil start. However, in the midst of this mundane routine, an unexpected bolt of agony struck his head. His grip on the cat food faltered, and it scattered across the floor with a soft thud.

Clenching his teeth, Eryx dropped to his knees, his world spinning into chaos. Waves of torment wracked his body, rendering him helpless. Amidst the suffering, an eerie and haunting voice pierced his thoughts.

Eryx.

He tried to respond, but the pain rendered his voice feeble, the words trapped in his constricted throat. His gaze darted around wildly, searching for the source of the voice that seemed to reverberate inside his skull.

"Who… Who's there?" Eryx rasped, his voice barely a whisper as the pain distorted his words.

There are dark forces at work that are about to come after you. Remember not to break.

The voice lingered, haunting and chilling, before gradually fading. As the pain began to ebb, Eryx found himself clutching the nearest wall for support. He panted heavily, struggling to regain control over his trembling limbs.

Slowly, he rose to his feet, his mind reeling with confusion and fear. Clutching Mr. Whiskers tightly to his chest, he found solace in the comforting purring of his feline companion.

After some time, Eryx managed to clean up the spilled cat food and proceeded to take a long, hot shower. The memory of the voice persisted, an enigmatic presence that refused to fade.

As the water cascaded over him, Eryx's thoughts returned to the warning. His mind raced with questions and anxieties.

Eryx shook his head, dismissing the ominous thoughts before they consumed him entirely. He couldn't afford to let fear paralyze him, not now.

With his shower finished, Eryx dried himself off and dressed, his mind a whirlwind of conflicting emotions. He couldn't shake the feeling that his peaceful life was about to be disrupted in ways he couldn't yet fathom.

Taking a deep breath, he swallowed a small pill to ease the persistent ache in his head—a constant companion he'd rather forget. As he adjusted his collar and prepared to face the day, Eryx couldn't help but wonder if this episode was just the beginning of a deeper and more perilous journey—one that he was reluctantly thrust into, whether he liked it or not.

Eryx found himself at a Starbucks conveniently nestled near the Shadowguards Headquarters. He approached the counter, placed an order for his usual latte, and joined the queue of eager caffeine seekers.

As he waited, Eryx's thoughts wandered, unable to escape the strange events of the morning. He wanted to forget, to let go of the mysterious encounter that had stirred him up inside.

Finally, his latte was ready, and Eryx carefully carried it to a cozy spot by the window. He settled into the cushioned chair, his fingers curling around the warm cup. The aroma of freshly brewed coffee enveloped him, mingling with the sweet scent of pastries displayed on the counter.

Eryx stirred his latte absentmindedly, his gaze fixed on the bustling Manhattan street outside. The soft buzz of conversation in the coffee shop provided a soothing backdrop. The hum of the espresso machine, the clinking of cups and saucers, all seemed to blend into a comforting melody.

He sipped his latte, feeling the creamy beverage wash over his senses. The taste was familiar, a small comfort in the midst of the whirlwind of emotions that had taken hold of him.

But there was no denying it; his thoughts kept drifting back to Alex.

His fingers tapped lightly on the table, a nervous habit he

couldn't shake. He took another sip of his latte, savoring the warmth and the bitterness, a bittersweet reminder of the morning's encounter.

As he gazed out the window, the play of sunlight on his latte cup caught his attention. It was like a glimmer of hope, a tiny spark that danced on the surface of his thoughts.

The aroma of baked treats from the counter wafted through the air, filling his senses with sweetness. It was as if the universe was teasing him, offering a taste of something he couldn't quite reach.

He took a deep breath, trying to steady his racing heart. There was something about Alex, something that defied logic and reason. It was a magnetic pull, an undeniable attraction that left him both exhilarated and uncertain.

He glanced down at his latte, the cup cradled in his hands. It was a simple pleasure, a moment of solace in the midst of chaos. But it was also a reminder that sometimes, the most unexpected encounters could lead to the most extraordinary discoveries.

Suddenly, a deep voice broke Eryx's thoughts, pulling him out of the swirling vortex of memories. He looked up and there was Landon, his ex-boyfriend, standing right there. Landon's smile, a blend of familiarity and something new, brought back a rush of emotions and memories of their shared past.

Eryx couldn't help but smile, surprised and a bit nostalgic. "Hi, Landon," he said, his voice warm but uncertain. He motioned to the chair in front of him. "You can sit here if you want."

Landon took the seat, a mix of curiosity and understanding in his eyes. Eryx noticed how Landon had changed since they last saw each other—the way his hair fell differently, the subtle shifts in his smile. Time had added layers to the person he used to know.

"I haven't seen you here before," Landon said, glancing around the cozy Manhattan Starbucks.

Eryx shrugged, trying to sound casual despite the swirl of emotions inside him. "Yeah, thought I'd explore this area a bit."

Landon, ever perceptive, saw right through him. Eryx cursed himself inwardly for not being better at hiding his true feelings.

"Checking out the Shadowguards Headquarters?" Landon asked with a grin, a hint of mischief in his eyes.

Eryx raised an eyebrow, surprised. "You know about them?"

Landon leaned back in his chair, a glint of amusement in his eyes. "Oh yeah, I know everything about this city."

Eryx chuckled nervously, feeling a bit exposed. "Okay, you got me. It's an interesting place, wanted to check it out," he said, as if he had never set foot inside.

Landon smiled, clearly understanding more than he let on. "Your sense of adventure always impressed me, Eryx. So, what's the real story? Some secret mission?"

Eryx pretended to be shocked. "You found out! I'm here to be a singing secret agent."

Landon laughed, the sound warm and familiar. It was a laugh that made Eryx feel better. "A spy by day, Broadway star by night?"

Their banter flowed effortlessly, as if no time had passed since they were last together. The conversation was easy, reminding Eryx of their old friendship. Despite the years that had separated them, there was still something special between them.

They talked about their lives since they parted ways, sharing snippets of their respective journeys. Eryx couldn't help but notice how Landon's eyes sparkled with enthusiasm when he talked about his new job in event planning. Landon, in turn, seemed genuinely interested in Eryx's recent travels and musical pursuits.

Eryx leaned back in his chair, studying Landon through the warm, diffused sunlight that streamed into the Manhattan Starbucks. Their history was a tangle of emotions he'd tried to forget, but seeing Landon again brought a mix of nostalgia and uncertainty.

"So, why are you here, Landon?" Eryx asked, a flicker of curiosity in his eyes.

Landon grinned sheepishly, his fingers tracing patterns on the table. "No big reason, really. Just drove by, saw you, and thought I'd catch up."

Eryx raised an eyebrow, a playful smirk tugging at his lips. He knew there was more to it. "Uh-huh, just a random thing, right?"

Landon chuckled, a soft sound that held a hint of nervousness. "Yeah, well, maybe not entirely random. I was just wondering if we are still friends."

Their breakup had been amicable, a mutual understanding that they wanted different things. Still, Eryx couldn't help but wonder about the true reason for Landon's visit.

Eryx's voice softened as he spoke, sincerity in his eyes. "Definitely! That won't change. You meant a lot to me, Landon. And our breakup wasn't awful."

Landon's smile softened too, and he met Eryx's gaze with a

hint of relief. "I was just unsure if you still felt that way. But thanks for saying that."

Their conversation flowed smoothly, like picking up an old book and finding it as familiar as ever. It was as if time had blurred, and they were back to being friends.

"Well, I should go now. Don't want to keep you," Landon said, starting to rise from his chair.

Eryx nodded, his emotions settling into a comfortable rhythm. "You too, Landon. Take care."

But just before Landon could make his exit, he paused. There was something more he wanted to do. He reached for a tissue on the table, scribbled a number on it, and handed it to Eryx.

"If you ever need anything, I mean anything, here's my new number," Landon said, a genuine offer in his eyes.

Eryx took the tissue and pocketed it with a nod. "Thanks, Landon. I'll call you sometime."

With a final wave, Landon left, disappearing into the bustling Manhattan streets. Eryx watched him go, feeling a sense of closure and gratitude for their conversation.

The Starbucks remained a sanctuary of familiar smells and cozy ambiance, but it held a new memory now—a reminder that connections could stay strong even when life changed. As he sipped his coffee, Eryx couldn't help but reflect on the evolution of their friendship.

The memories of their past experiences together flashed through his mind, like snapshots from another time. The first time they met at a crowded party, their shared laughter during a road trip, and the quiet moments of understanding they had shared.

Eryx knew there were unspoken feelings, lingering regrets,

but there was comfort in the fact that they had moved forward as individuals. It was a testament to their growth and resilience.

Eryx finished his coffee, a sense of contentment settling over him. Life had a funny way of bringing people back together.

After Landon left Starbucks, Eryx strolled along the Manhattan street, the city's hustle and bustle accompanying his every step. It was a sunny afternoon, with a gentle breeze ruffling his hair. His fingers were wrapped around his phone, and he couldn't help but hum along with the playlist he needed to rehearse for the upcoming concert.

As he walked, Eryx took in the sights and sounds of the city he called home. People hurried by in a blur of colorful attire, and the smell of street food wafted from nearby vendors. A street musician strummed a guitar on the corner, adding a musical backdrop to the urban scene.

But just as Eryx was getting lost in his thoughts and the rhythm of the city, his concentration was interrupted by an incoming call. The familiar ringtone jolted him back to the present moment. He didn't even check the caller ID before answering.

"Hello?" Eryx said, his voice laced with curiosity.

"Eryx! Where've you been?" The voice on the other end belonged to none other than Dion, his best friend since forever. Eryx should have known it was him.

"Just around. What's going on?" Eryx replied, a smile playing at the corners of his lips. He couldn't help but feel a surge of warmth at hearing Dion's voice. They had been through so much together, and their friendship was as steady as a lighthouse in a storm.

"I've been missing my buddy. How about dropping by my place? We can catch up," Dion suggested, his tone filled with genuine fondness.

Eryx had missed his friend too, so he decided that Mr. Whiskers, could wait a bit longer for his food. He chuckled softly at the idea.

"Yeah, sure. See you there," Eryx agreed, his excitement growing. There was something about catching up with Dion that always brightened his day.

With the call ended, Eryx continued his journey, making a mental note to return to the store for Mr. Whiskers' cat food later. The anticipation of reuniting with his best friend put a spring in his step.

As he walked through the bustling streets of Manhattan, Eryx couldn't help but think about the countless adventures he and Dion had shared. From childhood mischief to teenage escapades, they had been inseparable. Their friendship was a treasure, and Eryx cherished every moment spent with Dion.

Soon, Eryx reached Dion's apartment building. It was a familiar place, one he had visited countless times over the years. He climbed the steps to Dion's door, his heart light with anticipation.

Dion opened the door with a wide grin, his eyes lighting up as he saw Eryx. "Eryx, my man! Come on in!"

Eryx chuckled, his eyes crinkling with warmth. "Missed you too, Dion."

Dion flashed a grin and motioned for Eryx to follow him inside. "I've got some tea ready."

The moment Eryx settled onto the luxurious couch in Dion's Manhattan apartment, he couldn't help but sigh in contentment. "Seriously, I'm in love with this couch."

Dion's voice came from the kitchen, a playful lilt in his tone. "Sorry, it's a one-of-a-kind. You can't have it."

Eryx laughed, his relaxed demeanor contrasting with his earlier excitement. "I might just sneak it out while you're asleep."

Dion fired back with mock seriousness, "I'll break you if you dare."

Soon, Dion returned with two mugs of steaming tea. The cozy living room, adorned in warm hues of amber and burgundy, seemed to embrace them. The scent of the tea, a fragrant blend of chamomile and honey, filled the air.

Eryx accepted one of the mugs and took a slow, appreciative sip. "You know, this setup feels oddly familiar."

Dion raised an eyebrow, his curiosity piqued. "Does it?"

Eryx nodded, a fond smile playing on his lips. "Yeah, Ari and I used to sit on a couch and have tea. Although with her, I ended up adopting a cat."

Dion leaned back, his gaze fixed on Eryx. "So, what's new? Ari mentioned you're seeing someone, but she didn't spill the details."

Eryx's eyes sparkled with a mixture of excitement and affection as he spoke of his newfound romance. "His name's Alex."

Dion couldn't hide his curiosity. "Do you have a picture of him?"

Eryx pulled out his phone, a mischievous grin tugging at his lips. He glanced at a discreetly taken photo of Alex and handed the phone to Dion. "Here you go."

Dion's expression froze as he studied the picture, his brows furrowing with concern. "Are you sure?"

Eryx leaned in, his curiosity piqued. "Why? Do you know

him too?"

Dion chose his words carefully, his voice tinged with caution. "It's a long story. Just… be cautious, okay?"

Eryx set his tea down and stood abruptly, his excitement giving way to unease. "I should get going."

Dion tried to stop him, his hand reaching out in a futile attempt to hold Eryx back. "Eryx, wait!"

But Eryx was already out the door, his heart heavy with unanswered questions and a sense of foreboding.

As Eryx hurried down the city streets, the fading echoes of Dion's words lingered in his mind. He couldn't help but wonder about the warning from both Ari and Dion.

The city lights danced around him, casting long shadows that seemed to mirror the uncertainty in his heart. With every step he took away from Dion's apartment, Eryx's resolve to uncover the truth grew stronger. He needed to know what lay hidden behind Alex's smile and the cryptic warnings from his closest friends.

Eryx's steps echoed through Central Park as he strolled along the winding path, still reeling from the events at Dion's house. The vibrant green of the trees provided some solace, but his mind was a whirlwind of thoughts and emotions.

As he walked, the soft rustling of leaves overhead and the distant chirping of birds created a soothing backdrop. The warmth of the sun bathed the park in a golden glow, and families picnicked on the grass while children played on the nearby playground. It was a serene afternoon, a stark contrast to the turmoil inside Eryx.

Lost in his thoughts, Eryx hardly noticed the stranger who approached him. The man had striking grey hair, perfectly combed despite the warmth of the day, and he wore a tailored suit that seemed entirely out of place in the park's casual atmosphere.

The man's approach was discreet, his steps almost soundless on the gravel path. Eryx turned to find himself face to face with the enigmatic stranger. The man's pale blue eyes bore into Eryx's, and a faint, cryptic smile played on his lips.

"Good day," the man greeted in a tone that held an air of formality, a strange contrast to the park's relaxed ambiance.

Eryx raised an eyebrow, feeling a bead of sweat forming on his temple. "Can I help you?" he asked, his voice tinged with curiosity and a touch of wariness.

The stranger continued to smile, unfazed by Eryx's guarded demeanor. "A simple question, if you'll indulge me. What's your name?"

Eryx's brow furrowed. This encounter felt peculiar, and he couldn't help but wonder about the man's intentions. "Eryx," he replied cautiously.

The stranger's smile widened, and he nodded as if he had uncovered a hidden treasure. "Eryx, we'll meet again soon."

With that cryptic statement, the man turned and walked away, disappearing into the park's bustling crowd. Eryx watched him go, a sense of foreboding settling in his chest.

The atmosphere around him seemed to shift, imperceptibly but undeniably. The warmth of the sun felt less comforting, and a shiver coursed through him, despite the heat of the day. It was as if the encounter had left an indelible mark on his surroundings, a ripple of the unknown.

Eryx sighed, rubbing his temples as he tried to make sense of the strange encounter. He really didn't need any more surprises today. With a resigned shrug, he decided to continue with his original plan and headed to the nearest store to buy cat food for Mr. Whiskers at home.

Eryx couldn't help but replay the encounter in his mind.

Finally, he reached the store, grabbing a bag of cat food and a few other essentials. The mundane act of shopping offered a brief respite from the strangeness of the day, but the encounter in the park lingered in the back of his mind.

With his purchases in hand, Eryx made his way back home, the weight of the day's events pressing on his shoulders. He couldn't escape the feeling that this encounter with the mysterious man was just the beginning of something much larger, something that would test him in ways he couldn't yet imagine.

As he unlocked the door to his apartment and stepped inside, he couldn't help but wonder what other surprises awaited him on this day.

12

Alex

ALEX WAS IN THE MIDST of a grueling workout at the Shadowguards Training Facility. The weight of the world pressed down on his broad shoulders, or at least it felt that way as he sweated heavily. The repetitive motion of his training served as a temporary escape from the relentless thoughts that plagued his mind.

The case consumed his thoughts. The Order had been growing more brazen and powerful by the day. Their malevolent deeds were on the rise, and Alex's sense of duty drove him to understand why this malignant force was surging forward so rapidly.

As he pushed his body to its limits, his mind wandered to Eryx. The wards he had meticulously placed around Eryx's home remained steadfast, an impenetrable fortress against any with nefarious intentions. It was a source of comfort, knowing that he could sense any threat that dared approach.

A small, tender smile tugged at the corners of Alex's mouth as he reminisced about their date. It was as if their souls had recognized each other long before their paths crossed. His god soul had fallen silent ever since he had grown closer to Eryx. At first, he dismissed it as a mere coincidence.

Alex grappled with conflicting emotions. He yearned to be by Eryx's side, to provide safety and security, and to bask in his warmth. But the weight of his duty as a Shadowguard pulled at him, a relentless reminder of the responsibilities he bore.

Alex found himself questioning if there was a way to balance both worlds. Could he protect Eryx and fulfill his duty without compromising either? The answer eluded him, and his heart ached with the weight of his uncertainty.

His body moved mechanically, the repetition of exercises serving as a form of meditation. Sweat poured down his forehead, mingling with the tension that knotted his brow. The physical sensations mirrored the intensity of his inner turmoil, a relentless battle that raged within.

Out of the blue, Alex's thoughts were disrupted by a charge in the air. He turned quickly, almost stumbling off the treadmill. There, right next to him, was Hermes, running at a superhuman speed. The treadmill came to an abrupt stop as Hermes hit the brakes, halting effortlessly without a drop of sweat on his brow. It really wasn't fair.

Alex paused the treadmill and grinned at his nephew. They exchanged a look, a silent understanding that had developed over years of closeness. Hermes' smile was radiant, the kind that could make you forget all your worries. He really missed his nephew. Not being in the underworld had its cost, and not being able to see loved ones was one of those sacrifices.

The city's clamor seemed to fade into the background as they stood together.

"Damn, you're sweating like you've never faced the heat

of the underworld," Hermes teased, mischief gleaming in his golden eyes.

Alex chuckled, his breath still heavy from the workout. "Well, I try to keep my infernal heat in check when I'm not down in the underworld."

He stretched out his arms for a hug, but Hermes playfully danced out of reach. "Aw, come on, uncle. You're super sweaty," Hermes quipped.

Alex playfully chased Hermes around, mockingly pretending to catch him. They circled the training area for a while before finally flopping down on nearby mats.

"Surprisingly speedy, Hermes."

Hermes grinned back. "I am the God of Swiftness, remember? Got a reputation to maintain."

Alex rolled his eyes at his nephew. "And here I thought your legendary reputation was all about your fashion sense."

Hermes, with his wavy dark brown hair and piercing green eyes, looked every bit the god he was.

Alex couldn't help but be amazed by his nephew's fashion sense. Hermes was wearing casual clothes, but they screamed style. He had on a white t-shirt that seemed to fit him perfectly, and a pair of jeans that looked effortlessly cool with just the right amount of fading. His colorful sneakers added a fun touch. Hermes also had some cool accessories going on. He wore a couple of bracelets that added personality to his look, and a necklace that peeked out from his shirt collar. His watch looked like a work of art.

The echo of his nephew's laughter lingered in the training room, filling it with a youthful vibrancy.

Their bond, nurtured over centuries, was a profound one. Alex remembered the first time he had met Hermes, a mischievous child who had grown into the God of Swiftness. They had shared countless adventures and secrets, their camaraderie unbreakable.

Alex was in the middle of his workout routine at the Shadowguards Training Facility, the sweat glistening on his brow, when the door swung open, and in walked Hermes, his mischievous nephew. Hermes clutched his chest dramatically, a playful twinkle in his eyes.

"Ouch, uncle! That one hurt," he said, feigning injury as he approached Alex.

Alex chuckled, wiping his brow with the back of his hand. "Alright, so what brings you here? You don't usually drop by without a reason."

"You're right," Hermes replied, flashing a charming grin. "I've got a message from Zeus."

Alex's expression darkened at the mention of Zeus. He clenched his fists, the memory of past grievances bubbling to the surface. "What does that... person want?"

Zeus wasn't exactly on Alex's list of trusted gods these days.

Hermes chose his words carefully, knowing how touchy the subject was. "Zeus wanted to see you as soon as possible."

Alex's growl deepened. "And he couldn't show up himself?" Leave it to Zeus to avoid doing things for himself. Selfish jerk.

"You know how father is," Hermes said, a trace of exasperation in his voice. "He gets whatever he wants. Though I couldn't resist the chance to visit my favorite uncle."

Alex took a deep breath, tempering his anger. Hermes didn't deserve his frustration. He asked, "Where is he, then?"

"He's currently the Prime Minister of England," Hermes replied with a mischievous glint in his eye.

Alex couldn't help but let out a bitter laugh. "Your father really can't stand not being in the spotlight, can he?"

Hermes grinned. "He definitely has an insatiable hunger for power."

"That he does," Alex replied, his voice tinged with resignation. Zeus had an unending thirst for power. He was constantly looking for more, always aiming to be in the spotlight. His desire for control seemed limitless, and he used his charm and authority to influence others. It was like power was his oxygen, and he loved the way it made him feel.

As they spoke, Alex couldn't help but notice the theatricality in Hermes's gestures. He had a flair for the dramatic, much like his father, though he used it in a more lighthearted manner.

Alex's own expressions told a story of their own. His face had shifted from amusement at Hermes's arrival to irritation when discussing Zeus. Memories of Zeus's past actions, his betrayals and manipulations, weighed heavily on Alex's mind.

He knew that his strained relationship with Zeus had deep roots. It all began when Zeus had made promises and then broken them, leaving Alex to pick up the pieces. The scars of those betrayals still lingered, making it difficult for Alex to trust the god of thunder.

Their family history was riddled with conflicts, and Zeus had played a central role in many of them. His pursuit of power had often come at the expense of others, and he had shown little regard for the consequences of his actions.

Alex couldn't help but wonder what Zeus wanted now, what new scheme he had concocted. He couldn't deny that his curiosity was piqued, despite his reservations.

Hermes, ever the messenger and mediator, seemed caught

in the middle. He had inherited his father's charm and charisma, but he also possessed a streak of mischief that set him apart. It was hard to stay mad at him for long.

"What's happening around here?" Hermes inquired, his tone filled with genuine curiosity and concern.

Alex wiped the sweat from his brow with a towel, catching his breath. "It's been chaotic, Hermes," he replied, motioning for his nephew to join him. "We're dealing with a case involving the Stolen Souls. They've become a real nuisance lately."

Hermes raised an eyebrow, intrigued by the mention of the elusive Stolen Souls. "Sounds like you're pretty busy, uncle," he remarked softly.

"You've got that right," Alex admitted, his voice carrying the weight of responsibility. "But those Stolen Souls are really getting under my skin."

Hermes nodded in understanding. He had once played a crucial role in guiding the souls of the departed to the underworld, a task now undertaken by his son. "I can look around and see if I can assist," he offered, his willingness to help evident in his eyes.

Alex appreciated the offer, knowing that Hermes possessed unique abilities when it came to the realm of the departed. "Couldn't hurt," he said with a nod. "I'd like to visit, but the threats here are increasing. It's become a dangerous place."

"I understand, uncle," Hermes replied, his voice filled with empathy. "Trust me."

The two of them continued their conversation, shifting to a different topic that had been occupying Alex's thoughts recently. "So, this Eryx guy," Hermes began, curiosity dancing in his eyes. "Tell me more about him."

Alex leaned against a nearby pillar, a thoughtful expression on his face. He shared the story of Eryx, the mysterious individual who had captured his attention and the interest of the Fates themselves. "So yeah," he concluded, "he's been incredible, and he's been keeping me on my toes."

Hermes couldn't help but smile at his uncle's description. "Wow, he sounds like a great match for you. Though I do wonder why the Fates chose to protect him."

Alex chuckled softly. "You know the Fates. They enjoy their riddles and mysteries."

Hermes nodded, remembering the cryptic nature of the Fates' messages and their enigmatic presence whenever they appeared. Their answers were like puzzles with missing pieces, leaving more questions in their wake.

"True," Hermes agreed with a thoughtful expression. "I'm looking forward to meeting him, though."

"Me too," Alex admitted with a smile, his gaze fixed on his nephew. "I have a feeling you two will get along well."

Alex wiped the sweat from his brow as he finished another set of push-ups. It was a routine that brought him a sense of calm, a momentary escape from the complexities of his world.

"How's Marcus doing?" Hermes asked, sounding a bit worried. Marcus, their enigmatic teammate, had a background as intricate as a labyrinth, a mix of divine and mortal heritage.

Alex turned to face his nephew, offering a warm smile. "He's doing great. Marcus has turned into quite a capable force."

Hermes raised an eyebrow with a hint of a grin. "Taking after his powerful lineage?"

Alex chuckled, his gaze distant with fond memories. "Absolutely. He's got his father's determination and a touch of your mischief."

Hermes grinned, clearly proud of the unconventional mentorship he had inadvertently provided. "Well, that's a good combo."

Alex playfully nudged Hermes's arm. "Don't forget his talent for finding himself in unexpected situations."

Hermes laughed, reminiscent. "Ah, the days of youthful adventures."

Alex leaned closer, their bond evident in the ease of their conversation. "Marcus might even have us beat in the 'daring escapades' department."

Hermes mock-glared, his eyes dancing with amusement. "Really? Maybe I should've been his mentor."

Alex's smile softened, a hint of understanding in his gaze. "You did what you thought was best."

Hermes looked thoughtful for a moment. "Yeah, but I sometimes wonder…"

Alex offered his unwavering support. "It's natural to have doubts. But you're here now."

Hermes smiled appreciatively, grateful for Alex's reassurance. "You're right."

Alex assured him, "When the time is right, you and Marcus will find your way."

Hermes met Alex's gaze with renewed resolve. "I hope he'll understand."

"He will," Alex said confidently. "He's a mix of your strengths."

Hermes chuckled, his eyes sparkling with shared history. "And probably a bit of your stubbornness too."

Alex teased, "That's his human side showing."

Their laughter filled the air, a testament to the enduring camaraderie they shared.

"Hermes," Alex said sincerely, "just be there for Marcus when you're ready to talk. That's what matters."

Hermes nodded with determination. "I will. For Marcus."

In that moment, amid their chat and genuine words, they knew challenges might come. Yet, their friendship would guide them.

Hermes grinned. "Enough seriousness. How about a challenge? Who can do the most sit-ups in a minute? Winner gets unlimited ambrosia."

Alex laughed heartily, his deep voice echoing through the training facility. "Deal, Hermes. But remember, you're competing with the King of the Underworld."

Their laughter echoed, a reminder that through divine matters and everyday hurdles, their friendship remained steadfast and joyful. It was a bond that had weathered the test of time, and as they embarked on this lighthearted challenge, they celebrated not only their strength but the enduring connection that had shaped their lives.

Alex and Hermes said their goodbyes not long after that. Hermes told him that he was tracking an elusive Hesperides dragon that currently resides here in New York.

Alex's eyebrows shot up in surprise. "Really? He's here?"

Hermes nodded solemnly. "Yeah, Hespere said that he was here and glamoured as a human."

Concern crept into Alex's voice. "Did she say how he got here? Maybe we can help out."

Hermes hesitated for a moment. "No need, uncle. I've got it under control." He rubbed the back of his neck. "Hespere told me that he ran away like a rebellious teenager, and they haven't seen him since a couple of centuries ago."

Alex couldn't help but frown. The guardians of the Tree of Life were responsible for safeguarding the Golden Apple, believed to hold magical properties that granted immortality and immeasurable power. The presence of one of these guardians in the mortal realm raised serious questions and red flags.

"Who's helping them guard the Tree of Life now?" Alex wondered aloud.

Hermes sighed, his worry evident. "Erythesis and Aigle are still able to guard it. But they also told me that the energies in Hesperia were troubling them. When I got there, the energies seemed off, and we couldn't explain why it was acting the way it is. The sisters are concerned. That's why they wanted to find him before something catastrophic happens."

Alex placed a reassuring hand on his nephew's shoulder. "That does sound troubling. If you need any help locating the dragon, don't hesitate to call me."

Hermes nodded, a grateful smile crossing his face. "Thanks, uncle. I've got to get going. That damn dragon is fast."

Alex chuckled, the tension in the room easing slightly. "Okay. Take care, yeah?"

With a nod, Hermes backed away and, with a swift movement, conjured a portal that led him away from the training facility, leaving Alex alone once more.

Alex peeled off his sweat-soaked shirt and made his way to the nearby shower facilities. The conversation with Hermes had stirred a mixture of emotions within him—concern for the guardians, curiosity about the dragon's motives, and a sense of duty to protect the balance between the mortal realm and the mystical world.

After cleaning up, Alex dressed in fresh clothes and headed toward his office. The facility's corridors were quiet, a stark contrast to the energy of the training sessions.

Alex sat at his cluttered desk, his brow furrowed as he skimmed through the report Gabriel had sent about the Order's recent movements. The implications were troubling, and he couldn't shake the unease that gnawed at him. His concentration was broken by a knock on his office door.

"Come in," Alex called, setting the report aside.

The door swung open, revealing Marcus on the other side. "Sir, Director Hernandez is here and wanted to see you."

Director Daniel Hernandez, head of the Human Investigation Bureau, was a figure Alex had crossed paths with numerous times. He had a reputation for being kind as long as you didn't tread on his toes. The fact that Hernandez was here without scheduling a formal meeting raised a red flag.

"Let him in, Marcus," Alex ordered, his tone firm.

Marcus nodded and stepped aside to allow Director Hernandez to enter. The director's face was a storm of irritation, his brow furrowed, and his lips pressed into a thin line. It was clear that he was not pleased.

"Director, what can I do for you?" Alex inquired cautiously, his gaze locked onto Hernandez.

"Did you really take the case out of our hands?" Hernandez's voice carried an accusatory edge.

Alex didn't flinch. "Are you referring to the Rina Lane case? If so, then yes."

Hernandez's nostrils flared slightly as he responded, "That case fell squarely within our jurisdiction, Knight. You had no right to snatch it away without going through the proper channels. You know the protocol. Unless you know something we don't."

"The victims had their souls ripped from them, Hernandez," Alex retorted, his voice unwavering. "Would you have preferred your team to face a danger they're ill-equipped to handle? Think, Director. Even if I were in your shoes, I wouldn't want my team to meet a senseless demise."

Hernandez's anger seemed to ebb slightly, replaced by a grudging understanding. "You should have informed me beforehand, Knight."

"We didn't have the luxury of time," Alex explained, his gaze steady. "Right now, the Order's actions are escalating, and our focus must remain on countering their imminent threat."

The director's pointed finger lowered, though his expression still held a hint of irritation. "If you pull a stunt like this again, Knight, I won't hesitate to file a formal complaint against you. And believe me, I can make it stick."

"Understood," Alex replied, maintaining his composure. "Now, I need you to leave, and we will keep you updated on the case's progress."

Hernandez hesitated for a moment, his gaze locked with Alex's. Then, with a curt nod, he turned and exited the office, leaving Alex alone in the dimly lit room.

As the door closed behind the director, Alex leaned back in his chair, a heavy sigh escaping his lips. He knew that his decision to take on the Rina Lane case had crossed a line, but he couldn't allow his team to be put in harm's way. The Order was a threat unlike any other, and he couldn't afford to be bound by bureaucratic red tape.

He glanced at the cluttered desk before him, filled with reports, maps, and notes related to the Order's activities. The weight of his responsibilities pressed down on him, but he had chosen this path, and he would see it through, no matter the consequences.

Alex contemplated the implications of his actions. He knew that tensions with Director Hernandez might linger, but he had made the decision he believed was right for his team and for the safety of those they were sworn to protect. The Order's shadow loomed ever larger, and he couldn't afford to let protocol stand in the way of their mission.

Alex's office was a realm of organized chaos, a reflection of the man himself. He shuffled papers and neatly stacked documents, his mind focused on the mundane task of tidying up. The phone's familiar chime cut through his concentration, and he reached for it, the device's cool metal grounding him in the present.

"Hello?" Alex answered, a subtle note of relief slipping into his voice as he recognized Eryx's warm, velvety tone on the other end of the line.

"Alex? How's your day been?" Eryx's voice flowed through the phone, and a sense of calm settled over Alex, like a balm for his weary soul.

"Much better now that you've called," Alex admitted, a hint of fondness coloring his words. There was something about Eryx's presence, even through the phone, that had the power to soothe him.

Eryx's concern was palpable. "Want to talk about it?"

Alex appreciated the offer, but he wasn't ready to open up just yet. "Not right now, but I appreciate the offer. How about your day? How did it go?"

Eryx's response came after a brief pause, his voice carrying a mix of emotions. "It was alright." He sounded fatigued, as if the day had taken its toll on him. "Hey, Alex, can I ask you something?"

Alex sensed a shift in the conversation and grew attentive. "Of course, anything."

Eryx's sigh was heavy, laden with weariness. "Do you have any secrets you're keeping from me?"

The question caught Alex off guard, and a twinge of doubt crept in. "Where's this coming from?"

Eryx's voice sounded weary, as if he was grappling with something. "I visited Dion today. He and Ari mentioned knowing you, and they warned me to be cautious around you."

Alex's brows furrowed at the revelation. Those two were always stirring up mischief. He needed to have a word with them soon. "It's not what you think, Eryx. Can you trust me when I say that I'll tell you when I'm ready?"

"You don't happen to have a secret wife stashed away somewhere, do you?" Eryx's question caught Alex off guard, prompting an uncontrollable burst of laughter.

"No, no secret wife lurking around, I assure you," Alex replied, his tone carrying a light-hearted assurance. "I'd stake my life on that."

Eryx's voice held a mix of relief and playfulness. "Alright, I'll hold you to that, Alex. I don't want secrets between us. And just so you know, I really like you."

Alex's heart skipped a beat at Eryx's words. The urge to rush to Eryx's side was strong, but he managed to contain it. "You sound tired, sweetheart. Go get some rest."

Eryx's response was punctuated by a yawn. "Yeah, you're right. Goodnight, Alex."

"Goodnight, Eryx," Alex murmured softly, his heart feeling strangely full as he heard Eryx end the call. He leaned back in his chair, a small smile tugging at his lips. The mysteries and secrets of their lives could wait. For now, he relished in the warmth of Eryx's voice, the connection they shared, and the promise of tomorrow.

13

Eryx

"**A**RE YOU READY, ERYX?" Richard's voice cut through the buzzing anticipation in the room.

Eryx glanced up from tuning his guitar, finding Richard's gaze locked onto him. Tomorrow was the big day, and Richard, ever the considerate bandleader, had insisted on including Eryx in every rehearsal session, despite Eryx only being slated to perform two numbers—both the opening and closing acts.

No pressure, Eryx thought to himself, his fingers nimble as they adjusted the guitar strings. The whole band was gathered in Richard's living room, each member bustling about, busy getting their instruments ready for the final rehearsal.

The room hummed with activity, filled with the sounds of strings being tuned and drumsticks tapping in rhythm. The faint scent of wood and leather from the guitars wafted through the air, mingling with the underlying scent of coffee and excitement.

Richard strolled into the room, his presence bringing a

sense of familiarity and camaraderie. His easy smile was contagious, and it was clear that despite the upcoming concert, the band was in high spirits.

Eryx couldn't help but think about how much he was going to miss everyone once this was all over. They had become a close-knit group, connected by their love for music and the time they had spent practicing and playing together. The upcoming concert was more than just a performance; it was a reminder of the journey they had taken as a team.

"Huh?" Eryx was so focused on what he was doing that he didn't hear Richard.

Richard chuckled at him. "I was asking if you are ready to start."

Eryx rubbed the back of his neck and put his guitar down. "Yeah, I am ready."

"Are you okay?" Richard asked as Eryx stood up.

"Yeah. Just a lot in my mind is all."

"Hey, Eryx, you're not thinking of bailing out on us now, are you?" Joey, chimed in with a playful grin. He adjusted his drum kit, the metallic clinks and thuds accompanying his movements.

Eryx shot Joey a mock glare. "Do I look like a quitter to you, Joey?"

Sarah, laughed as she tested the keys of her instrument. "If you do, then I'm in trouble too," she added, her fingers dancing over the keyboard.

Chris, nodded in agreement. "We're a package deal, Eryx. No quitting allowed."

Eryx couldn't help but smile at their banter. Despite the looming pressure of the concert, the camaraderie within the band was unbreakable. They shared inside jokes, playful jabs, and an unspoken understanding that made them more than just a group of musicians.

Richard, always the backbone of the band, joined the banter with a wink. "That's the spirit, Eryx. Besides, you've got the opening and closing numbers. The rest of us are just here for the ride."

The room buzzed with excitement as they prepared to start the rehearsal. Eryx couldn't deny the mixture of nerves and anticipation bubbling within him. The responsibility of opening and closing the show weighed on him, but he was determined to rise to the occasion.

"Cool. Come on let's start." Joey said.

He mentally scolded himself for bringing down the mood. He didn't want to let down the people who had given him a chance and believed in him.

"We could always start later on once you're feeling better." Richard reassured him.

"No, it is fine. I just need to shake my nerves off and we can start."

"If you're sure then let's go." Richard patted his shoulder making him jump and they all chuckled.

As the first chords filled the room, Eryx's thoughts raced. He was living his dream, making music with friends who felt like family. The lyrics of the songs resonated with him, each note and melody carrying a piece of his soul.

With each strum of his guitar and every note he sang, Eryx poured his heart into the music. The band played on, their harmonies blending seamlessly, their passion for their craft evident in every chord.

In the midst of the music, Eryx couldn't help but think about the journey that had brought them to this point. The countless hours of practice, the gigs in tiny, smoky venues, and the auditions that had tested their resolve—all had led to this moment.

Despite the lighthearted banter and camaraderie, Eryx knew that the concert was a significant step for their band's career. It was a chance to showcase their talent to a larger audience, to make their mark on the music scene.

As the rehearsal continued, Eryx's fingers danced across the fretboard, his voice filling the room with raw emotion. The music flowed through him, a powerful connection that transcended words. He was in his element, doing what he loved most, and it was a feeling like no other.

But beneath the surface, a sense of anticipation lingered. Tomorrow, they would take the stage, and the world would listen. The stakes were high, and the pressure was real. Eryx knew that they had to give it their all, leaving no room for doubt or hesitation.

As the final chords of their closing number resonated through the room, a shared sense of accomplishment settled over the band. They exchanged nods and smiles, the unspoken understanding that they were ready for the concert.

Eryx couldn't help but feel a surge of gratitude for his bandmates and the music that had brought them together. The road had been long and challenging, but they had persevered, and now they were on the brink of something extraordinary.

The rehearsal had gone smoothly, the music flowing in harmonious rhythm, like a well-oiled machine. After the last chord had faded into the air, Richard, the band's charismatic frontman, motioned for Eryx to join him in a quiet corner of the room. Eryx, wiping sweat from his brow, followed, curiosity etching lines into his usually composed features.

As they moved away from the rest of the band, Eryx couldn't help but notice the exchanged glances and secretive smiles among his bandmates. His brow furrowed in confusion, and he couldn't resist asking, "What's going on, guys?"

Richard stepped closer, a mischievous grin dancing on his face. "We've got a little surprise for you, Eryx."

Eryx's eyes darted between the band members, their smiles and nods deepening his bewilderment. "A surprise? For me?"

Richard chuckled heartily, his enthusiasm infectious. "Yep, you've been such a great sport through all this, and we wanted to show our appreciation."

Eryx's lips curled into a playful smirk. "Appreciation, huh? Is this some sort of elaborate prank?"

Richard burst into laughter, his eyes crinkling at the corners. "No way, Eryx! No pranks, I promise. In fact, Chris here has something for you."

Chris stepped forward, his grin matching Richard's in magnitude. "Hey, Eryx, this one's from all of us."

He handed Eryx a beautifully wrapped gift, and Eryx accepted it with a mix of excitement and curiosity. "Oh, you guys really didn't have to."

Richard shook his head, sincerity in his eyes. "We really wanted to."

Eryx gave the gift a playful shake before carefully unwrapping it, unveiling the contents. His eyes widened in genuine surprise. "Whoa."

Richard's excitement bubbled over, and he urged, "Go on, open it!"

Eryx's fingers worked delicately as he unveiled the gift,

revealing a stunning Gibson Les Paul Standard guitar. The vintage beauty was a classic Gibson, known for its incredible sound, craftsmanship, and timeless design. Eryx's breath caught in his throat as he admired the gift in his hands. "Is this…?"

Chris beamed proudly. "A rare Gibson Les Paul Standard. We know you'll make the most of it."

Eryx was at a loss for words, his emotions swirling like a tempest. The gift was beyond his wildest expectations. He ran his fingers over the guitar's sleek body, marveling at the exquisite craftsmanship. "This is incredible. I can't believe you guys got this for me."

Richard clapped him on the back, a wide grin on his face. "You deserve it, Eryx."

Eryx looked around at his bandmates, gratitude flooding his heart. "Thank you, all of you."

Joey chimed in with a hearty laugh, "Well, Eryx, now you've got a guitar worthy of your talent!"

Sarah added, "And it's about time you had an upgrade from that old one."

"You're going to make some amazing music with this, Eryx." Chris said,

Eryx couldn't stop himself from strumming a few chords, the rich sound filling the room. The guitar felt like an extension of himself, a new chapter in his musical journey.

The band members exchanged proud glances, their bond stronger than ever. Eryx felt a surge of gratitude for these friends who had become family.

Eryx looked at his bandmates, his voice filled with warmth. "I don't know what to say, except thank you. You guys are the best."

Their shared excitement and happiness were palpable, their friendship deepened by this heartfelt gesture. In that moment, amidst the laughter and music, Eryx knew that no matter where their musical journey took them, they would always be united by the love of music and the unbreakable bond they shared.

As Eryx cradled the rare Gibson Les Paul Standard in his hands, he couldn't help but be in awe of the moment. The guitar was a masterpiece, its glossy finish reflecting the warm, ambient light of the Manhattan Club called Autumn. He ran his fingers along the smooth fretboard, marveling at the weight and craftsmanship of the instrument. It was a piece of art, a treasure that he never thought he'd possess.

"I don't know if I can get you guys anything that's more valuable than this guitar," Eryx admitted, his voice filled with genuine humility. His eyes shimmered with sincerity as he looked at his friends.

Richard shook his head, a warm smile on his face. "No need to worry about that, Eryx. We all chipped in because we wanted to. The only thing we're asking is for you to stick around and not be a stranger."

Eryx's lips curved into a grateful smile, his heart swelling with emotion. "Yeah, okay. I'm not going anywhere," he promised, his voice steady despite the emotions that threatened to overwhelm him. He didn't want to tear up in front of everyone, but the gratitude he felt was undeniable.

It felt surreal how quickly things had turned around. Just moments ago, Eryx had been uncertain if he would see these people again, and now they were extending their friendship and asking him to stay. The sense of belonging he felt warmed his heart, and he couldn't help but think that his found family was growing in the most unexpected yet beautiful ways.

Joey clapped Eryx on the back. "Man, that guitar is going to take your music to a whole new level. We can't wait to hear you play it."

"And we won't take no for an answer. You're a part of this band, Eryx." Sarah added with a wink.

"It's not just about the music, buddy. It's about us, too. You're family now." Chris chimed in.

Eryx nodded, his heart full. The weight of the Gibson Les Paul Standard in his hands was a tangible reminder of the trust and friendship he had found in these people.

As he continued to run his fingers over the guitar's fretboard, Eryx couldn't help but think back to his initial doubts and uncertainties. He had once questioned whether he belonged in this world of music and friendship, but now, he had the answer. He belonged here, with these incredible people who had shown him what it truly meant to be a part of something special.

Eryx and the band decided to wrap up their rehearsals with a visit to a Manhattan bar. The idea of navigating New York's bustling streets didn't appeal to him, so he happily accepted a ride with his fellow musicians. During the car ride, they bonded over singing along to radio songs and playful banter. It was one of those rare moments when they weren't in "music mode."

Once they arrived at the club, called Autumn, along the vibrant Manhattan strip, Eryx felt the city's electric energy pulsating all around him. Neon signs flickered above, and the sidewalks teemed with pedestrians, creating a lively backdrop to their evening. The bar itself exuded a warm and cozy vibe, with the gentle murmur of conversations and the faint hum of live music filling the air.

They were met by an imposing bouncer, who happened to be a rather huge ogre. Eryx couldn't help but notice the contrast between the bouncer's massive frame and the gentleness ogres could exhibit when they chose to. "ID," the bouncer demanded in a firm tone.

Eryx obliged, handing over his ID, which was checked and nodded at. The same routine followed for the rest of the band, each of them showing their IDs and receiving the nod of approval. It was a serious and efficient process, a mix of tough looks and necessary security.

Inside, Eryx pulled Richard aside, a plan forming in his mind. "Hey, Richard, do you mind if I invite someone over?"

Richard, always easygoing, flashed a grin over the loud music. "Sure! We'd love to meet your friends, too!"

Eryx pulled out his phone, heart racing a bit as he dialed Alex's number. The anticipation of hearing Alex's voice grew with each passing second. When Alex finally answered, Eryx couldn't help but smile. "Hey, Alex. How's your evening going?"

Alex's voice was like a comforting melody over the phone. "Hey, Eryx. It's been good. Just finishing up some work. What about you?"

The distant sounds of life in the background of the call made Eryx feel closer to Alex. "I'm at a club with the band. We wrapped up rehearsals and decided to hang out. It's been fun."

Curiosity and warmth colored Alex's voice as he responded. "Sounds like a great way to unwind. How's the band?"

"They're awesome, really welcoming," Eryx replied. He glanced at his bandmates engaged in animated discussions.

"Hey, I was thinking… would you want to join us? I mean, if you're not too busy."

There was a brief pause on the line before Alex spoke again. "I appreciate the offer, Eryx. But I'm not sure if I should intrude on your time with the band."

Eryx leaned against a wall, his thoughts and emotions swirling. "You wouldn't be intruding at all. In fact, I'd love for you to meet them. They've been really great, and I want you to be part of this."

A hint of hesitation lingered in Alex's response. "Are you sure?"

Eryx's smile carried into his voice. "Absolutely. It would mean a lot to me."

A warm chuckle emanated from the other end. "Alright then. I'll head over. Just text me the address."

Eryx's heart leaped with joy. "Great! I'll send it right over. See you soon, Alex."

As Eryx hung up, a sense of contentment washed over him. He was looking forward to introducing Alex to his newfound friends, the band that had quickly become like family. He couldn't wait to see how this night, filled with music and camaraderie, would unfold.

14

Alex

HIS TEAM WAS GATHERED AROUND the briefing room, their faces etched with a mix of anticipation and weariness. The clock on the wall ticked away the seconds, a constant reminder of the pressing task at hand. Alex wanted to know the updates on the case they were investigating, one that had taken a perplexing turn.

"Olivia, do you have any information regarding the boyfriend of Ms. Lane?" Alex asked, his piercing gaze fixed on Olivia.

Olivia was the only mage on their team, a woman of extraordinary power whose abilities transcended the realm of ordinary magic users. Alex was grateful to have her on the team. Her unique skills had often proven invaluable in cracking some of the city's most enigmatic cases.

"So far, sir, there is nothing on the man other than his identity. According to some of Ms. Lane's friends, the man's name is Sven Janssen. And he apparently owns the big tech company ChronoKeep." Olivia reported.

Knowing the company's reputation, Alex was wary. While

ChronoKeep held a prominent position in the tech industry of New York, rumors of dubious dealings and ethical breaches cast a shadow over its success. Beyond its impressive technology, there lingered an unsettling sense that there might be more to the story, tarnishing ChronoKeep's otherwise polished image.

"Did they say whether or not he's human?" Alex inquired, his mind racing with the possibilities.

"No, sir," Olivia replied, her eyes scanning the notes on her tablet, "they mentioned that Ms. Lane never really talked about him to them that much."

Alex nodded, absorbing the information. The mystery surrounding Sven Janssen deepened with each passing moment. He was a shadowy figure, lurking at the periphery of the victim's life, and Alex couldn't shake the feeling that he held a key to unraveling the enigma of Ms. Lane's murder.

"I want you to look further into this guy and pinpoint his location before the murder," Alex ordered Olivia, his tone resolute. They needed to bring Sven Janssen in for questioning, to peel away the layers of secrecy and unveil any connections he might have to the tragic events that had unfolded.

Turning his attention to Lucas, a tech genius with a penchant for bypassing digital barriers, Alex issued his next directive, "I want you to hack into the ChronoKeep's database to see if you can find anything."

Lucas, who had already prepared himself for this task, nodded and promptly sat down at his computer station. His fingers danced across the keyboard as he infiltrated the complex digital fortress of ChronoKeep. The screen illuminated his face with a bluish glow as lines of code scrolled rapidly.

"Sir, I'll need some time," Lucas said, sweat forming on his brow as he navigated through layers of firewalls and encryption.

"Take as much time as you need, but be discreet. We don't want to tip them off," Alex cautioned, fully aware of the potential consequences of poking into the affairs of a powerful tech giant.

Meanwhile, Marcus, provided his update, "Sir, the roommate is very elusive, but with the help of Gabe, we were able to find out his name. His name is Damon Shill, and we are currently tracking everything that he does."

"Good work," Alex acknowledged, a sense of satisfaction washing over him. They were making progress, each team member playing their part in this intricate puzzle. "Don't lose sight of him."

Gabe and Marcus, exchanged nods of determination. Damon Shill was a key figure in the timeline of events leading up to the murder, and they were determined to uncover his role in this chilling narrative.

With each team member in motion, Alex felt a sense of urgency gripping him. The investigation was becoming increasingly complex, and the stakes were higher than ever. They were delving deeper into the case, unraveling the layers of mystery surrounding Ms. Lane's murder, and the clock continued to tick, each second bringing them closer to the truth.

As the room buzzed with activity, Alex knew that they were on the precipice of a breakthrough. But he also understood that with each answer they uncovered, more questions would arise.

Not long after their briefing, Alex overheard Gabe talking to someone on his SHD. Curiosity piqued, Alex watched as Gabe approached him after ending the call, a look of concern in his eyes.

"Sir, Elder Lucius wants us at their Coven," Gabe reported, his voice tinged with uncertainty. "He mentioned that one of his coven members seems to have gone missing."

The mention of the Vampire Coven immediately brought a complicated mix of emotions to the surface for Alex. Their relationship with the vampire coven had always been a precarious one. The supernatural beings were known for their neutrality in most matters, but trouble often followed in their wake, especially when they needed to feed.

Unlike other covens, Elder Lucius had a more modernized approach to their operations, allowing humans to join their ranks in exchange for providing sustenance – the vampire saliva, which held magical properties that prolonged human life. It was a mutually beneficial arrangement, but it didn't mean their relationship was anything close to friendly.

Alex knew that Elder Lucius harbored deep suspicions about him. It wasn't because of their respective organizations but rather because of what Alex was – the ruler of the underworld and the one who could take away the magic that gave vampires their immortality. That knowledge fueled the elder's mistrust, and Alex could sense it every time they interacted.

Without hesitation, Alex gave a terse order. "Gabe, come with me."

Leaving the rest of the team to their own tasks, they made their way to the discreet location of the Vampire Coven in New York. The exterior was intentionally dilapidated, designed to deter anyone daring to enter. It was a clever facade that masked the true luxury that lay beyond those weathered walls.

As they entered, the contrast was stark. The opulence within screamed of old money and ancient power. The scent of age and history hung in the air, mingling with the faintest trace of blood, a reminder of the true nature of this place.

Alex couldn't help but feel the weight of their complicated history with the vampires pressing on him. He couldn't forget the time when he had saved their coven from a rogue supernatural threat or the countless negotiations and disputes that had occurred since.

Gabe, though always composed, wore a similar air of tension as they walked through the coven's hidden corridors. They passed grand chambers adorned with ancient tapestries and antique furnishings, giving the impression of stepping back in time.

They were greeted by a human servant named Erin, who led them through a discreet location in New York. Alex knew better than to underestimate the importance of discretion when dealing with vampires. Erin guided them with an air of deference to the Vampire Elder, Lucius.

Lucius's chamber was a sight to behold, a testament to centuries of wealth, refinement, and vampiric power. The room was adorned with opulent artifacts, intricate tapestries, and dark, antique furnishings. It exuded an air of sophistication that Alex found unsettling, given his plain attire.

"Elder. You wanted to see us regarding missing vampires?" Alex inquired as they entered the lavish chamber.

Lucius, with his commanding presence and piercing gaze, turned to face them. He looked as if he had a bone to pick, his anger evident. "Director Knight, please have a seat."

Alex exchanged a glance with Gabe, his trusted companion and witch, before taking a seat. His irritation was palpable. "Is this an urgent matter or a social call?" Alex asked tersely.

Lucius didn't offer any pleasantries. He rose from his ornate desk and leaned on it, his eyes narrowing. "The vampire that was missing had been turned recently. He was feeding in one of our weekly sessions in one of my clubs. As you already know, they were well supervised by one of my children. But as the night ended, the new vampire vanished without a trace."

"What's so special about this vampire that you want him to be found?" Alex's curiosity mingled with his frustration.

Lucius turned away, his gaze focused on something beyond the window. His voice took on a somber tone. "The vampire had a unique ability to nullify any sort of magic."

Alex was taken aback. He knew that vampires developed unique abilities after being turned, but someone who could nullify magic was a rarity. The only person he had heard of with such a power had died because she posed a threat to every living magic user around her.

"Why didn't you notify us of this?" Alex's tone was laced with anger.

Lucius turned to meet Alex's gaze, his eyes cold. "You should know by now, Director, that I can't just leave any of my children to suffer. I knew that if I gave him up, he would suffer the consequences, and I couldn't have that. My children are important to me."

Alex understood the sentiment but couldn't help but feel betrayed by the omission. "Do you have anything of his that we can use?" he asked after a moment of silence.

Lucius reached into a drawer and produced a pendant. It radiated power, a relic of old magic. He handed it to Alex without explanation. "This pendant was specifically made to conceal his abilities."

Alex examined the pendant, sensing the ancient magic imbued within it. "Where did you get this?" he asked.

"That doesn't matter," Lucius snapped, his impatience evident. "Are you going to help me find this vampire before it's too late or what?"

Alex clenched the pendant in his hand, his mind racing. The situation had taken an unexpected turn, and the weight of it pressed down on him. He knew the implications of a vampire with the ability to nullify magic. It could disrupt the balance of power in their world and pose a significant threat.

Gabe spoke up, his voice calm and measured. "We'll do what we can to find him, Elder Lucius. But we need more information. Where was he last seen? Were there any witnesses? And what are the potential consequences if this ability falls into the wrong hands?"

Lucius sighed, his anger momentarily giving way to concern. "He was last seen at Club Nocturne, one of our establishments. There were witnesses, but they claim to have seen nothing unusual. As for the consequences, you can imagine the chaos that would ensue if someone could nullify magic at will. Our world thrives on the balance of power, Director Knight, and that balance is at risk."

Alex possessed a unique ability, a power of the underworld that resided within him—a power known only to his team. He could track a person's core, the place where their magical signature lay. Today, that ability would be put to the test.

Closing his eyes, he focused on the pendant before him, the

same pendant that had belonged to the missing vampire. If the vampire still lived, Alex could glimpse his memories and, more importantly, his current location.

As he delved into the pendant's secrets, a shiver ran down Alex's spine. He tapped into the dark depths of his power, the sensation sending a chill through his veins. It was as if a door had swung open to a realm of shadows and secrets.

With a surge of energy, Alex summoned hellfire into his palms, its eerie glow casting an unsettling light. The smell of sulfur filled the air as he projected the vampire's memories into the space before them.

Lucius took a step back, his eyes wide with astonishment and a hint of fear. Gabe, ever the strategist, watched intently, his mind racing to decipher the images that materialized in the air.

Memories flashed before them like ghostly apparitions—a clandestine meeting, cryptic conversations, and the vampire lying unconscious in a dimly lit alley.

"What was that?" Lucius asked, his voice trembling.

"That was his memories," Alex replied, his voice steady despite the turmoil within him. "I wouldn't be able to see those if your child was dead. He's alive, but I also sensed something was wrong. We need to get to him, and fast."

Lucius's concern was evident as he inquired, "Where do you think he is?"

"He's somewhere close by," Alex stated, his gaze locking onto Gabe's. "Let's go. Lucius, are you coming?"

Lucius nodded, determination replacing his initial shock. The three of them would find the missing vampire and uncover the truth behind his disappearance.

Contrary to popular belief, vampires could withstand

sunlight, albeit for a limited time. With the urgency of their mission in mind, they couldn't afford to waste a moment. Alex hurled the pendant into the air, its silver surface gleaming. A ball of hellfire burst from his palm, colliding with the pendant and igniting it with an otherworldly fire.

The pendant, now engulfed in a vivid purple flame, emitted swirling purple smoke that beckoned to be followed. It danced in the air, an ethereal guide leading them on their quest. The pendant returned to Alex's palm, but the lingering smoke lingered, an eerie reminder of the path they must tread.

As they moved forward, the tension in the air was palpable. The trio knew that they were venturing into unknown territory, where danger and deception lurked in every shadow. The sun's rays grew stronger, casting their journey in stark relief against the morning light.

Lucius clenched his fists. Gabe analyzed their surroundings for potential threats. Alex led the way with a determined stride.

Alex and his companions hurried along, following the elusive trail until it finally came to a halt in an alley not far from where they had discovered Rina Lane's lifeless body.

They reached the alley and found the vampire sprawled on the ground. Lucius rushed forward to aid the unconscious vampire, but an uneasy feeling gripped Alex's gut.

It was a trap.

"Gabe, shield!" Alex's voice cut through the tension as he conjured a protective barrier. Gabe, swift as ever, mirrored his actions, their combined efforts reinforcing the magical shield. "Lucius, get in here."

Lucius didn't hesitate and retreated to the safety of the

magical barrier. It was just in time. An explosive eruption rocked the alley, flames roaring in the center where the vampire lay. Alex scrambled to extend his shield, desperate to save the injured vampire. But this wasn't ordinary fire; it was as potent as his hellfire.

With a deep breath, he tapped into the underworld, drawing upon its dark power to siphon away the divine flames. The fire burned fiercely, and sweat beaded on Alex's forehead as he wrestled with the fiery force. It was a taxing effort, one that drained him with each passing moment.

As the flames dissipated, leaving a trail of smoldering embers, Alex panted heavily, his chest heaving with exertion. "Is everyone okay?"

Gabe and Lucius nodded, their faces flushed from the ordeal. Gabe wiped a bead of sweat from his brow. "What was that?"

Alex's eyes darkened with worry. "Something tells me we're on the Order's radar."

Lucius, still tending to the unconscious vampire, added with urgency, "He's alive, but something's wrong. He's lost a lot of blood, and I can't sense his magic."

Their options were limited, but they had to get the wounded vampire to safety. Gabe stepped forward, his focus shifting to protecting their retreat. "Alex, we need a temporary ward for him to walk in the sun."

Gabe's conjured warding spell enveloped the unconscious vampire, creating a protective barrier against the sun's deadly rays. With their fragile ally now shielded, they made their way back to the coven.

Once back in Lucius's chamber, they carefully laid the injured vampire on a bed. Gabe couldn't hide his concern.

"Is he going to be okay?"

Lucius continued to watch over the vampire, his eyes never leaving the slumbering figure. "Yes, but I don't know what caused this. He's lost so much blood, and his magic has been drained."

Alex, deep in thought, finally broke the silence. "What we have on our hands is a threat unlike any other. This being is running amok, and we need to find out who and why."

* * *

"How is it going in Washington?" Alex asked Lily as she called.

In his Manhattan home, Alex stood in front of his mirror, cycling through different outfits in search of the right look for his upcoming meet-up with Eryx and friends. He was in the midst of trying on a red button-up shirt paired with faded jeans. As he took a glance at himself, a self-deprecating thought crossed his mind – he felt a bit like a plump tomato in this getup.

Alex's place in the city was quite the find – a converted warehouse that he had turned into his own creative haven. He had originally considered a quieter location, but the convenience of this spot had won him over. The open space, high ceilings, and exposed brick walls lent a unique charm to his home. Every corner reflected his personal touch, as he had meticulously designed the layout and decor himself.

Alex's home was a showcase of his design and woodworking talents. The open layout he created felt spacious, with high ceilings and brick walls lending character. His handcrafted furniture, including a worn leather sofa and a reclaimed wood coffee table, added a personal touch to the living area.

In the kitchen, his woodworking skills were evident in the wooden countertops and open shelves displaying ceramics. His home office corner featured a vintage desk he restored, surrounded by his intricate woodworking projects on the walls.

Even the bedroom bore his mark, with a bedframe he designed and nightstands he crafted. The bathroom maintained an industrial feel, but a custom wooden shelf showed his attention to detail.

Every corner of the house was a testament to Alex's creative abilities, making his warehouse home truly unique.

As he stood in the midst of his creative haven, Alex couldn't help but smile, despite the self-consciousness of his outfit. The scent of wood and sawdust hung in the air, a comforting reminder of the countless hours he had spent crafting each piece of furniture. The texture of the materials under his fingertips, the smoothness of the wooden countertops, the roughness of the exposed brick walls – all of it spoke to his passion for design.

The vintage desk in his home office corner held a special place in his heart. It had been a dilapidated find in a dusty antique shop, but with patience and care, he had restored it to its former glory. It was where he poured his thoughts onto paper, where he turned dreams into reality through the stroke of a pen.

In the kitchen, the wooden countertops bore the marks of countless meals prepared with love. The open shelves displayed ceramics, each piece a unique creation from his pottery classes. He had always been drawn to the tactile nature of ceramics, and the imperfections in each piece only added to their charm.

Alex's home was more than just a place to live; it was an extension of himself, a canvas where he expressed his creativity and individuality. It was a place where every piece of furniture, every design choice, told a story about who he was and what he valued.

Alex stood in front of his bedroom mirror, his brows furrowed in concentration. He was on a call with Lily, his trusted partner in the world of supernatural investigations. The chaos outside was in stark contrast to the calm of his room.

Lily's voice came through the phone, slicing through Alex's thoughts. "Don't bother asking. Things are chaotic. The government and those other alphabet agencies are in a frenzy."

Alex nodded, though Lily couldn't see him. "Why? Aren't they okay with us establishing a presence in Washington?" He reached for a different outfit, this time a bow tie, but dismissed it immediately. It made him look like a pompous jerk.

Lily's sigh crackled over the line. "They're concerned about more supernaturals and magic users gaining power. They're convinced it'll just lead to trouble."

Alex knew that despite having support from the government, some agencies opposed them due to their unconventional investigative methods. "What did you tell them?" he inquired.

"Nothing yet," Lily replied. "Themis advised me to hold off until we're certain about our position."

Themis, representing divine law and order, held the ability to function across different realms due to her status. Alex understood the gravity of the situation. "Well, if you need me there, just say the word. I'll be on my way," he offered, though he was currently preoccupied with his clothing dilemma.

"Will do. So, what's happening at your end?" Lily asked.

"I'm struggling with outfits for a date tonight," Alex confessed, not wanting to burden Lily with the details of their ongoing case. Lily had enough on her plate.

Lily's laughter tinkled through the phone. "And let me guess, you're failing miserably. Let's see what mess you're in, so I can help."

With an eye roll, Alex activated his camera, revealing his wardrobe conundrum to Lily. He had settled on a green shirt and red pants.

Lily couldn't contain her amusement. "Sweet heavens, you're like a messed-up Christmas present."

"Yeah, yeah. Are you giving a hand or just mocking me?" Alex grumbled, though he couldn't help but chuckle as well.

"I'm going to banish you to the underworld. I'm still your King, Persephone!" he teased, trying yet another outfit that made him look like a stripper.

Lily chuckled in response. "Calm down, Alex. I'm definitely helping. And don't forget, I'm still the Queen. Go for the classic black leather jeans and a black button-up, but leave the top two buttons undone."

Following her advice, Alex studied himself in the mirror. He looked impressive, though he'd never admit it to Lily. "It's passable."

"I'll accept Ambrosia as payment. You're welcome," Lily chuckled. "So, are you going to fill me in on who this person is?"

"Maybe. Let's wait until you're back. I want you guys to

meet face-to-face," Alex replied, hinting at the significance of the date.

"Serious stuff, huh?" Lily mused.

"Hopefully. Anyway, I have to run. Take care, Lily."

"You too, Alex. Enjoy yourself!" Lily's voice faded as the call ended.

With the outfit dilemma resolved, Alex felt a mixture of anticipation and nerves as he prepared for his date. As he headed out into the Manhattan evening, he couldn't help but wonder how this night would unfold.

Alex arrived at the club Eryx had mentioned, called Autumn. As he walked in, he couldn't help but notice that it was a mixed bar, welcoming both humans and supernaturals. The presence of an ogre bouncer at the door confirmed that fact, and the thumping bass of loud music greeted him as he stepped inside.

Navigating through the crowd, Alex began his search for Eryx. It didn't take him long to spot him on the dance floor, grooving with a man who had wavy brown hair. An inexplicable surge of jealousy coursed through Alex; he felt an urge to confront the guy for dancing with Eryx. It was a weird reaction, even to himself.

Fortunately, Eryx noticed him before he could act on his impulse, averting a potentially foolish situation in front of everyone. Eryx's eyes locked onto Alex's, and he broke away from his dance partner, making his way through the pulsing crowd.

"Alex, you're here!" Eryx's excitement was palpable as he reached Alex, giving him a passionate kiss right there, amid the crowd.

Alex responded with equal fervor, a grin tugging at his lips.

"Hey there, you look absolutely amazing," he complimented once they pulled back from the kiss.

Eryx chuckled, a playful glint in his eyes. "Says the one who's turning heads everywhere. It's like everyone's eyeing you as their next meal."

"Only yours to devour," Alex retorted, his tone affectionate as he winked at Eryx.

Eryx's smile deepened. "Promise?"

"Promise. Now, let's seal that with another kiss." And they shared another tender moment.

"Alright, come with me. I want you to meet the band," Eryx said, taking Alex's hand and guiding him toward the area where his friends were dancing.

They came to a halt in front of the man Eryx had been dancing with. As Alex drew nearer, a subtle feeling prickled at his senses, indicating that this individual was no ordinary human. Alex brushed off the sensation before it could escalate into something more.

"Alex, I'd like you to meet Richard Lane. Richard, this is my boyfriend, Alex." The word "boyfriend" caught Alex off guard, but he found himself warming to it – more than he expected.

"Boyfriend, huh? It's a pleasure to finally meet you," Richard said, extending his hand for Alex to shake.

Alex shook Richard's hand, and in that brief contact, he felt it – Richard was a demigod.

"Likewise. Maybe we can have a chat sometime," Alex replied with a touch of restraint.

"Absolutely. Just give Eryx the heads up," Richard murmured near his ear. "No worries, Hades. Your secret is safe." With a wink, Richard leaned back.

Alex couldn't fathom how Richard knew his true identity. Whoever Richard's divine parent was, they possessed considerable power to discern his aura.

"Why don't you continue dancing with your friends, sweetheart? I'll be over at the bar," Alex suggested to Eryx.

"Are you sure? You're welcome to join us if you want," Eryx offered.

"Yeah, I'm sure. I'll grab you a drink." Alex kissed Eryx before stepping away, leaving him to enjoy the company of his friends.

As Alex settled at the bar, he couldn't help but take in the eclectic decor that surrounded him. The bar's interior was a mix of vintage and contemporary, with mismatched furniture and dim, warm lighting. The walls were adorned with framed photos and artwork that seemed to tell a story of the bar's rich history.

The music playing on the dance floor was a lively mix of beats that drew people in like a siren's call. The scent of various cocktails and appetizers wafted through the air, creating an enticing aroma that added to the overall atmosphere.

His thoughts drifted back to Eryx dancing with Richard. Alex's jealousy had taken him by surprise, but he knew he had to navigate these emotions. He wanted to be the one who made Eryx smile, and seeing him with someone else stirred a strange mixture of emotions within him.

His heart raced, a mixture of jealousy and attraction making his chest tighten. It was absurd. He knew Eryx was his, but the sight of Eryx dancing with another still affected him deeply.

Alex tried to push these thoughts aside, focusing on the

moment instead. He ordered Eryx's drink and sipped his own, letting the flavors wash over him. The bar's vibrant energy was infectious, and he couldn't help but tap his foot to the music.

Eryx's friends were an interesting bunch, and Alex couldn't help but wonder how they fit into Eryx's life. Richard's knowing words lingered in the back of his mind, a reminder that there were secrets and mysteries he had yet to uncover.

Alex couldn't deny that he felt a growing connection to this unique group. The term "boyfriend" was starting to grow on him, and he found himself embracing it more than he had expected.

As he sipped his drink at the bar, he couldn't help but smile, looking forward to whatever adventures lay ahead in this intriguing world that Eryx had introduced him to.

Alex watched Eryx dance amidst the pulsating lights of the Manhattan Club. The music throbbed, and the memories of Apollo resurfaced, as they often did in moments like these. The pain of Apollo's loss still cut deep, a wound that refused to fully heal. With each day that passed, having Eryx by his side made it a little more bearable.

He leaned against the bar, his gaze fixed on Eryx's graceful movements on the dance floor. Eryx's presence in his life had been a soothing balm to his wounded soul, a chance at healing and happiness he never thought he'd find. Yet, he wasn't ready to let go of Apollo's memory. That fateful day when Apollo had fallen had planted seeds of doubt about the gods themselves, and those doubts lingered like a stubborn ache.

"Looks like things are getting pretty serious between you two," a voice interrupted his reverie.

Alex turned to find Thanatos casually leaning against the bar. "What do you want?" Alex asked, his tone clipped.

"Just passing along another warning from the Fates," Thanatos replied, lifting his drink to his lips.

Alex's eyes narrowed. "What's it about this time?"

"The Fates have foretold that Ares is in New York," Thanatos revealed, his voice carrying a hint of indifference.

Alex's expression soured at the mention of Ares. "Should have finished him off during the war."

"You might get another shot at it now," Thanatos mused, a dark glint in his eyes.

"What else did they see?" Alex pressed, his curiosity piqued.

"They glimpsed a hall with music playing. That's all they divulged," Thanatos replied cryptically.

"We'll need more than that," Alex sighed, setting aside the warning for the moment. At least it was a lead. "And what do you know about the stolen souls?"

There was a pause before Thanatos answered, his demeanor growing more serious. "A number of souls have gone missing, causing disturbances in the underworld's balance."

Alex's concern deepened. "The underworld is being affected?"

"The divine energy down there is fluctuating," Thanatos explained. "Zagreus and I haven't traced the cause precisely, but if I had to guess, it ties back to the stolen souls."

Before Alex could respond, a hand touched his elbow, and he turned to find Eryx, looking sweaty and tired from dancing. Eryx introduced himself to Thanatos, extending a hand for a polite shake.

"Hi, I'm Eryx," he said with a friendly smile.

Thanatos nodded. "Than. Nice to meet you, Eryx." He

turned to Alex. "See you around, Alex."

"Keep me updated," Alex instructed, his gaze following Thanatos as he departed.

Eryx, looking curious, inquired, "Old friend?"

"You could say that," Alex replied, his gaze now focused on Eryx. "Ready to head out? I can drop you off at your place if you want."

"Yeah, I am. Just let me grab the guitar the guys gifted me, and we can go," Eryx agreed with a smile. He gave Alex a quick, affectionate kiss before following him outside.

In the car, Eryx's energy waned, and he succumbed to sleep, emitting soft snores. Alex couldn't help but watch him, a warmth swelling in his chest. Eryx had brought light into his life in ways he couldn't have imagined, and he cherished every moment they spent together.

They arrived at Eryx's house just before midnight, and Alex gently roused him. "Eryx, time to wake up, sweetheart."

Eryx stirred, his eyes blinking open slowly. Alex assisted him with his belongings, escorting him to his front door. The surroundings were quiet, the night air cool against their skin.

As they stood at the entrance, Eryx turned toward him, a frown forming on his face. "Aren't you joining me inside?" he asked, his voice soft with anticipation.

"I really want to," Alex began earnestly, "but it's quite late, and you've had a few drinks. I won't take advantage of you in this state."

Eryx chuckled, a hint of agreement in his expression. "You're right. But what about tomorrow?"

"Tomorrow?" Alex raised an eyebrow.

"The concert, remember? Oops, I forgot to tell you about it." Eryx's eyes widened as he realized his oversight.

"Don't worry, I'll be there."

"It's going to be at Carnegie Hall. I'll see you then," Eryx said, sealing the words with a kiss.

"Good night, sweetheart," Alex murmured after they broke the kiss.

"Good night." Eryx closed the door, leaving Alex standing in the dimly lit street. As he walked back toward his car, a realization struck him like a bolt of lightning.

15

Eryx

"HEY, HOW IS IT GOING IN HERE?" Dion asked, stepping into Eryx's dressing room alongside Ari. The moment had arrived – Eryx was backstage at Carnegie Hall, ready to perform. It had come faster than he expected, but there he was, about to step onto one of the most prestigious stages in the world. He'd managed to secure backstage access for Ari and Dion, though he hadn't heard from Alex, who also had a pass.

"Maybe he's just busy at work. He'll be here like he promised," Eryx thought, finding some comfort in that assurance.

Eryx's dressing room was a haven of preparation. In one corner, a generously sized mirror stood surrounded by lights, reflecting his anticipation. A well-organized vanity held grooming items with precision, ready to transform him into the performer he needed to be.

A cozy couch occupied another corner, and a rack elegantly showcased his wardrobe choices. A wooden table offered refreshments – water, snacks, and a few deep breaths for his racing heart.

The room buzzed with gentle background music, setting a soothing backdrop for his jumbled emotions. Framed photographs and posters of past performances adorned the walls, serving as a reminder of how far he'd come.

"I'm doing okay, just a little nervous," Eryx replied to Dion, though 'nervous' was an understatement. He was downright terrified. The weight of not messing up this opportunity bore down on him; after all, he held the responsibility of both opening and closing the show.

Dion offered a teasing solution, "Don't worry, we're here for you. And if things get rough, you can always imagine the audience in their underwear."

Eryx playfully shoved Dion, a hint of gratitude in his eyes. "Any word from Alex?"

Ari and Dion exchanged a quick look before Ari answered, "I'm sorry, sweetheart. Alex hasn't shown up yet."

Eryx let out a sigh, disappointment evident in his demeanor. "He did promise he'd be here."

Dion chimed in, trying to reassure him, "He will be. You've still got a couple of hours before the show starts."

"I know. I just wanted to see him before stepping on stage," Eryx mused.

Ari added, "Come on, have a bit of faith in the guy."

Eryx's muttered response carried a tinge of humor, "This from the same folks who warned me about him."

"We apologize for that. And remember, we did say he's a great guy," Ari said.

Eryx asserted, "I appreciate it, but you don't have to fight my battles. I can handle myself."

Ari gently took his hand. "We know, sweetie. We were just

looking out for you."

Eryx nodded, appreciating their concern. "Now, please get out of here. The pre-show checks are about to start." He offered a grateful smile as his friends left.

As they exited, Eryx's thoughts drifted back to Alex. With Dion and Ari by his side, he knew he was not alone. Still, he couldn't help but hope for Alex's arrival, a familiar presence to calm his pre-performance jitters.

The hours leading up to Eryx's Carnegie Hall performance were a whirlwind of activity. Backstage, a skilled team of technicians worked diligently to fine-tune every aspect of the show. Eryx stood at the center, feeling a mix of excitement and nerves.

The technical crew carefully checked audio, lighting, and stage setups, making sure everything would come together flawlessly. Microphones were adjusted to capture Eryx's voice, and lights were calibrated to match the mood of his music.

During the sound check, Eryx's voice filled the hall, ensuring his vocals would carry throughout the venue. His fingers danced on his guitar, its strings perfectly tuned for harmonious sounds.

With the band, Eryx rehearsed on stage, getting a feel for the transitions between songs and how lights and sound would sync with his movements.

A wardrobe check ensured Eryx's outfits were impeccable. Accessories were chosen with care, and every detail was attended to.

In a final run-through, Eryx sang his setlist, connecting with the lyrics and melodies he'd soon share.

As the show approached, a mix of excitement and nervousness filled Eryx. The careful preparations and anticipation merged into the moment he had long awaited for.

With the pre-checks completed, Eryx found himself back in his dressing room at Carnegie Hall, the grandeur of the venue contrasting with the simplicity of his thoughts. The show was a mere half-hour away from its start, and he couldn't help but feel a mixture of excitement and nerves coursing through him. As he adjusted his crisp shirt, the sound of a knock reached his ears.

"Come in," Eryx called out, turning to face the door. He knew the moments before a performance were crucial, and any unexpected visit could either soothe or shatter his concentration.

The door swung open, revealing Richard's presence. Eryx met his gaze, a tinge of curiosity in his eyes. Richard was his long-time friend and manager, a reassuring figure in times of chaos.

"Richard, everything all right?" Eryx asked, his pulse quickening. The unexpected knock had disrupted his pre-performance ritual.

"Everything's fine. I'm here because someone is looking for you," Richard replied, causing Eryx's heart to skip a beat. He knew that tone—Richard had something up his sleeve.

"Who is it?" Eryx inquired, his curiosity further piqued. He couldn't help but wonder who would seek him out at this crucial moment.

Without a spoken response, Richard moved to the side, allowing Alex to enter the room. Eryx's heart raced at the sight of him. Alex looked striking in his snug v-neck shirt and denim jacket, despite the hint of weariness in his eyes.

"I was worried you might not make it," Eryx admitted, a

mixture of relief and happiness washing over him. He had missed Alex more than he cared to admit.

"I promised, didn't I? And we also went over a few things at the office," Alex shared, a hint of something unspoken in his words. Eryx decided to let it slide for now; there would be time for questions later. "Feeling nervous?" Alex asked him.

Eryx's words tumbled out, "Yeah, I mean, it's normal to feel jittery before a performance. But playing in front of you? It's a whole different kind of nervousness."

Alex's chuckle was a balm to Eryx's nerves. "No worries. You'll be fantastic. Remember, I've heard you play before."

Their conversation was momentarily interrupted by the crew's announcement, indicating only five minutes remained before Eryx took the stage. The reminder of the impending performance brought a renewed surge of adrenaline.

"I'll be in the front row. Just give me a glance if nerves start creeping in, okay?" Eryx found comfort in Alex's presence, a source of strength to lean on in his final moments of preparation.

Backstage at Carnegie Hall, the bustling crew worked diligently, attaching sound equipment to Eryx's outfit. His heart raced with nervous anticipation as he stole a quick glance toward the auditorium. In the front row, he spotted Alex, Ari, and Dion, their smiles a source of both comfort and anxiety.

"Tonight, you're going to shine," Richard said beside him.

Eryx's doubts clung to him like a stubborn shadow. "You really think so?"

Richard flashed a reassuring smile. "Absolutely. You're already famous, but this will take you to a whole new level."

Eryx nodded hesitantly, trying to steady his nerves. The

backstage environment buzzed with activity as the crew finalized their preparations. The stage equipment gleamed under the harsh, warm-toned lights, and the scent of fresh wood and warm electronics filled the air.

With a final announcement from the crew, Eryx knew it was time to take that daunting step onto the stage. His heart hammered in his chest, and his palms felt clammy.

As he approached the stage's entrance, he couldn't help but think about the significance of this performance. It wasn't just another show; it was a milestone in his career, an opportunity to showcase his talent on one of the world's most prestigious stages.

Taking a deep breath, Eryx stepped onto the stage. The soft hum of the audience's anticipation reached his ears, and he could feel their eyes on him, the weight of their expectations pressing down.

The spotlight illuminated him as he stood before the eager audience, his guitar in hand. He felt the weight of the moment, the realization that he was about to share his music with a crowd at Carnegie Hall.

The first chords of his song reverberated through the hall, and Eryx's voice filled the air. His rich, soulful vocals intertwined with the melodies he strummed on his guitar, creating an intimate atmosphere despite the grandeur of the venue. The audience's attention was captivated, their eyes fixed on him as he poured his emotions into the lyrics.

As he sang, he stole glances at Alex, Ari, and Dion. Their presence reassured him, their supportive gazes giving him the boost of confidence he needed. Eryx was no longer just singing for the crowd – he was singing for them, for the people who believed in him.

Midway through his performance, something unexpected happened. Richard joined him on stage, a guitar in hand. Eryx's surprise was evident, but he quickly adapted, their instruments harmonizing effortlessly. Their voices blended, creating a unique and mesmerizing duet that resonated through the hall.

As Richard and his band continued to play, Eryx stepped back slightly, allowing the spotlight to shift onto them. Richard's dynamic presence and his band's energy electrified the audience. The crowd was captivated by their performance, the music weaving a spell that drew them into the rhythm.

With a final flourish, Richard and his band wrapped up their set, leaving the stage to Eryx for the closing act. The audience erupted into applause, acknowledging the seamless transition between the two performers.

Eryx took a deep breath, feeling a mix of emotions – gratitude, excitement, and a hint of nervousness. He stepped back up to the microphone, ready to close the show on a high note. The spotlight once again centered on him, and he launched into his final song.

His voice soared, filling the hall with a mixture of power and vulnerability. The lyrics carried weight, telling a story that resonated with the audience's hearts. Eryx's passion radiated from every note he played, his fingers dancing across the strings of his guitar.

As he reached the crescendo of his performance, Eryx felt an overwhelming sense of accomplishment. The cheers and applause from the audience were a testament to the connection he had forged through his music. And as the final chords echoed through Carnegie Hall, Eryx knew that he had left a lasting impression, closing the show with a performance that would be remembered for years to come.

Just as Eryx was about to step off the stage, the lights went out, plunging Carnegie Hall into darkness. His heart raced as he groped for a sense of what was happening. Moments later, the hall erupted in screams, and the acrid smell of smoke filled the air. Fire flickered to life, casting eerie shadows as figures darted and clashed in the chaos.

Eryx's eyes locked onto Alex, battling against the shadowy assailants with frantic desperation etched across his face. But all Eryx could see were the frantic movements of their lips.

"This can't be real," Eryx thought, his mind struggling to comprehend the nightmare unfolding before him. The chaos mesmerized him, and he didn't notice the man with a spear charging at him until it was too late.

The assailant was a blur, moving with inhuman speed. Eryx's heart pounded in his chest, and fear surged through him as the menacing figure closed in for the kill. But in a flash, everything around Eryx turned blindingly white.

Eryx, a voice called out, its familiarity striking a chord of recognition within him.

Startled, Eryx replied, "Who's there?" His voice quivered with nervousness.

No time to explain. Ares is on the brink of killing you, the voice conveyed urgently.

"Ares? What in the world is going on?" Eryx's confusion was palpable.

Eryx, do you want your friends to perish? The voice's urgency grew.

"No!" Eryx's response was immediate and fervent.

Then follow my lead. The man's directive was unwavering. As he stepped into the light, Eryx finally saw him—a mysterious figure clad in intricate metal armor, an enigma wrapped in mystery. *Take my hand*, the instruction was clear, and Eryx complied. *Now, embrace your destiny*, the command resonated.

"Destiny? I don't understand," Eryx's bewilderment deepened.

Eryx! It's the sole path to safeguarding your friends. The man's insistence was resolute.

Eryx hesitated for only a moment before declaring, "Alright, I accept!" His resolve was unwavering. Suddenly, the world around him erupted in blinding brilliance. It was the last thing he recalled.

The chaos, the screams, and the fire all faded into oblivion as Eryx's senses were overwhelmed by the dazzling light. His mind whirled with questions and doubts, but he held tight to the stranger's hand, trusting in the promise of safeguarding his friends.

16

Alex

"GABE, GATHER EVERYONE IN MY OFFICE RIGHT AWAY," Alex's voice carried a sense of urgency as he dialed up the tension in the room. Time was slipping through their fingers like grains of sand. Realizing that Ares intended to disrupt the concert, he sprang into action, calling for an emergency morning meeting. Eryx's safety was non-negotiable.

In a matter of minutes, the team assembled in Alex's office, a mix of concern and readiness evident on their faces. Alex stood before them, his posture rigid, his eyes focused on the task ahead.

"Thank you all for being here so early," he began, cutting straight to the chase. "We're facing a serious crisis that we can't ignore."

Gabe spoke up, his brow furrowing with determination. "Whatever it is, we're ready to tackle it, sir."

"I've received word that a someone is planning to attack tonight's concert at Carnegie Hall," Alex revealed, the weight of the news settling heavily on his shoulders.

"Isn't that where Eryx is performing?" Marcus sought clarification, his voice tinged with worry.

"Yes, and that's exactly why we can't take this lightly," Alex emphasized, his gaze unwavering.

"Do we know if this being is connected to the Order?" Emma asked, her concern mirroring that of the team.

"It is highly possible," Alex replied, acknowledging the ominous possibility. "But our main focus is Eryx's safety and the safety of everyone at the concert."

"What's the plan, then, sir?" Emma inquired, her voice steady, a hint of determination in her eyes.

"To survive," Alex declared, his words stark and unyielding. His tone might have sounded dramatic, but he knew the extent of Ares' threat and wasn't willing to risk anything.

Tension hung in the air, palpable and suffocating. Each member of the team grappled with the weight of the situation in their own way. Gabe's jaw was clenched, his mind already working through strategies. Marcus shifted from foot to foot, his impulsive nature itching for action. Olivia clenched her fists, her eyes revealing a hidden well of power. Lucas was busy running scenarios through his mind, his gaze focused on the holographic screen in his hand. Emma's concern for Eryx was evident.

He knew that not everyone might agree with his approach or assessment of the situation, but there was no time for debate. Their mission was clear: protect Eryx at all costs.

As the team began to discuss their strategy, ideas and suggestions flowed like a torrent. They considered everything from enhancing security at Carnegie Hall to setting up magical wards around the venue. Each member's expertise was put to use, and the room buzzed with a sense of purpose.

He glanced out the window, the evening sun casting long shadows across the city. The concert was hours away, and they had a lot of work to do. He couldn't allow his emotions to cloud his judgment, but deep down, he knew that tonight, they were fighting for more than just a successful mission.

As the meeting came to a close, the team's commitment to the mission was unwavering. They had a formidable opponent in Ares, and the challenges ahead were daunting.

With a final nod, Alex rallied his team. "Let's move out, everyone. Time is running out, and Eryx's life depends on us."

The room erupted into action, a sense of urgency driving each member to do their part. The tension remained, but it was a powerful motivator, pushing them forward into the unknown. Tonight, they would face Ares, and they would do whatever it took to ensure that the concert at Carnegie Hall would end in success, not tragedy.

As they arrived at Carnegie Hall, a palpable sense of urgency hung in the air. The grandeur of the iconic venue loomed before them, its majestic façade illuminated by the warm, evening sun. Inside, the bustling audience, unaware of the impending threat, whispered in hushed tones, their anticipation thickening the atmosphere.

Alex wasted no time, turning to Gabe with a steely determination etched across his features. "Gabe, we need to shield the entire building."

Gabe nodded, his gaze sharp as he assessed the monumental task. Geomancy was his specialty, and while warding Carnegie Hall was no small feat, he had the skills to do it.

Across the hall, Marcus, their speedster, moved with a blur of energy. His superhuman speed allowed him to patrol the surroundings swiftly, his keen eyes scanning for any signs of danger. He was always the first to react, the embodiment of controlled chaos.

Emma stood gracefully, her hands poised in a fluid gesture. Her magic flowed from her fingertips, a soft, shimmering light enveloping the team one by one. It was a protective veil, a layer of defense that would shield them from harm.

At Alex's side, Lucas and Olivia stood vigilant, their expressions resolute. Lucas, the tech genius, was armed with an arsenal of gadgets, and Olivia, had a mastery over her own brand of magic. They were the final line of defense, ready to unleash their powers at Alex's command.

Alex watched his team with a mixture of pride and determination. They were a well-oiled machine, each member contributing their unique abilities to the task at hand. Their trust in each other was unshakable, a bond forged through countless missions and battles.

With his team focused on their preparations, Alex left them briefly to visit Eryx. It was an eventful encounter, and he felt a wave of relief wash over him as he saw that Eryx was unharmed. He hadn't shared the details of the looming threat with Eryx, wanting him to perform without the burden of worry.

Eryx, oblivious to the danger that loomed over the grand hall, was called onto the stage. Alex couldn't help but feel a mixture of emotions. He wanted to protect Eryx, to shield him from harm, but he also knew that Eryx had a performance to give, a moment that meant everything to him.

The tension in the hall was palpable as Eryx took the stage, his presence commanding the attention of the audience. Alex watched him from the shadows, his heart pounding in his chest.

As he settled into his designated seat, Alex noticed Ari and Dionysus occupying the chairs beside him. It had been a while, and he couldn't help but feel a mix of emotions as he looked at his old friends.

He cleared his throat, his stoic demeanor giving way to a hint of concern. "How's your magic?" he asked Ari, who sat on his right. She sighed, her expression troubled.

"I'm still not back at full strength," Ari admitted, her voice tinged with weariness. She glanced at Dionysus, whose name had become a mystery these days. "Dion, how about you?"

Dionysus, or Dion as he might prefer to be called now, turned to Alex with a thoughtful expression. "Why are you asking?" He seemed guarded, as if old wounds still lingered beneath the surface. "Hades. It's been a while."

"It's Alex," Alex responded, a hint of nostalgia flickering in his eyes. "Just answer the question. Are you guys able to fight? I need to know now."

Ari leaned forward, her concern evident. "Why? What's going on, Alex?"

Alex wasted no time in delivering the news that weighed heavily on his mind. "Thanatos warned me that Ares was spotted in New York by the Fates."

Ari's eyes widened in realization. "Are you saying that Ares might attack at any moment?"

"Yes," Alex replied tersely. "We don't have time for this. Can you fight or not?"

Dion chimed in, his voice tinged with regret. "We'll do our best, but our magic has been depleted."

Alex's brow furrowed in concern. "For how long?"

Ari hesitated for a moment before answering, her voice carrying the weight of a revelation. "Since we started concealing Eryx's true nature."

Alex's confusion flared, and he couldn't help but let his frustration seep into his tone. "What the fuck are you talking about, Ari?"

Before Ari could respond, the room's lights dimmed slightly, signaling the beginning of the performance at Carnegie Hall, where Eryx was about to take the stage.

"This isn't finished," Alex growled, his frustration unabated. "If we make it through this alive, the two of you have a lot of explaining to do."

With that, he took a deep breath, determined to focus on the impending threat and the task at hand. As the music began to fill the room, he couldn't help but feel a sense of pride and awe wash over him.

Eryx, on the stage, commanded the audience's attention with a presence that was nothing short of captivating. He owned every inch of the stage, connecting with the audience on a deep and emotional level. Each note carried a weight of sincerity, each lyric told a story that resonated with those in attendance.

Alex's gaze remained fixed on Eryx, and for a moment, he forgot about the impending danger, the unresolved tensions with his old friends, and the mysteries surrounding Eryx's true nature. The music transcended the chaos of their world, and he found himself swept away by the beauty of the performance.

As the songs unfolded, Alex couldn't help but be reminded of the power of art. Eryx's music created a bond, not only between the artist and the audience but also between himself and Eryx.

The concert had reached its electrifying crescendo, leaving the audience in a state of euphoria as Eryx's final notes reverberated through Carnegie Hall. Applause thundered through the grandiose space, echoing in the hearts of those who had gathered to witness the spectacle. However, before Eryx could take his leave from the stage, the lights abruptly plunged into darkness.

Chaos erupted within the concert hall as screams filled the void left by the extinguished lights. Panic spread like wildfire among the spectators, a sea of faces contorted with fear and confusion.

Alex's SHD device blinked to life, a beam of eerie blue illuminating his stern features. He wasted no time connecting with Gabe, his voice a low growl amidst the chaos. "Gabe, what the hell is going on? Why didn't your wards work?"

Gabe's voice crackled with urgency on the other end. "Sir, the wards are still up. It seems like whatever is attacking was able to bypass them."

As the chaos continued, Alex sprinted into action alongside Marcus, Ari, and Dion, his heart pounding with a potent mixture of determination and dread. It was then that the Shadow Figures materialized, their eerie presence sending shivers down his spine.

Shadow wraiths, he realized with a curse.

"Dion, Ari, watch your backs. Shadow wraiths are in play. Channel some magic from me so you can fight," Alex ordered, his voice edged with urgency. Dion and Ari nodded, their bond as family members and bloodline magic users allowing them to draw upon his energy.

With Olivia's arcane power, the concert hall was briefly

awash in a soft, pale glow. It revealed the haunting visages of the Shadow Figures, their malevolent forms swaying ominously. Lucas, alert and resolute, positioned himself as a shield for the panicked crowd, ready to protect them until Marcus could lead them to safety.

"Emma, I want you to help people who have been evacuated. Make sure they're okay," Alex instructed through his SHD, his tone unwavering.

As he prepared to engage the shadow wraiths, Alex's hands crackled with dark energy, an ominous power drawn from the underworld. Hellfire danced in his palms, casting an eerie light across his determined face. The wraiths were formidable adversaries, and the only person who could defeat them was dead. The responsibility fell to him and his team to take down whoever had brought them here.

Around him, chaos reigned as the audience struggled to find safety amidst the flickering emergency lights. The sounds of screaming and panicked footsteps filled the air, punctuated by the occasional hiss of a shadow wraith. The emergency lights cast eerie, uneven shadows that seemed to dance with the malevolent creatures.

As the battle raged on, the identity and motives of their attackers remained shrouded in mystery. The shadow wraiths seemed to serve a purpose, but their purpose was yet unknown. Alex's mind raced with questions, but he couldn't afford to be distracted. The immediate threat had to be dealt with first.

The concert hall itself became a battleground, with the stage and lighting equipment serving as both obstacles and opportunities. Shadows danced and intermingled with the play of magic, creating an eerie tableau of light and darkness.

Every move was a calculated risk, and every decision held the weight of lives at stake.

Alex's heart pounded in his chest as he faced the encroaching Shadow Wraiths. They materialized before him, their shapes twisting and contorting like shifting shadows, their eerie eyes glowing with malevolence. Whispers, eerie and unsettling, filled the air, a symphony of lost souls and haunting echoes.

His instincts kicked into overdrive, and he reacted with a blend of defensive maneuvers and powerful spells. Each movement was precise, a testament to years of training and experience. Fear gnawed at the edges of his mind, but he couldn't afford to let it consume him.

Beside him, Ari and Dion fought with determination, channeling their magic through him despite not being at full strength. Together, they held their ground against the advancing wraiths. Sweat soaked their brows, and their breaths came in ragged gasps, but they didn't waver.

Alex couldn't help but think of Eryx and the others facing this same danger. The thought of their safety, or lack thereof, hung heavily in his mind. Yet, he couldn't afford to lose focus, not in the midst of this chaotic battle.

He pressed forward, his attacks growing sharper, his magic surging in response to the threat. With every wraith he neutralized, his determination only grew stronger. His team relied on him, and he wouldn't let them down.

From the corner of his eye, he caught sight of Richard wielding a scepter, the gemstone at its apex glowing with a brilliant intensity. "Richard! What the fuck are you doing? Are you trying to get yourself killed?" Alex's voice rang out, frustration seeping into his words.

"What does it look like? I'm lending a hand!" Richard shouted back, his focus still on battling the shadowy wraiths. His determination mirrored Alex's own.

Alex kept an eye on Richard, and he couldn't help but marvel at the way the scepter emitted a radiant aura that pushed back the encroaching darkness. It was an unexpected but welcome aid in their struggle.

"Watch out behind you!" Olivia's urgent voice pierced through the chaos, and Alex's instincts kicked in. He spun around just in time to see a spear hurtling toward him with breakneck speed. Adrenaline surged through him as he narrowly evaded the projectile, feeling the rush of air as it whizzed by.

Somewhere amidst the chaos, slow applause echoed, a sinister note in the midst of the battle's tumult. "Well, well. What a fascinating reunion we have here. Hello, dear brother. It's been quite a while." The voice was familiar, chilling in its self-satisfaction.

"Ares, where the fuck are you hiding?" Alex's voice carried frustration and anger, his eyes scanning the shadowy battlefield for any sign of his enigmatic brother.

In response to Alex's question, Ares materialized before him as if he had been there all along. His presence exuded menace, his features twisted in a self-satisfied grin. "Such a pity I have more pressing matters to attend to," Ares remarked cryptically.

Alex attempted to tap into his magic, only to find it utterly unresponsive. Panic and anger surged within him as he realized the extent of Ares's interference. "What have you done to my magic?" His voice growled with an undercurrent of fury.

Ares looked at him with a triumphant expression, savoring the moment. "You have your allies, and I have mine," he replied enigmatically before vanishing from Alex's view.

The battle raged on, the wraiths relentless in their assault. The team fought with unwavering determination, their fear buried beneath layers of resolve. Each spell, each strike, was a testament to their strength and unity.

The atmosphere in Carnegie Hall grew more oppressive with each passing moment. The darkness, both physical and metaphysical, pressed in on them, threatening to overwhelm. And amidst the chaos, the presence of Ares lingered like a looming storm.

As they battled on, Alex's thoughts were a whirlwind of frustration, anger, and determination. The odds were stacked against them, and their enemy remained elusive. But they were Shadowguards, and they would fight to the end, no matter the cost.

Incensed, Alex tracked Ares' movements, his heart pounding in his chest as he watched his brother close in on Eryx. The evening air in Carnegie Hall crackled with tension, and the audience's cheers had turned into terrified gasps.

"Eryx! Look out!" Alex's voice rang out, a desperate plea as he sprinted toward Eryx's location. His footsteps echoed through the grand hall, but his sprint fell short, and he could only watch helplessly as Ares raised his spear, ready to strike.

The clash of powers filled the air, a deafening symphony of magic and might. Eryx turned to him, his eyes wide with terror, but before Alex could reach him, a blinding supernova of light engulfed everything. Eryx's body became the epicenter, radiating an intensity that eradicated most of the lingering shadow wraiths.

Alex's eyes squinted against the brilliance, but he still caught a glimpse of Ares attempting to strike through Eryx, only to be thwarted by the blinding light. "This isn't over!" Ares's defiant voice echoed before he vanished, taking the shadow wraiths with him.

With the bright light fading, Alex found Eryx's unconscious form sprawled on the stage floor, the remnants of their battle scattered around them. He rushed to Eryx's side, his heart pounding with a mixture of relief and protectiveness. He couldn't bear the thought of anything happening to the person who had become the center of his world.

Kneeling down, Alex conducted a quick assessment of Eryx's condition. Relief washed over him as he detected Eryx's steady breathing. A touch on his shoulder drew his attention, and he looked up to find Dion beside him, offering a reassuring squeeze.

"Let me take a look at him," Dion's voice broke through the tension, his experienced eyes scanning Eryx's prone form. He exchanged a cryptic glance with Ari, whose presence had remained enigmatic throughout the ordeal, leaving Alex puzzled and anxious.

"What's going on?" Alex demanded answers, his voice taut with concern.

"Calm down, Alex. Eryx is okay," Dion assured him, his tone soothing as he continued to examine Eryx.

"We'll take him to my place. It's safer," Alex decided, his leadership resolute. The others nodded in agreement, trusting his judgment implicitly.

Alex tapped his SHD to communicate with his team, the device crackling to life. "Is everyone alright? Have all the people been evacuated?"

"Yes, sir," Gabe's response came through, reassuring and steady. "Everyone is accounted for, and all the attendees are safe."

"Good. Manage the HIB when they arrive and regroup at my place," Alex instructed, his voice reflecting his determination to see this through.

"Will do, sir," Gabe confirmed, and Alex could sense the unwavering support of his team even through the digital connection.

Richard approached them, his presence steady and reassuring. "Alex, I'll check up on Eryx later. Right now, I need to take care of some matters here."

Alex nodded in acknowledgment and gratitude, knowing that Richard's expertise would be invaluable in handling the aftermath of the supernatural battle.

"Come on," Ari suggested, her tone carrying a sense of urgency. "Let's get out of here. We've done what we can."

Alex and the others agreed, stepping away from the chaotic aftermath of the confrontation. The evening had taken an unexpected and dangerous turn, and the mysteries surrounding Ares' motivations and the true nature of the battle hung heavy in the air.

As they left Carnegie Hall, Eryx's unconscious form in their care, Alex couldn't help but feel a renewed sense of determination. Protecting Eryx had become more than just a mission, it was a deeply personal commitment. And as they navigated the uncertain path ahead, Alex knew that their bond would be tested like never before.

17

Alex

GENTLY, ALEX PLACED ERYX ON HIS BED, his movements careful and deliberate. The sight of Eryx in his house filled him with a sense of rightness, as if a missing piece of his life had fallen into place. He brushed a strand of hair away from Eryx's handsome face, his touch light and warm. The room was bathed in the soft glow of evening light, casting long shadows that danced on the walls.

Eryx's skin felt warm against Alex's hand, and the room was filled with the subtle scent of lavender from the scented candles Alex had lit earlier. The air was thick with a mixture of emotions—relief, worry, and an underlying sense of mystery that hung in the room like an unspoken question.

Alex couldn't help but smile as he looked down at Eryx. His heart swelled with a complex mix of emotions. He wanted to keep Eryx here, in the safety of his home, indefinitely. The events that had transpired earlier still echoed in his mind, the memory of Eryx's otherworldly glow etched in his thoughts.

It wasn't a glow like that of a magic user or a supernatural being whose latent powers were being awakened. No, it was something entirely different, something he couldn't quite put his finger on. It had radiated from Eryx, enveloping him in an ethereal light that had both fascinated and unnerved Alex.

As he continued to watch Eryx, Alex's mind drifted back to a memory, a moment that had left a lasting impression on him. He remembered the first time he had met Eryx, the way their eyes had locked through the chaos of the debris. It had felt like the universe had conspired to bring them together, and in that mom ent, everything else had faded into the background.

The memory brought a bittersweet ache to Alex's chest. He had known, from the very beginning, that there was something extraordinary about Eryx. And now, as he lay unconscious in Alex's bed, that truth was more apparent than ever.

Alex leaned in closer, his gaze never leaving Eryx's face. He whispered softly, as if afraid to disturb the fragile peace of the moment. "You've always been a mystery, Eryx. But now… now you're an enigma I can't ignore."

The room seemed to hold its breath, as if waiting for Eryx to wake and provide answers to the questions that swirled in Alex's mind. But Eryx remained still, his breathing steady and peaceful.

Alex couldn't help but feel torn. Part of him wanted to know the truth, to unravel the secrets that lay hidden within Eryx. Yet, another part of him feared what he might discover, the implications of Eryx's otherworldly nature.

The sound of Eryx's breathing filled the room, a reminder of his vulnerability. Alex's protective instincts surged, and he vowed to keep Eryx safe, no matter what challenges lay ahead.

Alex remained by Eryx's side, his thoughts a whirlwind of emotions and unanswered questions.

In the aftermath of the war, the world had irrevocably changed. The once-blighted landscape had transformed into something almost surreal. Fields that had been scorched by the fires of battle now teemed with vibrant, otherworldly flora. Rivers, once stagnant and polluted, flowed with crystal-clear water. The very air was charged with a newfound energy, crackling with an unseen force.

For mortal humans, the war's end had brought an unexpected and extraordinary gift. They had awakened to newfound abilities. Shape-shifting had become commonplace, and magic coursed through their veins, manifesting in unpredictable ways.

Alex couldn't help but marvel at the transformation that had taken place in the world. The Fates, had foreseen this shift long before it had occurred. Their cryptic visions had hinted at a momentous event, but the details had remained veiled in ambiguity.

Through these stories, Alex had come to understand the role of Apollo's sacrifice in this miraculous transformation. The god's luminous act had held an unimaginable power, one that had the capacity to awaken the dormant magic residing within people's souls. It was as if the world had been reborn, and humanity had become the custodians of this newfound magic.

As Alex pondered these extraordinary changes, he couldn't help but think of his neighbors and friends who had experienced this transformation firsthand. Each individual had their own unique gift, a testament to the diversity of human potential.

The newfound abilities had not come without their challenges and conflicts. As more and more people embraced their powers, a complex web of ethics and responsibilities had emerged. Power struggles were inevitable, and the consequences of misusing these newfound abilities weighed heavily on society.

Cultural shifts had also rippled through the world. Some cultures had readily embraced the changes, viewing them as a divine gift. Others clung to tradition, fearing the unknown. Tensions had arisen between those who sought to protect the old ways and those who saw the transformation as an opportunity for progress.

The mysteries of the Fates' foresight continued to baffle Alex. Their knowledge had been a guiding force throughout this transformative period, yet their motives remained elusive. It was as if they had orchestrated a grand symphony, and humanity was merely a participant in their intricate composition.

Lost in thought, Alex sat in his room until the door swung open, and Ari walked in, closely followed by Dion. Ari held a steaming mug of coffee, which she handed to him with a small smile. The warmth of the mug was a comforting contrast to the weight of the conversation that hung in the air like a storm about to break.

Alex accepted it gratefully, feeling the heat seep into his hands. Ari and Dion settled on the other side of the bed, their expressions serious yet comforting.

Alex didn't waste any time. He needed answers. "What happened out there?" he inquired, his gaze shifting between his two friends.

Ari took a deep breath before speaking. "Do you remember

what the Fates mentioned about Apollo's soul returning?"

A brief pause hung in the air as Alex processed her words. "Yes, I do. What about it?"

Ari's eyes met his. "We believe that Apollo's soul has found a home in Eryx."

The realization hit Alex like a lightning bolt, illuminating the pieces of the puzzle he hadn't connected. "That's probably the reason why my god soul was acting up when I'm around him."

Ari nodded, understanding evident in her eyes. "Apollo's soul carried that connection, even if you two weren't fully aware of it."

Turning his attention to Dion, Alex searched his face for answers. "And you, what role did you play in all of this?"

Dion's gaze met Alex's, his expression honest. "Before the battle in Elysium, Apollo approached me. He asked if I could safeguard his god soul. It was a risky ritual, but it succeeded. However, it took time for his soul to find its rightful place."

A mix of emotions swirled within Alex. "Did he explain why he wanted this?"

Dion's smile was tender as he met Alex's gaze. "He didn't say much, but he once asked me if I'd risk my life to save someone I loved. I knew he was thinking of you."

Tears welled up in Alex's eyes, emotions bubbling beneath the surface. "You were quite the fool, Apollo," he whispered softly, his fingers brushing Eryx's cheek with a gentleness he hadn't known he possessed. "How did you find out about Eryx hosting his soul?"

Dion's admission was straightforward. "I secretly cast a tracking spell on Apollo's god soul during the ritual. I couldn't bear the thought of losing it."

"Once the Fates realized Eryx's true nature, they tasked us with protecting him," Ari added.

"Is that why your magic was drained?" Alex's question was laden with understanding.

Ari nodded solemnly. "Yes, concealing a potent god soul like Apollo's took a toll. Both of us expended a significant amount of magic to shield his true self from prying eyes."

Regret filled Alex as he thought of his absence during this time. "I should have done more to protect him."

Dion's voice was gentle yet firm. "You can do that now."

Determination surged within Alex. "That's exactly what I plan to do. What comes next?"

Ari's honesty was evident in her response. "To be honest, we're not entirely sure. The Fates didn't provide a detailed account of what occurs when his god soul awakens."

Alex pondered this, his mind racing with possibilities. "We'll have to tell him everything when he wakes up."

Their synchronized nods affirmed his words. "Whenever you're ready, let us know. It's time he knows the truth. Keeping secrets from him weighs on us as well," Ari added.

Alex received an alert on his SHD. It was from Gabe, informing him that the team had arrived.

"The team's here. Will you all be okay in here?" Alex inquired.

"Yes, we'll be fine. Go ahead and update your team," Ari replied softly.

Alex nodded and left, heading to update his team while leaving Ari and Dion with Eryx.

When Alex entered his living room, his five team members stood there, expectant faces turned toward him. He knew that the time had come to reveal the truth. With Ares' looming threat and potential others aligned against them, honesty was their best weapon.

Marcus was the first to speak, concern etched in his voice. "Sir, how's Eryx holding up?"

"He's on the path to recovery. And how is everyone else doing?" Alex inquired, genuinely interested in their well-being.

"Minor scratches, nothing serious, sir," Gabe replied, offering a reassuring nod.

"Good. I assume those who were evacuated are being attended to as well as the media?"

"Yes, sir. The Human Investigation Bureau (HIB) has taken care of that," Gabe confirmed, and Alex nodded his approval.

Lucas voiced the team's curiosity, "What were those shadowy figures? We've never encountered anything like them before."

"They are what we term as Shadow Wraiths," Alex revealed after a moment's pause.

Olivia's gaze locked onto Alex's. "And who do you mean by 'we,' sir?"

"The gods." Alex stated with a gravity that hung in the air.

"But gods are mere myths, aren't they?" Emma interjected, skepticism evident in her tone.

"Some myths are steeped in reality," Alex replied before taking a deep breath, mentally preparing himself. It's now or never, he thought. "My real name is not Alex. It's Hades."

The team's reactions were a mix of shock, disbelief, and curiosity. Marcus blinked, his mouth agape, unable to process the revelation. Olivia's eyes widened as if she had just witnessed a miracle. Lucas stared at Alex. Gabe maintained his composure, though his eyes betrayed a flicker of uncertainty. Emma, ever the skeptic, seemed torn between doubt and fascination.

Alex watched their reactions, his own emotions concealed behind a mask of stoicism. He had carried this secret for far too long, and now, its weight had shifted to his team.

The room was charged with tension, and the truth hung in the air like an unspoken promise of change.

Then, Olivia broke the silence, her voice contemplative. "The man with the spear referred to you as his brother. Is he a god too?"

Alex's jaw clenched involuntarily as he considered how much to reveal. "Indeed, that was Ares."

Lucas leaned forward, his eyes wide with intrigue. "For how long have gods been living among us?"

Alex met their gaze unflinchingly. "We've existed for more than a couple of millennia, some among you and some beyond the aether."

A collective hush settled over the room as the weight of his revelation sank in. The team exchanged glances, their disbelief evident.

"If what you say holds true, then who oversees the underworld now that you are here?" Olivia's inquiry revealed genuine interest in their world, her eyes searching for answers.

"My son, Zagreus, now oversees the realm as my proxy," Alex replied, observing the nods of understanding from his team.

Gabe, always the strategist, redirected their focus to the immediate challenges ahead. "Where do we stand now? Do we have any certainty that Ares is aligned with the Order?"

Alex's expression hardened as he considered the implications. "For the moment, we must prioritize Ms. Lane's case. That remains our primary concern. I want each of you to continue with your assigned tasks before the events at the concert. Return home, rest, and stay vigilant."

As his team agreed and began to disperse, Marcus stopped and looked at him with a sense of genuine concern. "Keep us informed of Eryx's condition, please."

"Of course," Alex replied, conveying their shared commitment before they left the room.

The door to his room opened, and Ari stepped out, her expression a mixture of worry and relief. "How did it go?" she asked, her eyes searching his for answers.

"Better than I expected," Alex sighed, feeling a weight lift from his shoulders. "How's he doing?"

"He's stable and still sleeping. You can go in if you want. I'll make some food," Ari offered, her concern for both Eryx and Alex evident in her voice.

"Thanks, Ari," Alex said, appreciating her support. He knew she understood the complexity of his responsibilities and the sacrifices he had to make.

Entering the room, he felt a mixture of anticipation and relief wash over him. Eryx lay on the bed, his face serene in slumber. His injuries, though severe, were slowly healing, thanks to the supernatural resilience of his kind.

Alex pulled up a chair beside the bed and watched Eryx's steady breaths. He couldn't help but wonder about the challenges that lay ahead, the unknown threats posed by Ares and the Order. His mind raced with thoughts of his team, the mission, and the world he had left behind in the underworld.

As he sat there in the dimly lit room, the weight of his responsibilities pressing down on him, Alex knew that the path ahead was fraught with danger. He would have to navigate a world where gods and mortals collided, where ancient rivalries resurfaced, and where the fate of not just one life but many hung in the balance.

But for now, in this moment of quiet reflection, he found solace in the knowledge that his team was by his side, ready to face whatever challenges lay ahead. And as he watched over Eryx, his thoughts turned to the uncertain future and the battles yet to come.

18

Eryx

*W**AS HE FLOATING? IT CERTAINLY FELT LIKE IT.*

Eryx's attempt to move his legs yielded no results; it felt like he was floating in a vast, empty space. Slowly, his eyes blinked open to confront an unyielding expanse of blackness that enveloped him. It was as if he'd been plunged into a bottomless pit.

A peculiar presence lingered nearby, its existence undeniable. An instinct he couldn't explain compelled him to navigate through the void toward it. "Hello?" he called out tentatively, his voice carrying an echo that bounced into the abyss. The response was silence, but there was an unusual, calming vibration resonating in the darkness.

Desperate for answers, Eryx continued forward. "Who's there?" he asked again, a mix of confusion and anticipation coloring his voice.

This time, a reply came, faint but distinct. "You're getting closer, Eryx. Just a bit more."

Recognition rippled through him, his heart quickening in response. Encouraged, he pressed on through the unknown. The inky darkness gradually gave way to a faint, door-shaped light in the distance.

"Am I dead?" he pondered aloud, his thoughts steeped in disbelief. The situation spiraled further into the surreal with each passing moment.

"No, you're definitely not," the voice chuckled, amusement threading through its words.

Eryx's emotions were a whirlwind. His initial curiosity morphed into anxiety, the unease of his surroundings weighing heavily on him. Yet, amid the uncertainty, a sense of excitement grew as he recognized the familiar voice.

Navigating through the void, Eryx's senses remained heightened. The temperature around him was neither hot nor cold but held a peculiar neutrality that sent shivers along his spine. There was no solid ground to touch, leaving him with an eerie sensation of weightlessness. The faint vibration he'd initially felt now hummed through his being, creating an odd sense of connection with this enigmatic realm.

As he journeyed further, hints of mystery and intrigue whispered through his mind. Eryx couldn't shake the feeling that this encounter was tied to something significant, a puzzle piece in a larger, unknown picture.

The voice that guided him was warm and comforting, its timbre reminiscent of forgotten memories. It was as if it resonated with his very soul, igniting a spark of recognition and nostalgia. Eryx couldn't place it, but it was a voice he'd known intimately, one that had been a part of him.

Rationalization eluded him, the surreal nature of it all defying explanation.

Flashes of memories flickered at the edge of his consciousness, tantalizing glimpses of his past and the enigma of this present moment. *They were fragments of a puzzle, pieces he couldn't yet fit together.*

As the dizziness subsided, Eryx found himself surrounded by the ethereal beauty of the place. Before him stood a man, his presence awe-inspiring. With locks of golden hair cascading like sunlight, eyes the mirror of Eryx's own blue gaze, and a form sculpted to divine perfection, the man seemed to radiate a timeless grace. He was clad in silver armor and bore wings as pure as newly fallen snow. In his skilled hands, he plucked a lyre, weaving a melody that resonated deep within Eryx's soul.

Drawn by the enchanting tune, Eryx hummed along, his voice blending seamlessly with the man's melody. Their harmonious union created a musical tapestry that transcended the boundaries of time and space.

As the music swelled to its crescendo, the scenery around Eryx shifted once more. He found himself in the heart of a breathtaking field, the scent of blooming flowers caressing his senses. Soft grass cradled his feet, and the distant song of birds filled the air. A sense of tranquility washed over him, and for a fleeting moment, the burdens of his reality lifted.

"It's beautiful, isn't it?" the man's voice, tinged with both sorrow and warmth, broke the serene moment. Eryx turned to him in awe and nodded. "The never-ending sun brings contentment and peace to the souls who find their way here," the man continued.

"It truly is," Eryx replied, his gaze still fixed on the captivating vista. Curiosity stirred within him. "Who are you?"

The man met Eryx's gaze, sadness and warmth reflecting in his eyes. "My name is Apollo. I've been waiting for you, Eryx."

Baffled and intrigued, Eryx's mind raced with questions. "Where are we?"

"This is Elysium," Apollo explained, a touch of melancholy in

his voice. "Once, it was a paradise for souls, serene and beautiful."

Eryx's eyes traced the horizon, realization dawning upon him. "What happened to it?"

"It was destroyed during the war with Kronos and Morvain," Apollo revealed, regret heavy in his voice. "In a desperate attempt to protect the mortal realm, we brought the battle here to minimize casualties."

Eryx processed the revelation, his thoughts carefully shaping his next question. "Why have you brought me here now?"

Apollo's hand rested reassuringly on Eryx's shoulder. "I wanted you to witness the beauty of this place before its fall, to share a moment outside the chaos of war." He turned to Eryx, his eyes intent. "Our time here is limited, so ask what you need to know."

Eryx took in the vibrant colors of the flowers, the gentle rustling of leaves, and the distant laughter of unseen children. He marveled at the paradise that had once been, now reduced to fragments of memory.

"Tell me, Apollo," Eryx began, his voice steady. "What role do I play in all of this?"

Apollo's gaze deepened with both sadness and determination. "You carry a burden, Eryx, one that is intertwined with the destiny of both realms. As the bearer of my soul, you are the key to restoring balance and healing the wounds caused by the war."

Eryx's heart quickened as he tried to grasp the weight of Apollo's words. "But how? What must I do?"

Apollo's response was cryptic yet filled with purpose. "The path ahead will be treacherous, filled with trials and choices. Your journey will be one of self-discovery, where you must embrace your destiny and the power that resides within you."

Eryx's skepticism hung heavy in the air like a thick fog. He couldn't quite wrap his head around what Apollo was telling him.

It felt like a bizarre dream, but one he couldn't simply wake up from.

"How can I possibly achieve that? I don't possess any form of magic," Eryx's voice was laced with doubt, his eyes narrowing as he studied Apollo.

Apollo, however, exuded quiet confidence, his presence almost ethereal. "You do, Eryx. The medication that you've been taking has been blocking it from manifesting."

A torrent of questions flooded Eryx's mind, and he couldn't help but voice them, his voice tinged with disbelief. "Assuming I believe you, what kind of magic am I supposed to possess?"

Apollo's reply was cryptic yet intriguing, his eyes locked onto Eryx's. "Considering I'm a part of you, our magic is likely the same."

Eryx's curiosity piqued further. He leaned in slightly, his voice lowering to a hushed tone. "A part of me? Those dreams and nightmares... those were your memories, weren't they?"

Apollo confirmed his suspicion with a nod, his expression filled with a strange mix of emotions. "Yes, they were mine. Merging with another soul as a vessel brought unforeseen consequences."

Eryx's mind raced, connecting the dots like pieces of a complex puzzle. "So, you reside within me?"

Apollo's gaze held a certain intensity as he answered, "Yes, now that my soul has reawakened, I'll guide you. You have all my godly abilities, and learning to control them won't be easy. But I have faith you'll manage, especially with Hades by your side."

"Hades?" Eryx's brows furrowed, his mind struggling to grasp the enormity of what he was hearing.

"You may know him as Alex," Apollo clarified, and a sense of revelation washed over Eryx. The pieces of the puzzle were slotting into place.

Eryx ventured further into uncharted territory with his questions. "So, you're saying I can talk to you whenever I want?"

Apollo's response was unwavering. "Yes, our connection will be constant."

Eryx processed this avalanche of information, feeling both daunted and reassured. He leaned back, his mind a whirlwind of thoughts and emotions. "I want to help, but I'm overwhelmed. This much change can't be healthy."

Apollo's gaze met his, brimming with determination and empathy. "I'll be with you, as will Hades. Dion and Ari will also lend their support."

Eryx couldn't help but seek clarity. "Dion and Ari? What do they have to do with this?"

Apollo's final words hung in the air like an urgent plea. "Listen to your heart's music, Eryx. It will guide you. We're out of time."

Desperation laced Eryx's voice as he reached out, his fingers trembling slightly as Apollo began to fade away. "Apollo? Apollo?!"

Eryx slowly regained consciousness, his senses mired in disorientation. It felt as if his body had been transformed into an anchor, each movement a herculean task. He was aware of a voice, distant and comforting, calling his name. A gentle shake accompanied the sound.

"Eryx, sweetheart. You're okay. It's just a dream."

The voice belonged to someone he knew, someone who had become his refuge in this world of uncertainty. With great effort, he willed his heavy eyelids to flutter open. The world that met his gaze was a blurry mosaic, save for a pair of deep brown eyes that held unwavering warmth and reassurance.

"A… Alex?" His voice emerged as a croak, his throat aching as if it had endured more than it could remember.

As he attempted to sit up, a strong and warm hand gently held him back. "Easy there, you're not fully healed yet."

Gradually, the fog surrounding him began to lift, revealing the soft contours of Alex's face, bathed in the gentle glow of the room. It was Alex's tender smile that gave Eryx solace in this bewildering moment.

"How long was I out for?" Eryx inquired, his voice steadier than before but still marked by vulnerability.

"You've been out for nearly a full day, sweetheart," Alex replied, his hand offering a reassuring squeeze.

Eryx's senses began to sharpen, allowing him to perceive more details of his surroundings. The scent of the room was familiar, a comforting blend of Alex's cologne and the subtle fragrance of the linens.

Beyond the confines of the room, he could hear faint sounds—a distant hum of city life, the occasional passing car, and the soft rustling of leaves in the evening breeze. These auditory cues slowly anchored him to the reality of the present.

His emotional confusion began to subside as recognition solidified. He had been trapped in the labyrinth of a vivid dream, its tendrils still haunting his thoughts. The moment he had heard Alex's voice, the lines between dream and reality blurred, and it was Alex who had gently guided him back to consciousness.

Eryx's body, once weighed down by leaden fatigue, began to cooperate more readily as he eased back against the pillows. His gaze never wavered from Alex, whose presence was a lifeline in this sea of uncertainty.

Alex's concern for Eryx was evident in his every gesture and the soothing cadence of his words. "You gave us quite a scare. But you're safe now."

The tenderness in Alex's eyes mirrored the tenderness of his touch as he brushed a lock of hair from Eryx's forehead. It was a silent reassurance, a promise that Eryx was not alone in this bewildering journey of waking up from the dream.

As he attempted to sit up, pain coursed through his body, and he winced.

As the door creaked open, Ari, Dion, and a large, friendly dog entered the room, gathering around his bedside. The bed he lay on was remarkably soft and comfortable, a stark contrast to the chaos of the night before. It was clearly not his own.

"Where am I?" Eryx's voice struggled out, his throat parched from the ordeal.

"In my house," Alex explained, his eyes showing a mix of concern and relief. "We decided it'd be safest for you to recover here. Would you like some water?"

Eryx nodded weakly, his gaze shifting to Ari. She held a glass of water to his lips, her expression caring but tinged with worry. "Just small sips," she instructed gently.

After a few sips, Eryx turned his gaze to Dion, who stood silently by the bedside. "How's everyone? Richard? The concert?"

"Everyone is safe and unharmed," Ari reassured him, her voice soothing. "You're the only one we're concerned about."

Eryx sighed, his gaze dropping to his lap. "I'm sorry."

Dion's voice was compassionate. "Sorry for what?"

"I'm not sure," Eryx confessed, his voice barely above a whisper. "I just feel like this is my fault."

Alex's voice was firm yet comforting. "No need for such thoughts. You couldn't have foreseen any of this. And honestly, if anyone should apologize, it's me."

Eryx looked puzzled. "For what?"

"We knew about the attack," Alex sighed, guilt weighing on his shoulders. "That's why I was late to the concert."

Eryx's brows furrowed as he processed the revelation. Despite his weakened state, he couldn't let Alex shoulder the blame alone. "Everyone's alive, right?" he checked, and Alex nodded.

"Then you fulfilled your duty," Eryx insisted, managing a weak but reassuring smile. "Without you all, it could have turned out much worse."

Ari and Dion exchanged a glance, their eyes reflecting gratitude and relief. They had all been through a harrowing experience, but their bond remained unbroken.

Eryx turned his gaze back to Alex, his voice earnest. "You did what you had to do to save everyone, and I'm grateful for that."

Alex nodded, a hint of a smile tugging at the corners of his lips. "Thank you, Eryx."

As the room settled into a moment of quiet, the tension that had hung in the air since Eryx's awakening began to ease. The weight of responsibility and guilt slowly lifted, replaced by a shared understanding that they had done everything in their power to protect those they cared about.

Eryx leaned forward, his eyes locked on his friends, Alex, Ari, and Dion, as he finally revealed what he had seen in his dream. "I saw you all fighting too. I didn't realize you had those skills."

"We did take self-defense classes, remember?" Ari chimed in, but Eryx sensed a tension in the air, a hint of unspoken truths lingering between them.

"Guys, please," Eryx urged, his voice soft but firm. "No more secrets. I know you're not just human. Apollo told me everything."

His words hung in the air, heavy and pregnant with revelation. Silence fell, a stunned hush that seemed to swallow the room whole.

"You've met Apollo?" Alex's curiosity sparkled in his eyes, and Eryx nodded, his expression tinged with weariness.

"At first, I thought he was merely a part of a dream, something unreal," Eryx admitted, his voice filled with uncertainty.

Dion leaned forward, intrigued. "What did he tell you?"

Eryx sighed, running a hand through his hair. "He shared enough, but frankly, I'm still struggling to understand half of it. So, please, I need the whole truth. No more secrets."

Ari and Dion exchanged a glance, their hesitation evident. But ultimately, they nodded, deciding it was time to reveal the hidden truths they had guarded for so long. They began to share everything, from the ancient war to how Apollo's soul had found its way to Eryx.

As he listened, Eryx felt a whirlwind of emotions. Confusion, awe, and a sense of being thrust into a world he never knew existed. His gaze eventually settled on Alex, who had been watching the revelation unfold with a mixture of apprehension and vulnerability.

"So, you're Hades, huh?" Eryx's voice was tinged with humor, a faint smile playing on his lips as he tried to lighten the heavy atmosphere. Alex nodded, his shoulders slumping slightly, a hint of weariness in his eyes. "And no."

"No?" Alex questioned, raising an eyebrow.

"Nothing changes between us," Eryx replied. "To me, you're

Alex, and that's all that matters. Regardless of me being a king or not."

Alex leaned in, pressing a gentle kiss to Eryx's forehead. "Thank you."

He turned his attention back to Ari and Dion, his voice soft but genuine. "And you two, thank you for telling me everything."

Ari's concern was evident as he asked, "Are you angry with us?"

Eryx shook his head, his expression one of understanding. "No, just disappointed that you kept this from me. However, I understand your reasons, and that's what matters most."

With those words, Eryx extended his arms, inviting his friends to join him in a warm and reassuring hug. It was a moment of unity, a silent understanding that their bonds ran deeper than the secrets they had harbored.

But exhaustion was beginning to set in, and Eryx's head spun with the weight of newfound knowledge and emotions. Alex's voice broke through his thoughts, brimming with concern. "Eryx, are you all right?"

Eryx admitted, "Just feeling tired, I guess."

"Let's get you back lying down," Alex suggested, his protective instincts kicking in. "Do you want Cerberus with you?"

"Cerberus?" Eryx's eyes widened with surprise. "You mean the real Cerberus?"

Alex chuckled, his voice warm and reassuring. "Yes, the real Cerberus."

Eryx nodded, his heart warmed by the thought. As he settled into the bed, Cerberus hopped up beside him, his adorable presence undeniable.

Eryx turned to Ari, a flicker of worry crossing his face. "Ari, Mr. Whiskers. I totally forgot about him."

Ari offered a comforting smile. "No worries. We'll check on him and bring him here if you'd like."

But before Eryx could respond, he felt himself drifting into unconsciousness. It was a gentle descent, a surrender to the weight of the revelations and the exhaustion that had finally caught up with him. As his vision blurred and his thoughts fragmented, he knew he was safe.

19

Alex

ALEX WAS IN THE MIDST of preparing food for Eryx when a knock echoed at his door. He hadn't been expecting any visitors, and it couldn't be Ari and Dion since they had just left to check on Mr. Whiskers.

Pausing what he was doing, Alex readied his magic, ready for any potential threat, before opening the door.

Before him stood Dr. Sloane, and his presence left Alex thoroughly bewildered. He hadn't called the doctor, so this unexpected visit left him puzzled. Alex lowered his magical guard, sensing no danger.

"Doctor? I don't recall calling you in," Alex said, his confusion evident.

"Yeah, I know, but someone wanted to see you and didn't know where you lived," Dr. Sloane explained with a hint of hesitation.

Just then, a familiar face appeared around the corner, causing Alex's surprise to deepen. The HIB's medical examiner, Leo, was standing there.

"Leo, what brings you here?" Alex asked, intrigued.

"Dr. Sloane let it slip that you've been dealing with four wolves who've had their souls stolen, and I believe I might have a way to help," Leo replied.

Alex nodded, welcoming them inside his home. They shed their coats, and Alex led them to the kitchen.

"Is it alright if I check on Eryx?" Dr. Sloane asked respectfully.

"Yes, please. You'll probably do a more thorough job than I could," Alex agreed, and the doctor headed to check on Eryx.

Dr. Sloane nodded, "I'll leave you two to talk."

"You're suggesting you can assist the wolves. How exactly do you plan to do that?" Alex inquired as he engaged in conversation with Leo.

"I am a necromancer, as you might have sensed. But what you may not know is that I'm also a soul tracker," Leo revealed.

Alex was taken aback by this revelation. Soul tracking was a highly intricate and mystical art practiced by only the most powerful necromancers. It involved skillfully manipulating the ethereal connections between souls and the mystical energies that pervaded the spiritual realm. Through this technique, necromancers could locate and trace lost souls across the vast expanse of the afterlife. Soul tracking demanded a deep understanding of the underlying structure of the spiritual realm and a mastery of necromantic magic.

"I believed that soul trackers were a thing of the past. Are you suggesting that's not the case?" Alex questioned as he prepared tea for both Leo and himself.

"Only a few of us remain. Many master necromancers were hesitant to pass down the intricate knowledge of soul tracking due to the risks involved in its training," Leo explained, and Alex could sense the truth in his words.

"Is that why you concealed your aura from the HIB?" Alex inquired as he poured hot water into the teacups.

"Partially," Leo admitted with a sigh. "I needed a break from wielding my magic. Necromancy takes a toll on a person."

Alex nodded in understanding. The toll of necromancy could be physical and psychological, including a potentially shortened lifespan.

"Just so you know, I won't let you take any risks that endanger your life," Alex stated as he carried a cup of tea to Leo.

"I understand, but I felt compelled to do this. After all, what good am I if I can't use my soul tracking abilities?" Leo replied.

Alex heard the door of his room open as Dr. Sloane stepped out.

"How is he?" Alex asked the doctor.

"Eryx is doing just fine. His body is almost completely healed," Dr. Sloane replied, offering a gentle smile of understanding.

"Is he awake? I was preparing his food before you guys arrived," Alex inquired.

Dr. Sloane shook his head. "Eryx passed out after I completed a thorough check-up on him. He'll be alright."

Alex nodded and turned his attention to Leo. "Are you absolutely certain about going through with this?" he asked.

"I'm sure, and besides, we have a doctor in the house," Leo said, glancing at Dr. Sloane, who Alex noticed was turning a bit red in the face.

Interesting, he thought. It seemed our resident doctor might not be single for much longer.

"Dr. Sloane, I'd like you to contact the team and instruct them to bring the wolves here to my home," Alex instructed the doctor.

Alex went to his room and tucked in Eryx, giving him the much-needed attention before he headed out. He then called the Alpha of the Hansen pack.

"Hello?" Alpha Hansen answered.

"Alpha, how quickly can you get here?" Alex asked, not wasting any time.

"Have you found their souls?" Alpha Hansen asked hesitantly.

"Not yet, but that's why I want you here. We may have a way to retrieve them," Alex said, determined that Leo would get the job done.

"Send me the address, and I'll be there," the Alpha answered right away. Alex provided him with the necessary directions and ended the call.

The team arrived not long after Alex called the Alpha. They were all dressed casually.

"Thank you, team, for bringing them over. Now, if you want to leave, you can. What you are about to witness is a ritual that hasn't been performed in more than a couple of centuries. However, you are also welcome to stay if that's your preference," Alex ordered.

His team looked at each other and silently agreed. "We're staying here, sir," Alex nodded.

"Then you'd better get out of the way before the ritual takes your souls," Leo said from where he was preparing.

"How much longer do you need? The Alpha will be here soon," Alex inquired.

"Won't be long. I just need Dr. Sloane to be right behind

me," Leo said, and the doctor nodded.

Alpha Hansen arrived half an hour later, seeing his mate and packmates in the middle of the room. He looked tired but hopeful.

"Are we ready, Leo?" Alex asked once more.

Leo nodded. "Ready. You'd better step back, people. Things can get nasty."

Leo had taken his position at the center of the room, his eyes closed in deep concentration. The rest of the team was gathered around, their collective energy creating an almost palpable tension in the air.

Leo's hands began to move, his fingers tracing intricate patterns through the air. The room seemed to respond to his movements, a subtle shift in energy that sent a shiver down Alex's spine. The very atmosphere hummed with an otherworldly resonance. *"Astra et ignes, nexus et umbrae, per vias aeternas vos revoco."*

A soft glow emanated from Leo's hands, casting a gentle luminescence that painted his features in a surreal light. His closed eyes fluttered beneath his eyelids, as if navigating a realm unseen by mortal eyes.

Then, as if responding to an invisible call, a flicker of ethereal light danced around the room. It was subtle at first, like the shimmer of a distant star, but it grew in intensity until it took form.

The forms of four wolves materialized before them, their outlines hazy and translucent. But there was something different about them, a darkness that clung to their ethereal figures like a shroud. They radiated an aura of anger and turmoil, their eyes blazing with an unholy fire.

"Something's not right." Alex said.

Beside him, Dr. Sloane watched with a mix of fascination and concern, his presence more of an observer than a participant in this perilous ritual.

Leo's voice took on a new intensity, his incantation rising in both power and urgency. The air seemed to vibrate with energy, as if the very fabric of reality was being woven anew. *"Anima ad vitam, per tenebras et lucem, vos remitto."*

The wolves' ethereal forms writhed and twisted, as if in agony. The darkness that surrounded them seemed to resist Leo's efforts, as if it were a malevolent force with a will of its own. *"Invenio vos."*

Leo's chant grew louder, his voice a desperate plea. The room pulsed with the rhythm of his words, every syllable resonating with a struggle against the dark magic that had ensnared the souls of the wolves.

One by one, the spectral wolves gained substance, their presence becoming more defined with each passing moment. But their anger only intensified, their snarls and growls echoing through the room like a chorus of malevolent spirits.

"Leo, be careful! They're not themselves." Alex said anxiously.

Leo's posture strained as he fought against the resistance of the dark magic. Sweat trickled down his forehead, his face a mask of determination mixed with exhaustion. Dr. Sloane, too, seemed to struggle with a sense of helplessness, unable to intervene in this battle of magic.

The room was filled with a profound tension, the air crackling with opposing forces. The wolves' eyes glowed with a sinister light, their rage fueling the very darkness that ensnared them.

Finally, with a collective roar of defiance, the wolves fully materialized. Their bodies were solid, their forms radiating with both anger and vitality. They stood before Alex and the others, their eyes glowing with an unholy fire.

"No! This isn't right!" Alex noticed.

Leo's voice quivered, his incantation faltering under the weight of the dark magic. He staggered, his strength waning as he struggled to maintain control. *"Socii... adiuva me..."*

Despite Leo's weakening efforts, the darkness began to recede. The wolves' forms wavered, their angry snarls becoming more desperate as they fought against the magic's influence.

In the midst of the chaos, Dr. Sloane stepped forward. His presence was a calming influence, his aura mingling with the currents of magic. With a determined expression, he chanted a phrase in Latin under his breath, his voice a counterpoint to Leo's struggle. *"Lux in tenebris, revoca animas!"*

The combined efforts of Leo and Dr. Sloane seemed to shift the balance. The dark magic's grip on the wolves loosened, allowing Leo's incantation to regain strength. *"Socii... adiuva me..."*

The room seemed to hold its breath as the tide turned. Slowly, the darkness began to recede further, replaced by a warm, golden light that surrounded the wolves.

With a final surge of willpower, Leo's voice soared, his incantation reaching its crescendo.

"Socii, vos revoco!," Leo roared.

The wolves let out a final, mournful howl, their forms convulsing as the dark magic relinquished its hold. The golden light enveloped them, and in an instant, they collapsed to the ground, their bodies human once more.

The room fell silent,

the tension dissipating like smoke in the wind. Alex rushed forward, followed by the rest of the team. They knelt beside the unconscious forms of the wolves, relief washing over them like a tidal wave.

"Leo, you did it." Alex said

Leo's shoulders slumped, his energy spent from the battle against the dark magic. He nodded weakly, his breathing heavy as he gazed at the wolves.

"It was touch and go there for a moment." Leo panted.

Dr. Sloane joined them, his expression a mix of exhaustion and triumph. He placed a hand on Leo's shoulder, a silent gesture of gratitude.

Dr. Sloane "Your magic and mine… we managed to break the hold of that darkness."

The wolves began to stir, their human forms slowly regaining consciousness. As they opened their eyes, their gazes were clear and free from the malevolent rage that had consumed them.

"Welcome back." Alex said to the wolves.

Leo's voice was soft, filled with a mixture of relief and exhaustion. "We did it."

As the wolves opened their eyes, the room seemed to fill with an unwavering energy. Alpha Hansen stepped forward, gratitude filling his gaze as he looked at Leo, Alex, and the rest of the team. Then, his eyes landed on the unconscious form of Henry, his alpha mate. With a nod, he moved to Henry's side, gathering him in a tight embrace. He turned to his other packmates, hugging them with equal fervor.

Once Leo managed to steady himself and stand without the risk of stumbling, Alex pulled him aside. He had lingering questions about the ritual that he needed to address.

"Are we certain that they're going to be okay?" Alex inquired, his voice tinged with concern, as he gazed at Leo.

Leo responded with a reassuring smile. "If you're asking whether they are now themselves again, then yes."

Curiosity piqued, Alex probed further, "How did you manage to accomplish that?"

"In the ritual, I connected with their inner essence, locating their core soul energy. I guided that energy back to its original state before it was stolen," Leo explained. This revelation was new to Alex, and he appreciated learning more about the intricacies of Leo's abilities.

"I can't thank you enough for rescuing these wolves," Alex expressed his gratitude sincerely. He knew that this act of recovery was no small feat.

Leo's response was lighthearted. "It's nothing much. Just make sure your doctor pays me a visit in the morgue more often."

Amid their conversation, the topic shifted to a pressing matter. "Speaking of the morgue, have you made any discoveries?" Alex inquired, detecting a change in Leo's demeanor.

Leo's expression shifted, becoming more serious. "There's been something unusual with the bodies. If possible, could you come and examine them?"

Alex nodded, delving further. "What's your initial assessment?"

"I suspect the individual responsible used dark magic. The bodies show no signs of decay," Leo responded. The mention of dark magic heightened the concern; the combination of undecayed bodies and dark magic hinted at a potential magical nightmare.

"I'll come to investigate tomorrow. For now, go home and get some rest. I know how much that ritual took out of you," Alex directed Leo before bidding him farewell.

Alex entered the living room, where everyone had gathered, and made his way toward the group of wolves. Placing a comforting hand on Alpha Hansen's shoulder, he drew the Alpha's attention.

"Alpha, I want you to take your mate and pack mates back home. They need rest," Alex spoke, his tone reassuring, as he noticed the fatigue etched on the Alpha's face.

Alpha Hansen released a weary sigh, the weariness in his eyes slowly giving way to a glimmer of hope. "Thank you. Your team member Gabe inquired if I could bring the wolves to your headquarters so they can provide an account of what happened before they vanished."

Alex's response was understanding. "Yes, we would prefer that. However, for now, let them return home and recover. When they're ready, then you can bring them to us."

The Alpha nodded in agreement, and after a moment, he gathered his mate and fellow pack members, leaving to let them find some much-needed rest.

With his team still gathered in his house, Alex saw it as a perfect opportunity to gather updates on the ongoing case.

"Marcus," he addressed, capturing Marcus's attention. "How's our progress with the roommate?"

"I managed to establish contact, sir. We're set to have dinner in a couple of days," Marcus replied.

"Good. Just exercise caution, alright? Emma, you'll accompany him," Alex instructed. Both Marcus and Emma nodded in agreement.

Turning his focus to the next aspect, Alex inquired, "And

what about the boyfriend? Any developments on Sven Janssen?"

"We're making headway, sir. I'm planning an infiltration of the company to gather more information," Olivia reported.

Acknowledging the effort, Alex nodded. "Very well. Keep up the good work, team. For now, you're all dismissed. Make sure to get some rest."

His team left one by one, and just before the last of them could depart, Ari and Dion entered the house with Mr. Whiskers in tow.

Once the house was cleared of their presence, Alex settled onto a couch, Ari and Dion joining him.

He wasn't used to having so many people around for such an extended period, and he felt the weight of exhaustion pressing on him. But he knew he needed to push through.

Ari was the first to break the silence. "What was all that about?"

Alex proceeded to recount the events that had transpired in the living room, watching as their expressions shifted in response.

"Stolen souls? That's a new one," Dion commented, his brow furrowed. "So, what's the plan?"

Alex leaned back, considering their question. "As of now, it's a task for me to handle. Your focus should be on supporting Eryx and helping him settle in. Leave the matter of the stolen souls to me."

Ari chimed in with a reassuring smile. "Don't worry, Alex. Even though our magic reserves aren't fully replenished, we're here for you."

Nodding in gratitude, Alex understood their dedication. "I appreciate that. But for now, you guys can head back home.

You have your own lives to tend to."

Dion shook his head, affirming their commitment. "True, but remember, we're just a call away."

With the conversation concluded and everyone having departed, Alex finally had a moment to himself. Taking a deep breath, he made his way to his room to check on Eryx, Mr. Whiskers following inquisitively at his heels.

20

Eryx

L*ICK, LICK, LICK.*

Eryx felt his face being licked by a pair of sandpapers. Plural. There were two of them. He also heard chuckling nearby.

Eryx opened his eyes to see Cerberus' tongue lolling up and down in front of him, and Mr. Whiskers licking himself. And, of course, he found Alex laughing at his predicament. He could see his tombstone now, reading, *Eryx Ross - Cause of Death: Adorable Animals.*

"Are you just going to let them eat me?" Eryx teased, his voice still a bit rough from sleep.

"Well, you do look delicious," Alex teased back, and Eryx groaned.

"You're horrendous," Eryx said and pulled the furry dorks closer for a cuddle.

Feeling the bed dip, Eryx turned his head to see Alex smiling down at him. *Man, he's gorgeous,* he thought.

"How are you feeling?" Alex asked him.

Eryx thought about that for a moment as he assessed his

body. "I actually feel good. Like I can do more than what I used to on a regular day." He genuinely felt better and was eager to move.

"Do you think you could stand up?" Alex asked softly.

"I think so." Eryx nodded and attempted to sit up, carefully placing Cerberus and Mr. Whiskers on the floor. Sitting up wasn't painful, so he decided to try standing. Alex was by his side, ready to assist if needed.

He managed to stand up without any help, and Alex smiled, hugging him tightly. Alex smelled good, and Eryx wanted to bask in it.

"Come on, I got us breakfast," Alex said as he broke the hug.

"Is it okay if I shower first? I'm pretty sure I smell," Eryx said, and Alex chuckled.

"Sure, I'll just take these two suckers out for a walk," Alex said, and Eryx highly doubted that Mr. Whiskers would walk, but it wasn't fun telling Alex that. "Ari and Dion brought you clothes before leaving Mr. Whiskers here yesterday evening. I'll take some out for you." Alex continued.

Eryx appreciated Alex's thoughtfulness before he headed to the bathroom.

When Eryx walked into Alex's bathroom, his eyes widened in awe. The space felt like a modern sanctuary with a cozy touch. The contemporary design was softened by wooden accents, giving it a rustic warmth.

The white tiles in the shower area sparkled under the soft lighting, reflecting the steam rising from the warm water. The showerhead, a sleek chrome fixture, stood ready to provide comfort and relaxation.

But what really grabbed Eryx's attention were the wooden shelves and countertops. The natural wood tones contrasted beautifully against the clean white surroundings. Potted plants on the shelves added a hint of nature, making the space come alive.

A wooden-framed mirror hung above the sink, its frame a blend of simple elegance and intricate detailing. The patterns etched into the wood showed expert craftsmanship, revealing the care put into every detail.

Eryx shifted his gaze to the wooden vanity, where grooming essentials were neatly organized. The mix of modern containers with the warmth of wood created a balanced and inviting setup.

As he explored the bathroom, Eryx spotted a small wooden stool tucked in the corner, adorned with neatly folded towels. The stool seemed like a cozy spot to unwind, adding a touch of comfort to the room.

Eryx got into the shower, feeling the warm water wash over his tired muscles. The gentle spray was soothing, rinsing away the last traces of sleep and the foggy feeling from his dreams.

Eryx's attention shifted when he heard the door open and recognized the familiar footsteps drawing near. He opened his eyes and found Alex entering the bathroom, his gaze fixed on Eryx. The steam from the shower enveloped them in a cozy mist.

Alex's lips curved into a gentle smile as he reached out, pulling Eryx closer. The warmth of the shower mixed with their body heat, and Eryx felt a surge of gratefulness.

"That was quick," Eryx remarked to Alex.

"Well, I had to make them. I can't miss an opportunity to do this," Alex replied with a mischievous grin, giving Eryx a playful squeeze on his ass

"A… Alex," Eryx moaned, his voice catching.

"What is it, baby?" Alex teased, a smug smile playing on his lips.

"Please… I need you inside me," Eryx pleaded urgently.

Eryx felt the press of Alex's body against his own, their connection sending a jolt of anticipation through him. Eryx couldn't help but notice Alex's considerable size, a realization that only heightened his excitement. Eryx's hand found its way to Alex's firmness, stroking him slowly, evoking a passionate moan of pleasure.

"Want your mouth on me, sweetheart," Alex moaned.

Eryx kissed Alex passionately, his lips eager as they enjoyed each other's taste. Moving downward, Eryx continued with purpose, a determined look in his eyes. Despite Alex's larger size, Eryx's determination pushed him forward; he wasn't one to give up easily. Taking Alex into his mouth, he showed a practiced skill that made it look easy. The sensation of Alex's cock brushing his throat sent tingles down his spine.

"Fuck baby. If you keep on doing that I am going to come." Alex panted

Eryx stopped what he was doing and kissed Alex again. Alex pulled Eryx closer and pressed him against the wall. Eryx felt Alex kneel down and start eating him out like he was dessert.

Eryx moaned as Alex's tongue slide over his hole.

"Please… Fuck me," Eryx begged Alex, unable to hold back his desire.

Eryx sensed Alex standing up behind him, Alex's cock pressing between his cheeks

Alex's warm breath tickled Eryx's ear. "Are you ready for me, baby?" Eryx was too overwhelmed to answer with words, so he just nodded in response.

Eryx sensed Alex positioning himself at his entrance, and he couldn't resist pushing back eagerly.

"So needy," Alex chuckled.

"Alex…" Eryx moaned, his voice heavy with desire.

Eryx was just about to push back further when he felt the fullness of Alex's girth filling him completely. Alex's thrusts grew stronger and faster, driving Eryx into a state of pure bliss. He knew he wouldn't be able to hold on much longer.

"Alex… I'm going to come," Eryx moaned, his pleasure building to its peak.

"Come for me, baby. I'm close too," Alex panted, the urgency in his voice echoing Eryx's own need.

After a few more intense thrusts, Eryx felt his release cascade through him as Alex came inside him.

They held each other for a while before cleaning each other up. Once done, they moved back to the bedroom and have a quick change of clothes before heading to the kitchen.

Eryx entered Alex's kitchen with wide eyes, taking in the sight before him. The room was a mix of modern and rustic styles, like a perfect blend. The clean lines of modern design matched with the coziness of wooden touches, making it feel inviting.

The kitchen island caught Eryx's attention, its shiny surface illuminated by soft lights. The sides of the island had intricate woodwork, showing off careful craftsmanship.

Pendant lights above the island cast a gentle glow, making the space feel warm. Eryx looked at the wooden shelves on the walls, holding a mix of modern gadgets and handcrafted items that gave a personal feel.

Eryx discovered the dining table brimming with food, and

his mouth watered instantly. He noticed Cerberus and Mr. Whisker sleeping beside each other. *Don't get used to it*, he thought.

"Did you make all of this?" Eryx inquired of Alex, who was next to him.

Alex chuckled, "No, I ordered before you woke up. I'm not that skilled at cooking, and I wanted you to have a good breakfast."

"You didn't have to do that," Eryx expressed his gratitude.

"I wanted to. What kind of boyfriend would I be if I didn't take care of you?" Eryx blushed, his cheeks turning a deeper shade. He had a habit of speaking his mind, especially when he had a few drinks.

"You remembered that?" Eryx's blush deepened even further, realizing that Alex had not only heard but also remembered his candid confession.

"Of course. How could I forget?" Alex smiled. "Now, come on, let's eat." He gently took Eryx's hand, leading them to the dining table.

They settled down with Alex seated across from Eryx. The moment Eryx tasted the food, a satisfied moan escaped him. "This is so good. Thank you."

"You're welcome," Alex replied, reaching for Eryx's free hand and holding it affectionately.

Curiosity tugged at Eryx. "So, what happened yesterday while I was out of it?" he asked, noticing the concern on Alex's face.

Alex's expression darkened as he recounted the events of the previous day. Eryx was taken aback by how much he had missed.

"Are the wolves going to be okay?" Eryx inquired, his

concern directed toward the wolves who had attacked him.

"Yeah, Leo said they'll be back to normal. They just needed some rest," Alex reassured, and Eryx felt relieved. He didn't want to cause the wolves any more pain. From what he gathered, they had been acting out of character.

Changing the subject, Eryx asked, "So, what's on your agenda for today?"

"I need to visit the morgue before I head to the office," Alex replied solemnly.

"Can I come to the morgue with you?"

"Why?" Alex questioned.

Eryx contemplated for a moment. "I just want to see you work, I guess. Plus, you can drop me off at Ari's place on the way to work."

"Sweetheart, you've just recovered from an attack, and the morgue might not be the best place for you," Alex expressed concern softly.

Understanding Alex's worry, Eryx persisted, "I'll be careful. I won't be in your way, I promise."

Alex sighed, his resolve wavering. "Alright, but if you start feeling uneasy or uncomfortable, you're out of there. Understand?"

"I promise. Now, let's go," Eryx declared, eager to get moving.

They quickly prepared to leave but not before Eryx set out some food for Cerberus and Mr. Whiskers. Eryx was touched to see that Alex had gotten Mr. Whiskers his own cat food and bowl.

They drove to the morgue in Alex's car, Eryx appreciating the comfort of the ride. They remained quiet during the journey until Eryx decided to break the silence.

"So, can you like, pop in and out of places? You know, like a portal?" Eryx asked, his curiosity evident.

Alex chuckled at the question. "Technically, yes. We can portal in and out of places, but it's an extremely rare magic that only gods and a few magic users possess."

"Do you think I'll ever be able to do that?" Eryx wondered aloud after a pause.

Alex placed a reassuring hand on Eryx's thigh and gently rubbed it. "I don't know. But for now, don't stress about it too much, okay?" Alex's comforting touch eased some of Eryx's uncertainty, even though he wished for a clearer answer on how to access his newfound magic.

"I think Apollo's soul made a mistake," Eryx confessed, his confusion still lingering about why he was chosen as its host.

"Why do you think that?" Alex asked with genuine interest.

"I don't know… I mean, I'm not really the strongest person out there," Eryx admitted with honesty.

Eventually, Alex parked the car in front of a modern-looking building, likely where the morgue was located. He turned to Eryx and spoke before they got out.

"You're one of the strongest people I know. After everything you've been through, I'm surprised you're still holding it together and not running away," Alex said, reaching for Eryx's hand and placing a gentle kiss on it. "Now come on, Leo's waiting."

Eryx nodded, pushing aside his doubts for the time being. Just as he was about to step out of the car, he felt a surge of something within him.

He's right, you know, a familiar voice echoed in his mind, the voice of Apollo.

Apollo? You weren't kidding about us being connected, were you? Eryx mentally asked, feeling a mixture of awe and amusement.

No, I wasn't. You'll get used to it, Apollo replied with a chuckle, his presence bringing a momentary surge of magic within Eryx, before it subsided.

They entered the morgue, and there stood a young man in a lab coat who seemed to be around twenty-something. "Hey, you must be Director Knight. I'm Jason. Follow me, please. Dr. Rodriguez is waiting for you," Jason said and guided them further inside.

As they walked deeper, the temperature dropped noticeably. The hallways were cold, and after a bit, they reached a room filled with big metal lockers for holding bodies. Alex looked at Eryx, probably checking if he was okay. Eryx held Alex's hand gently to show he was fine.

A door opened, and a tired-looking man appeared. "Director Knight, thanks for coming," Alex greeted, and then Leo's attention turned to Eryx. "And you must be Eryx. I'm Leo Rodriguez, the medical examiner," Leo introduced himself, shaking Eryx's hand from his lab coat. "Come this way," Leo continued, leading them farther in.

Approaching the bodies in the morgue, Eryx started feeling something strange. It was like his connection with Apollo's soul was making him sense things in a different way.

Do you feel that too? Eryx silently asked Apollo.

Yes, something's not right, Apollo's voice replied.

Eryx also noticed a faint humming sound that seemed out of place – like an odd energy in the air. The presence of Apollo's soul within him seemed to be making him more aware of it, and it made him feel uneasy. Eryx and Alex exchanged worried glances, sensing that the morgue, usually quiet and calm, was now charged with an unsettling feeling.

Eryx's gut told him that something was off. This special link he had with Apollo's soul was giving him the ability to sense things others might not. It was both eerie and interesting as he tried to understand what was happening by combining his feelings with the ancient soul's presence within him.

They arrived at the spot where the bodies lay, and Eryx's senses continued to go haywire. Leo signaled for them to stay where they were as he moved forward to uncover the bodies. Eryx had a hard time keeping his composure when he saw the gruesome state they were in – a sight that almost made him lose his breakfast.

"Are you okay? Remember, you can step out if you need to," Alex turned to him, concern in his eyes.

"Yeah, I'm okay," Eryx replied, taking a deep breath to steady himself.

"As you can see, there's something peculiar about their condition," Leo began, his tone grave. "There's an element inside their bodies that's slowing down the natural process of decay."

"Dark Magic," Alex said with certainty.

The strange humming sensation seemed to intensify, now even more palpable. Eryx felt it vibrating in his bones, creating a discomfort he couldn't ignore.

"Exactly, but this kind of dark magic is intricate and complex," Leo continued, noticing Eryx's confusion. "Usually, dark magic users leave the victims mostly ash but these bodies are still in tact."

Eryx's head began to ache, but he pushed through, determined to understand what was happening.

I sense something in their bodies, Apollo's voice echoed in his mind. *I want you to get closer to the bodies, Eryx.*

Are you crazy? Eryx was about to dismiss the idea, but Apollo persisted.

Listen, Eryx. Close your eyes and listen, Apollo instructed. *Center yourself and focus on the vibrations you're sensing.*

Eryx hesitated but followed Apollo's guidance. He closed his eyes, took a moment to calm himself, and started to focus. At first, there was nothing, but slowly the vibrations grew stronger. He felt like he could see the waves where they were emanating from – all the bodies were emitting them.

I need you to get closer, Apollo urged.

With a sense of trust, Eryx moved closer to the bodies. Alex and Leo exchanged puzzled looks, clearly unsure of Eryx's intentions.

"What are you doing, Eryx?" Alex asked, trying to approach him, but Eryx halted him.

"Step back, both of you." Eryx ordered.

Now what? Eryx asked Apollo.

Raise your hand above them and focus on your inner light to pinpoint the source, Apollo instructed.

My inner light? Eryx questioned, uncertain.

Yes, the light within you. Search for it deep in your soul, Apollo reassured him.

Eryx closed his eyes once more, envisioning the soft, radiant light he associated with Apollo. It was a symbol of ancient wisdom and strength, now intertwined with his own being.

That's it, Eryx. Hold onto it. Now open your eyes, Apollo guided him.

Eryx opened his eyes, surprised to see his hands emitting a bright glow. He moved his hands as if guided by an invisible force, zeroing in on something.

I'm actually doing it, Eryx marveled.

You are. Now let the magic flow around the bodies, Apollo encouraged.

Eryx channeled the energy within him, and a brilliant yellow light enveloped the bodies. The light granted him an X-ray-like vision, revealing an entity emitting a dark glow within the chest of each body.

Do you see it? Eryx asked Apollo.

Yes, bring the light back, Apollo instructed.

Eryx retrieved the light, feeling a bit unsteady afterward. Alex stepped forward, steadying him.

"What was that?" Alex asked, his concern evident.

"There's something inside them. Something dark. But I think you can remove it," Eryx looked to Leo for confirmation.

"Leo, are you able to do that?" Alex turned to Leo.

Leo nodded and proceeded to follow Eryx's guidance. As he cut into the bodies, Eryx felt a mixture of disgust and determination.

Eryx saw Leo remove a piece of metal from the bodies and present it to them. A curse escaped Alex's lips upon seeing it.

"Do you recognize this? There's something off about this metal," Leo spoke up.

Alex nodded. "Leo, I want you to extract all of them and send them to us. We need them as evidence."

Leo seemed hesitant, but ultimately nodded, understanding the importance of the situation.

As they departed from the morgue, Eryx's curiosity got the better of him, prompting him to turn to Alex with questions about what they had just encountered.

"What in the world was that thing?" Eryx's curiosity burned as he directed the question to Alex.

They paused just outside the morgue's entrance, the weight of their recent discovery settling between them.

"Not the right place or time. I'll tell you soon, alright?" Alex replied, his expression serious.

Eryx couldn't suppress a sigh. "Yeah, I get it."

In a tender gesture, Alex caressed Eryx's face and pressed a gentle kiss to his forehead.

"Are you certain about going to Ari's house? If you want, I can drop you off at home if you want. It might be safer," Alex proposed, concern lacing his words.

Eryx took a moment to contemplate this option. "Yeah, I think that's the right call." He hesitated before continuing, "Do you truly think there are people after me?"

A weary sigh escaped Alex's lips. "I'm afraid so. Ari and Dion had their reasons for concealing your true nature. All I want is for you to be out of harm's way. I can't bear the thought of losing you."

"I promise I'll be cautious. Now, let's go. After we're done here, I'll ask Ari to drop me off at your place," Eryx assured him.

"Alright, but no matter what, if anything seems off, promise me you'll call me," Alex insisted.

Eryx met Alex's gaze and nodded solemnly. "I promise."

With their understanding silently reaffirmed, Eryx and Alex left the morgue behind, the weight of the recent events making Eryx long for a cleansing shower.

21

Alex

CELESTIAL STEEL.

Alex was still thinking about what they found in the morgue.

Their visit to the morgue had been to find answers, and answers they had indeed found. But instead of feeling satiated, the newfound knowledge had ignited a fresh inferno of questions.

To even attempt to wield a Celestial Steel weapon, one had to possess a profound affinity with magic, a connection that went beyond mere knowledge or skill. It required a soul that resonated with the mystical energies of the universe, capable of channeling and directing those energies with precision and control.

When a compatible wielder touched a Celestial Steel weapon, a resonance occurred, as if two notes in a cosmic symphony had found their harmonious counterpart. This resonance went beyond the superficial, diving deep into the very essence of the person's being. Their magical energy intertwined with the celestial magic of the metal, creating a fusion of power that was greater than the sum of its parts.

This connection was not easily established. It demanded a profound understanding of one's own magical nature, a deep meditation on the weave of their soul's magic, and a conscious alignment with the elemental forces of the universe. Only through this harmony could a person begin to tap into the immense potential of Celestial Steel.

When successfully bonded, the weapon became an extension of the wielder's magic, responding to their thoughts and intentions as effortlessly as an extension of their body. The strength of the connection influenced the potency of the weapon's abilities, allowing the wielder to channel their magic through the Celestial Steel to perform feats that would otherwise be inconceivable.

Adding to the mystery, Alex found himself puzzled by Eryx's unique ability to sense celestial steel's presence. Even Apollo lacked this magical capacity, leaving Alex wondering if Apollo's essence merging with Eryx's soul had granted him this new perception.

Alex was sure they had wiped out every trace of celestial steel. After the war, they had meticulously collected each fragment, gathering them before burning the pieces in the depths of the underworld.

The fire they used was far from ordinary; it was forged from the merging of celestial and infernal forces. It stood as a bridge between realms, a fusion of magical energies from celestial steel and the underworld.

Now, with celestial steel reappearing, Alex grew more convinced that Morvain, the sinister right hand of Kronos, had returned to manipulate events. Morvain's dominion over shadows granted him power rivaling gods, and his web of spies orchestrated moves, leaving even deities exposed.

Alex's fists pounded the punching bag in a relentless rhythm, each strike an outlet for his frustrations. Sweat dripped down his face, mingling with the intensity of his efforts. He had to stay sharp, vigilant, and focused on the task at hand. Protecting the realm demanded nothing less.

Amid the relentless barrage of punches, Marcus barged into the training room, his voice urgent and alarmed. "Sir, we have an emergency. We tried calling your SHD, but you were not responding."

Alex's brow furrowed in realization. His SHD, a critical communication device, was turned off. Damn it, he hadn't noticed how deeply he'd been lost in thought.

Removing his boxing gloves, he turned to face Marcus. "What's the situation, Marcus?"

Marcus's eyes darted with anxiety as he relayed the news. "The HIB found bodies in the middle of Times Square."

Alex's muscles tensed. He needed more information. "How many bodies are we talking about?"

Marcus's voice quivered with concern. "They haven't given us an exact number. They just instructed us to get there as soon as possible."

Alex nodded, his mind racing as he processed the gravity of the situation. "Let me finish up here and inform the team to gear up. We'll be heading out in five."

With a sense of urgency, Marcus left the room to relay the orders to the rest of the team. Alex wasted no time, taking the quickest shower of his life before finding his team assembled in the lobby, ready to respond to the crisis.

His team stood prepared for whatever lay ahead. They knew the stakes, and they trusted Alex to lead them through any challenge.

Without wasting a moment, Alex addressed them. "We've got a situation in Times Square. The HIB has discovered bodies. We don't have all the details yet, but it's likely connected to the Order."

Gabe, his trusted strategist, nodded in understanding. "We'll be ready, Alex. Let's get there and assess the situation."

The team's determination and unity were palpable as they geared up and headed for the exit. They had trained for scenarios like this, but each mission carried its own uncertainties.

As they emerged from the facility into the bustling afternoon of Times Square, the transition from their controlled training environment to the chaotic city streets was jarring. The neon lights and towering billboards seemed almost surreal against the backdrop of the emergency call.

Their arrival at the scene was met with a sea of flashing lights, sirens wailing, and a crowd of onlookers held at bay by the police. The unmistakable aura of tension hung in the air as they approached the HIB agents already on site.

Alex and his team moved with purpose, their training taking over. The dynamics between them were fluid and seamless, each member knowing their role and executing it with precision. They gathered information from the HIB agents and observed the eerie scene in Times Square.

"Marcus, assist the HIB in managing the crowd. Emma, set up a distraction ward around the scene," Alex commanded, his voice carrying authority honed through countless missions.

Marcus didn't miss a beat, swiftly moving to coordinate with the Human Investigation Bureau officers. Emma, began weaving the ward, her focused expression highlighting the seriousness of their situation.

The distraction ward took effect, shielding their investigation from prying eyes. Spectators continued to mill about, oblivious to the strange events unfolding within its boundaries.

As Alex and his team crossed the yellow tape marking the perimeter of the incident site, Detective Collins, a seasoned officer, spotted them and approached.

"Director Knight," Detective Collins greeted with a nod of respect.

"Detective, tell me what you guys have," Alex ordered, his demeanor unwavering.

Detective Collins relayed the grim details, his voice tinged with unease. "The call came in this morning. The caller said they spotted a group of people dropping all of the bodies. When one of the officers got to the scene, they found all four bodies like this."

As they conducted their initial assessment, Alex couldn't shake the sense of foreboding that clung to him. The bodies lay sprawled in the midst of the iconic square, a stark contrast to the lively atmosphere it usually exuded.

The tension built as the team continued their investigation. Alex's thoughts raced, the weight of responsibility pressing down on him. He had to lead his team through this, no matter how grim the situation.

Gabe's voice broke the silence, drawing Alex's attention. "These wounds… they're not ordinary. It's as if some supernatural force was at play here."

Alex nodded, his mind racing with possibilities. They were dealing with something more sinister than they had initially thought. The mystery deepened, and the team braced themselves for the challenges that lay ahead.

Their mission had just begun, and the city held its breath, unaware of the darkness that lurked beneath the surface.

Alex's steely gaze remained fixed on the crime scene. "Was this person able to identify the individuals who brought the bodies here?" Alex asked the Detective.

"No, but he said that they didn't seem human. More like shadows," Detective Collins replied.

"Shadow wraiths," Olivia, their arcane mage, murmured, her knowledge of the supernatural world lending insight.

"What did Leo find?" Alex inquired, referencing their forensic expert.

"He said that the bodies were marked the same way as Rina Lane's body was," Detective Collins answered, referencing a previous case that had haunted their team.

"Do you think it's the Order, sir?" Gabriel, their strategist and witch, voiced the question that hung in the air.

Before Alex could reply, he sensed it—an unsettling surge of magic amidst the chaos of Times Square. His instincts sharpened, and his focus narrowed.

He scanned the area and pinpointed a woman who, despite the distraction ward, remained fixated on the scene. Her presence sent shivers down his spine, and his magic tingled in response, detecting the telltale taint of dark magic.

"You there, stay where you are!" Alex's voice boomed, cutting through the bustling square.

In a heartbeat, the woman bolted, her sudden flight catching everyone off guard.

Of course, they always run, Alex thought, his determination setting his course.

Sending Marcus in pursuit crossed his mind, but the risk of exposing Marcus to the dark magic's taint held him back. This was his chase, his responsibility.

Alex gave chase, his agile form weaving through the crowd with precision. Detective Collins directed his officers to follow, recognizing the urgency of the situation.

The woman's speed was impressive, but Alex was relentless. His powerful strides ate away at the distance between them.

"Stop! Goddamnit!" he roared, his voice filled with frustration and determination.

The woman's desperate scream pierced the air, echoing through the surroundings, sending shivers down the spines of those who heard it.

She's a fucking Banshee.

Her eerie scream fueled her escape, and Alex's senses sharpened. He knew the danger of confronting a Banshee, their wails capable of causing harm to those who heard them.

He pushed forward, determined to catch her before she could unleash her deadly power. The chase intensified, the chaotic backdrop of Times Square providing obstacles and opportunities alike.

People shouted and scattered as Alex closed the distance, his determination unwavering. The Banshee's pale figure weaved through the crowd like a phantom, her long hair billowing behind her.

In the narrow alley of Time Square, Alex, his features etched in determination, gave chase to the elusive Banshee. Her appearance was haunting; her skin had an otherworldly pallor, and her eyes shimmered with a malevolent light. An aura of ethereal menace clung to her, making her presence undeniable.

As they closed in on her, the Banshee's escape routes dwindled. Alex knew their quarry was far from ordinary; her strength hinted at an unsettling power. "Stand back, all of you!" he commanded his team of officers, who promptly complied. "Olivia, illuminate her path. Gabe, create a shield to block her escape." Alex's voice held a steady intensity as he led the pursuit.

In the confined space of the alley, the Banshee found herself cornered. Olivia summoned a fierce column of fire that encapsulated her, and Gabe erected a shimmering barrier, sealing her fate.

Drawing closer, Alex harnessed his hellfire, conjured from his very essence, to further confine the Banshee. His eyes, dark and unwavering, locked onto her. "Who sent you?" he demanded, his voice dripping with urgency.

The Banshee's lips curled into a sinister smile, and from them emerged an eerie, otherworldly sound that sent shivers down their spines. "You will die, Hades. You and that vessel will suffer the consequences of our Master's grand plan," she taunted cryptically.

Alex's patience wore thin; Eryx's safety was non-negotiable. "Tell me your Master's identity before I send you to the depths of the underworld," he growled, the flames of his hellfire intensifying in his grasp.

"Inflict your worst, Hades. My task here is done," the Banshee retorted defiantly.

Enough was enough. Alex focused his hellfire, channeling its potent energy toward the Banshee. But he wouldn't grant her the mercy of swift incineration. Instead, he melded his magic with the fabric of the underworld, opening a portal behind her in the same instant. The Banshee's form was engulfed in the inferno as she was banished to the underworld.

Alex sensed Detective Collins catching up to them, the lingering scent of the underworld still tainting the air. The detective's exhaustion was palpable as he approached.

"Where did you send her?" Detective Collins asked, his voice heavy with fatigue.

"To a place you don't need to know about," Alex replied bluntly.

"We needed her statement, Alex! She could be key to this case!" The detective's frustration was evident.

"I don't care. Remember, you're not in charge of this investigation anymore, Detective. Would you prefer to have a Banshee running amok, potentially causing more deaths, or do you want the threat eliminated?" Alex's words were edged with impatience.

The detective sighed, conceding reluctantly. "Could you at least assist us in transporting the bodies to the morgue?"

Alex nodded, his expression unyielding. "Gabe, Olivia, lend the HIB a hand with the bodies. I need to make a call."

His team members acknowledged the orders.

As the Banshee's cryptic message hung in the air, Alex couldn't help but feel a growing unease. The reference to "Hades" and the ominous mention of a "vessel" suggested a larger, more sinister plot. He knew they had only scratched the surface of a deeper supernatural conflict.

In the backdrop of the narrow alley, the setting sun cast long shadows, deepening the sense of foreboding that clung to the scene. The flickering of hellfire painted eerie patterns on the walls, and the scent of burning magic lingered like a sinister perfume.

Internally, Alex grappled with his emotions. Eryx's safety was paramount, and he was willing to go to any lengths to protect him. The use of his hellfire, a power born from his very essence, weighed heavily on him, for it always came with consequences that lingered.

As he continued to assist with the investigation, Alex's thoughts were clouded with the Banshee's cryptic message. Who was this "Master," and what was their "grand plan"?

With each passing moment, the tension between law enforcement and the supernatural grew, and the shadows deepened, revealing only glimpses of the larger, more complex supernatural world that lay beneath the surface.

Alex retrieved his phone, dialing a familiar number. "I need you to get to London."

* * *

Exhaustion seeped through Alex's bones as he managed to slip back into his house. The weight of the day hung heavy on his shoulders, and all he wanted now was the comfort of being with Eryx. He closed the front door softly, not wanting to disturb the peace of their home.

As he entered, a delightful aroma wafted to his senses, drawing him to the kitchen. The soft, warm glow of the pendant lights above illuminated the cozy space. The walls were painted a soothing shade of pale blue, and the wooden cabinets exuded a sense of rustic charm. The scent in the air was a symphony of herbs and spices, tantalizing his tired mind.

There stood Eryx, clad in only an apron and boxers, focused on cooking. Alex leaned against the doorway, quietly watching the man he loved. Eryx was a vision of domesticity, his dark hair tousled, and his lean form moving gracefully around the kitchen. It was a sight that never failed to make Alex's heart skip a beat.

"I didn't know that you could cook," Alex finally spoke up after a while, his voice a low rumble in the peaceful ambiance.

Eryx jumped slightly at the unexpected voice, almost dropping his spatula into the sizzling pan. He turned to face Alex, his brown eyes widening in surprise. "Alex! You scared me." His tone held a mix of relief and amusement.

Chuckling softly, Alex slowly approached Eryx, the exhaustion in his bones momentarily forgotten. He wrapped his strong arms around Eryx's waist from behind, relishing in the feeling of being close to him. Eryx's body was warm and familiar, a welcome sanctuary after a long day.

Eryx leaned back into Alex's embrace, his body fitting perfectly against Alex's chest. The subtle scent of Eryx's cologne mingled with the tantalizing aroma of the dish he was preparing. "I wanted to surprise you," he admitted, his voice soft and filled with affection.

Alex nuzzled Eryx's neck, planting a gentle kiss there. "You certainly did. And it smells amazing in here."

This feels so right, Alex thought to himself.

"What are you cooking?" Alex inquired, wrapping his arms around Eryx from behind, pulling him in close.

Eryx leaned back into Alex's embrace, his shoulders relaxing as he spoke. "I am making my famous chicken burgers. And yes, I can cook. I did bake you cookies that one time." He bopped Alex's nose with his finger, a playful glint in his eyes, before quickly retreating it to his mouth. "A…Alex. Stop it. Food first."

Playfully, Alex couldn't resist giving Eryx's backside a light spank, eliciting a surprised yelp from Eryx. "Fine, can I help?"

Eryx turned to face him, a smirk dancing on his lips. "You can set up the dining table. This won't be long."

Alex nodded, releasing Eryx, who turned his attention back to the sizzling chicken burgers on the stove. The sizzling sound and the tantalizing aroma filled the kitchen, making Alex's stomach growl with anticipation.

In the dining room, Alex meticulously arranged the plates, silverware, and glasses. He couldn't help but think about how much his life had changed since Eryx had entered it. The once solitary existence he had grown accustomed to was now filled with warmth and laughter, thanks to the man in the kitchen.

When everything was ready, they sat down at the dining table. Eryx placed the food before them, the chicken burgers perfectly cooked, with a side of crispy fries.

"Dig in!" Eryx exclaimed, taking his seat.

Alex picked up one of Eryx's homemade chicken burgers and took a bite. The first taste sent a burst of flavor through his senses, and he couldn't help but moan in delight. "Oh my god. This is better than sex."

Eryx raised an eyebrow, a playful annoyance in his tone. "Are you saying my ass isn't good enough for you?"

Alex chuckled, a twinkle in his eye as he replied between bites, "Your ass is amazing, but this burger is life-changing."

As they ate, their conversation flowed easily. They exchanged glances filled with warmth and affection, their gestures and actions revealing the chemistry that had grown between them over time. Eryx reached out to steal a fry from Alex's plate, and Alex responded by swiping one of Eryx's burger toppings. It was a playful dance, a testament to their connection.

The dining room, bathed in soft, warm light, held an air of intimacy. The colors and decor reflected their shared tastes and memories, creating a cozy atmosphere that enveloped them. It was a space where they could simply be themselves, where the outside world and its complexities faded away.

In the midst of their banter and laughter, Alex couldn't help but reflect on their journey together. He remembered the first time they had met, the way their lives had gradually intertwined. There had been challenges and obstacles, but those moments had only served to strengthen their bond.

Alex leaned back in his chair, a contented sigh escaping his lips. He couldn't help but feel grateful for the man sitting across from him, for the love and happiness they had fo

Alex reached across the table, his fingers finding Eryx's, their hands intertwining in a gentle but meaningful gesture. They sat there, in the quiet of the dining room, their hearts and souls bared to each other.

Their relationship was far from perfect, but it was real, and it was theirs. And as they sat together, savoring the simple joy of a shared meal, Alex couldn't help but feel that it was enough, more than enough.

"How was your day?" Eryx asked, turning to greet Alex with a warm smile.

Alex took a sip of water, his eyes meeting Eryx's as he considered his response. "Do you want to travel to London with me?"

Surprise flickered across Eryx's face, his brows furrowing slightly. "Why? What's going on?"

Alex sighed, the weight of his thoughts evident in his

posture. "My brother wants to see me, and I think he could help us with the case."

Eryx nodded, understanding the gravity of the situation. "When do you plan on leaving?"

"Tomorrow," Alex replied. "I already informed my team about it. They'll manage things here while we're away."

Curiosity danced in Eryx's eyes as he inquired further, "What made you decide to go now?"

Alex leaned against the kitchen counter, his gaze distant as he recounted the events of what had transpired in Times Square earlier that day. "There was an incident. A strange and powerful presence. I need answers, and my brother might be the key."

Eryx considered this information, concern for Alex evident in his expression. After a moment, he spoke, his voice resolute, "I'll try to call Sam and see if he needs me. I also need to go back to my place to pack some clothes."

Alex's eyes met Eryx's, a mixture of surprise and gratitude in his gaze. "Really? You're coming?"

"Of course," Eryx replied with a soft smile. "I can't let you handle this alone. Besides, if it involves me, I need to know everything. Now, let's finish up so we can make a plan."

As they continued their meal preparation, their body language spoke volumes. Eryx's surprise at the sudden decision to travel was evident in the way his hands moved more deliberately, his gaze occasionally drifting to Alex as if trying to read his thoughts.

Alex, on the other hand, displayed a mix of determination and uncertainty. He couldn't help but worry about Eryx's safety, even as he appreciated his partner's unwavering support.

Their cozy kitchen provided the backdrop for this important conversation, with the soft glow of overhead lights casting a warm ambiance.

Thoughts swirled in Alex's mind as he considered the upcoming journey. He knew the risks, the potential dangers that awaited them in London. But he also knew that facing them together with Eryx made the challenges more bearable.

Unspoken tensions hung in the air, a reminder of the complexities of their partnership.

"I don't want you to get hurt," Alex finally admitted, his voice tinged with vulnerability.

Eryx turned to him, his eyes filled with understanding. "I know, Alex. But we face risks every day and we're facing this together."

Alex nodded, his gratitude for Eryx's unwavering support evident in his gaze. "Thank you."

Their conversation shifted to practical matters as they discussed their plans for the trip. They considered potential obstacles they might encounter, the need to gather information, and the importance of staying vigilant in the unfamiliar territory of London.

As they finished their meal, a sense of unity and purpose settled between them. They were a team.

With their plans in motion, Eryx rose from the table, a determined glint in his eyes. "Let's make this trip count, Alex. We'll face whatever comes our way together."

Alex smiled, the weight of his concerns lightened by Eryx's presence. "Together," he echoed.

With that word hanging in the air, they cleared the table and began packing for their journey. The unknown awaited them in London, but with their love as their anchor, they were ready to confront whatever challenges lay ahead.

As they finished their preparations, their senses were filled with the familiar and comforting details of home—the warmth of each other's presence, the taste of a shared meal, and the promise of a future where they faced the mysteries of their world hand in hand.

22

Eryx

A S THEY LANDED IN LONDON HEATHROW, Eryx couldn't help but feel the warmth of London's summer air embracing him. It was a welcome change from the bustling streets of New York. He half-jokingly nudged Alex and quipped, "You know, we could've just teleported into the city, right?"

Alex chuckled, his laughter melding with the city's symphony. "No, love, it's not that simple. Our powers work differently. Plus, traveling with strangers can be quite an experience," he had said earlier, his voice carrying a touch of amusement that made Eryx grin.

Walking along the bustling pavement, Eryx's curiosity got the better of him. He turned to Alex, a playful glint in his eye. "You've been keeping our place to stay a secret for so long. Are we secretly camping in Hyde Park?"

Alex's laughter rang out, warm and melodious. "No need to worry, darling. We won't be roughing it. We're staying at the Savoy."

Eryx's eyebrows shot up in genuine surprise. "The Savoy?

Seriously? Having connections must be handy."

A mischievous twinkle danced in Alex's eyes, and he leaned in closer. "You're right. Lily and I have a unique friendship with the owner. Although, I should mention he's not exactly human — he's an insatiable fae."

Eryx's curiosity grew, and he couldn't help but smile. "An insatiable fae, huh? Sounds like quite the character."

Alex's laughter filled the air once more, blending seamlessly with the city's symphony. "You nailed it. He's truly one of a kind. Meeting him will be an adventure, for sure."

Eryx couldn't hide his smirk. "So, I'll either be charmed in seconds or left wondering what just hit me?"

"You got it," Alex confirmed with a wink. "But you know, a little unpredictability makes life more exciting, don't you think?"

Eryx couldn't help but notice the way Alex confidently navigated through the crowds, his stride purposeful yet relaxed. It was evident that Alex was in his element here. Eryx, on the other hand, embraced the newness of it all.

As they continued their walk through the bustling halls of London Heathrow, Eryx's thoughts shifted. "By the way, since you're our designated driver in this foreign land, do you know how to drive on the right side?"

Alex pretended to be offended, a playful grin tugging at the corners of his lips as he placed a hand dramatically over his heart. "Doubting my driving skills, huh?"

Eryx raised an eyebrow in mock seriousness. "Let's just say I have a bit more experience in that department."

"Really now?" Alex responded, a competitive spark gleaming in his eyes.

Eryx nodded, his grin widening. "Yes! So tell me, who are

we meeting here?"

But before he could hear Alex's reply, a car honked at them from the nearby curb. The car's windows rolled down, revealing a striking woman dressed casually, her long hair flowing in the wind. Eryx's jaw nearly dropped as he took in her appearance.

"Hey Alex, and you must be Eryx," she greeted them, stepping out of the car gracefully to assist with their luggage. "I'm Lily, or Persephone in the underworld."

Eryx blinked in surprise, momentarily speechless. "Y… You're Alex's wife."

Lily chuckled, her warm laughter filling the air. "Not exactly his wife anymore. So if you're worried about me stealing him back from you, don't be." She gave Eryx's shoulder a reassuring squeeze, her touch light and friendly.

Alex, who had appeared around the corner with a smug grin on his face, chimed in, "I overheard you two talking about me."

Eryx couldn't help himself and playfully smacked Alex on the shoulder. "You didn't mention that your wife would be the one picking us up."

"Like Lily said, not married anymore. So calm down," Alex reassured him with a chuckle, and Eryx relaxed.

"Come on, let's head to the hotel," Lily suggested, her voice warm and inviting.

As they settled into the car, Eryx couldn't help but steal glances at Lily. She was a vision of casual elegance, her brown hair cascading down her back in loose waves, and her attire, though simple, exuding a natural charm. Her smile was genuine and welcoming, and Eryx couldn't deny the undeniable chemistry between her and Alex, even if they were no longer married.

As they drove through the bustling streets of London, Eryx couldn't shake the curiosity that gnawed at him. He wanted to know more about Lily, about her past with Alex, and how they had come to be where they were now. But he also sensed that some things were better left unasked, at least for the moment.

The conversation flowed naturally, a mix of laughter and light banter, as they navigated the city together. Eryx observed the easy camaraderie between Alex and Lily, the way they shared stories and exchanged knowing glances. It was evident that their bond ran deep, despite the changes in their relationship.

The car smoothly navigated through the vibrant streets of London, seamlessly blending into the ebb and flow of the city's traffic. The bustling thoroughfares were a mosaic of motion, where cars, buses, and bicycles interwove in a choreographed dance. The traffic lights transitioned from red to green, orchestrating a synchronized movement that allowed vehicles to proceed in a rhythmic pattern.

The symphony of honks and the murmur of distant conversations added to the backdrop of the urban scene. Pedestrians crisscrossed the sidewalks, hurriedly traversing the zebra crossings while occasionally pausing to admire the historic architecture that adorned the cityscape.

As the car meandered through the maze of lanes, Eryx caught glimpses of iconic landmarks, their presence a testament to London's rich history. Towering monuments, charming storefronts, and the occasional red double-decker bus painted a vivid portrait of a city that seamlessly blended the old and the new.

"So whose brother are we meeting?" Eryx's curiosity pierced the silence that hung in the car, his voice laced with palpable interest.

"We're meeting Zeus," Alex replied, his tone a mixture of seriousness and anticipation.

"The king of the Olympians?" Eryx's question lingered in the air, seeking confirmation. Alex nodded in response, his grip on the steering wheel tight and unyielding.

As they navigated the winding road, Eryx's thoughts meandered to the impending encounter with the ruler of the Olympian gods. Uncertainty gnawed at him, its teeth sinking into his mind as he wondered about the nature of this meeting. His gaze shifted to Alex, who seemed to bear the weight of the world on his shoulders.

Breaking through the tension, Lily's voice echoed from the backseat, her presence a soothing balm. "Alex, any idea where Zeus has been hiding?"

Eryx extended his hand to rest on Alex's thigh, a wordless gesture of support.

"Hermes informed me that he's been posing as the current Prime Minister," Alex revealed, his voice measured and taut. "We've got a meeting scheduled with him tomorrow morning."

Eryx couldn't hide his surprise. "Wait, you mean he's Winston Thorne? That guy looks like he could eat a dragon for lunch."

Lily's reassuring touch on Eryx's shoulder conveyed warmth and comfort. "We're taking precautions, Eryx. Your safety is our top priority."

The determination in Alex's voice was tinged with caution. "Lily's right. Despite the family connection, I can't fully trust him."

Eryx sensed that there was more beneath the surface—details that Alex wasn't ready to divulge. Respecting Alex's decision, Eryx silently acknowledged the unspoken truths that lay between them.

The car smoothly pulled up in front of the Hotel Savoy, and Eryx's eyes widened in awe as he took in the modern marvel before him. The building's sleek glass exterior sparkled under the city lights, capturing London's lively nightlife. The hotel seamlessly blended innovative architecture with a contemporary style, creating a world of luxury.

Tall, geometric pillars framed the entrance, shining with a metallic glow. The entrance was adorned with a simple awning, radiating an elegant charm. Stepping out of the car, Eryx looked up, tracing the building's design that soared high with urban sophistication.

Inside, the lobby oozed modern opulence. Crystal chandeliers hung from the ceiling, casting a warm glow. The interior had clean lines and stylish furniture, reflecting a modern design. The air smelled fresh, adding to the sensory experience.

Eryx's attention was drawn to a staircase with glass railings that added to the feeling of openness. Chic furnishings and modern art decorated the lobby. Soft conversations and gentle music created a tranquil atmosphere.

As he walked further, Eryx reached the reception area. Instead of traditional desks, sleek touchscreen monitors stood. The digital displays seamlessly blended with the modern décor. Eryx's fingers brushed over the smooth surface as he approached, connecting him to the hotel's modern world.

The Hotel Savoy was a masterpiece of modern design and architecture. Eryx felt like he had stepped into a realm where the future met luxury, a fusion of fast-paced modernity.

"Unreal is an understatement," Eryx marveled as they stepped into the lobby of the Hotel Savoy. His eyes widened as they took in the futuristic design, from the sleek chrome accents to the holographic displays that adorned the walls.

A smooth voice broke the moment. "Well, it's the world's most popular hotel for a reason." Eryx turned to see the speaker, momentarily stunned by the man's appearance. Long, dark hair framed striking features, and his captivating blue eyes seemed to hold secrets of the universe.

Alex's growl and grumbling cut through the air, but Eryx was entranced by the stranger. Clearing his throat, Eryx managed to stammer, "Hi, I'm Eryx."

"Chris, good to see you." Alex introduced Eryx, his tone begrudgingly polite. "This is Eryx, our guest."

Eryx couldn't help but whisper incredulously to Alex, "Chris? This is Chris?"

Chris, with an amused glint in his eyes, interrupted. "Something wrong with Chris? Simple and effective, right?" He took Eryx's hand, pressing a kiss to it. "Chris Claremont, nice to meet you, Eryx."

Eryx blushed at the unexpected gesture. "Nice to meet you too," he managed to say, still slightly taken aback.

Amid the playful moment, Alex's territorial instinct flared, his irritation evident. "Enough distractions. Do we have a room or are we here for the view?"

Chris, with a charming grin that could melt glaciers, signaled a hotel staffer to lead the way to their room. "You're still the same old prickly Alex," he teased, his magnetic presence impossible to ignore.

Alex's patience wore thin, his impatience showing in the way he scowled. "Let's get to the point."

With a chuckle, Chris waved dismissively. "Sure thing. Just follow my staff here, folks. Enjoy your stay. I'll be in touch." With that, he left the trio, leaving Eryx both amazed and amused.

Turning to Alex, Eryx's eyes sparkled with amusement. "Well, that was unexpectedly entertaining."

Alex huffed, his irritation adding a layer of humor to the situation. "Yeah, just what we needed – more entertainment."

As they followed the hotel staffer, Eryx couldn't help but glance around in awe. The Hotel Savoy was a masterpiece of modern design. The walls shimmered with shifting holographic images, creating an ever-changing atmosphere. The lighting was soft and warm, creating an inviting ambiance that contrasted with the stark, futuristic architecture.

Alex, on the other hand, seemed to be immune to the hotel's charms. His stoic expression didn't waver as he navigated the sleek corridors. Eryx couldn't help but admire Alex's ability to remain composed in any situation.

The penthouse at the Hotel Savoy was a luxurious haven that combined sophistication with modern elegance. As the elevator doors opened onto the private floor, Alex, Eryx, and Lily entered a world of luxury that exceeded their expectations.

Eryx took in the opulence with wide eyes, the plush carpets beneath his feet feeling like a cloud. He couldn't help but run his fingers over the smooth marble of the coffee table, marveling at its cool touch. The room had a faint scent of expensive perfume and the soft, inviting aroma of a distant fireplace. The city's distant hum and the occasional car honk wafted through the open windows, reminding them they were still in London.

The living area was a lavish retreat, with floor-to-ceiling windows offering stunning views of London's skyline. The city lights bathed the room in a golden glow, contrasting with sleek furnishings. Plush sofas encircled a marble-topped coffee table, inviting relaxation.

"Wow," Eryx breathed, his voice barely above a whisper. He exchanged a quick glance with Alex, and he could tell that his partner was equally awed.

A sleek fireplace added coziness, and Eryx could almost feel its warmth despite the distance. On the other side, a state-of-the-art entertainment system awaited, but it paled in comparison to the real-life spectacle outside.

The dining area had a chic glass table surrounded by elegant chairs with gold accents, the setting fit for royalty. A modern, fully-equipped kitchen with minimalist design invited culinary adventures, though it seemed unlikely that they would be cooking tonight.

Passing through the hallway, they discovered plush bedrooms. The master bedroom featured a luxurious king-sized bed with pristine, white linens that looked impossibly soft. The en-suite bathroom was a spa-like escape with a deep soaking tub and a rainforest shower that promised indulgence.

A second bedroom with a queen-sized bed had its own en-suite bathroom, just as extravagant as the first. The highlight was the terrace that stretched along the edge, featuring a seating area and a private plunge pool. The sight of it took Eryx's breath away.

Alex and Eryx exchanged a look filled with wonder and anticipation. The Hotel Savoy's penthouse was an unforgettable blend of modern design and timeless beauty.

"You two can have the Master Bedroom," Lily smiled knowingly, breaking their reverie.

Eryx looked at Alex, surprised and grateful for Lily's thoughtfulness. He hadn't expected such consideration from a goddess. He nodded. "Thank you, Lily."

Lily chuckled. "Of course. Have a good night, both of you. I'll see you in the morning."

After Lily went to her room, Eryx's heart raced. He looked at Alex, a mix of excitement and nerves filling him. Without words, Alex held his hand and guided him to the main bedroom.

As they entered the room, Eryx couldn't help but notice the softness of the luxurious linens against his fingertips. The bed beckoned with promises of comfort and intimacy, and the soft lighting cast a warm and inviting glow over the room.

Their eyes met, and Eryx saw the desire in Alex's gaze, mirrored by his own. They didn't need words to communicate their feelings, their connection spoke volumes. Their hands entwined, and they shared a lingering, heartfelt kiss, sealing the unspoken promise of the night ahead.

When the kiss broke, Alex's voice was low and intense. "You're mine, Eryx. Don't forget that."

Eryx's heart swelled with feelings — desire, warmth, a sense of belonging. His voice trembled as he answered, "Yours."

Their lips met again, sensations flowing. Fingers explored, igniting desire.

As their kisses deepened, their bodies moved together, passion growing with every heartbeat. Electricity sparked with each touch, their connection growing stronger.

Breaths mingled as they looked into each other's eyes, saying more than words could. Vulnerabilities were embraced, their feelings clear in their closeness.

In the soft light of the penthouse, city lights painted patterns on the windows. Alex and Eryx stood together, their connection strong. Anticipation buzzed, fueling every touch.

Eryx's fingers brushed Alex's, gentle as a whisper. Alex's hand cupped Eryx's cheek, their eyes locked, silently promising.

Exploration continued, clothes disappearing with each kiss, each touch. Eryx found himself on the bed, a place for their closeness.

Gazes locked again, showing feelings beyond words. Eryx traced Alex's torso, remembering every inch. Lips met, expressing longing and warmth.

Their movements flowed like a dance, their connection powerful, leaving only them in their world.

Soft words filled the air, secrets shared in the quiet. Bodies moved with a gentle force, feelings unfolding with every touch.

Outside, lights and shadows played. Alex and Eryx found comfort in each other's arms, their connection strong. The room became a place for their passion, where they felt truly close.

23

Alex

ALEX WOKE UP AND SAW AN EMPTY PILLOW BESIDE HIM. Moonlight filled the room through the curtains. He felt a mysterious pull, urging him to the balcony. Eryx was there, silhouetted against the city lights.

Without thinking, Alex went to the balcony. He found Eryx leaning on the railing. Alex hugged Eryx from behind, feeling the warm summer air.

Breaking the silence, Alex's voice cut through the night air. "Penny for your thoughts?"

Eryx turned to face him, his lips curving into a soft smile. "Just lost in thought, I guess."

"Care to share?" Alex's gentle tone invited Eryx to open up.

Eryx looked out at the city lights for a moment before meeting Alex's eyes again. "I've been thinking about a lot of things."

Alex leaned against the balcony railing, mirroring Eryx's posture. "Like what?"

Eryx took a deep breath, as if gathering his thoughts.

"Remember when you asked me about the pills I was taking? The ones for sleep?"

Alex nodded, his expression attentive. "Yeah, I remember."

"I told you they were for sleeping better, but there's more to it," Eryx admitted, his gaze steady.

Alex's brow furrowed slightly, concern flickering in his eyes. "You don't have to tell me if you're not ready."

Eryx reached out and placed his hand on top of Alex's. "No, I want to. I want you to know everything about me."

He looked out at the city lights again, as if drawing strength from them. "Ever since I was a kid, I've had these recurring nightmares. They were always the same — scenes of destruction, people screaming, and a forest engulfed in flames. But after I met you, they started changing."

Alex's curiosity was piqued. "Changing how?"

Eryx turned to face Alex fully, his eyes reflecting a mixture of emotions. "They started becoming about you. I thought it was just my mind playing tricks, but Apollo confirmed they were memories."

Alex's eyes widened in surprise. "Memories? Memories of what?"

Eryx's voice grew softer, laden with a vulnerability he rarely showed. "They were Apollo's memories merging in to mines. Memories of us, in another time."

A heavy silence settled between them, the weight of Eryx's revelation sinking in. Alex's heart ached for the depth of what Eryx had carried all this time.

"Do you still have these dreams?" Alex finally asked, his voice gentle.

Eryx shook his head. "No, not anymore. Since I woke up in your house, they've stopped."

Alex let out a small sigh of relief. "I guess Apollo's soul awakening inside you must have had something to do with it."

Eryx nodded slowly, a mix of emotions playing across his features. "Yeah, I think so."

A hint of doubt lingered in Eryx's eyes, and Alex couldn't ignore it. But he waited.

Eryx hesitated, his gaze searching Alex's. "I'm worried that you're with me because of Apollo's soul, not because of me."

Alex's heart ached at Eryx's honesty. He reached out, gently cupping Eryx's face in his hands. "Eryx, listen to me. From the moment I met you, before I even knew about Apollo, I was drawn to you. It's you that I want. Your soul, your heart."

Eryx's eyes glistened with unshed tears, his vulnerability laid bare. "Really?"

Alex's thumb brushed away a tear that escaped Eryx's eye. "Really. Not because of Apollo or anything else. Just you."

A smile quivered on Eryx's lips, a mix of relief and gratitude. Alex leaned in, pressing a gentle kiss to Eryx's forehead.

"Come on," Alex murmured, his voice tender. "Let's continue this conversation somewhere more comfortable."

He took Eryx's hand in his, leading him back into the room. They settled onto the bed, wrapped in each other's arms, as the weight of Eryx's revelation continued to melt away in the warmth of their connection.

Wrapped in the comforting cocoon of their bed, Alex held Eryx close, his touch a gentle anchor amidst the uncertainty of the world. With a soft sigh, he pressed a tender kiss to the side of Eryx's head, his affection wordlessly conveyed.

Eryx's voice broke the tranquil silence, "Do you think the Order wants me only because of Apollo's soul?"

Alex's fingers traced soothing patterns on Eryx's arm, his response a gentle reassurance. "I sense that might be a part of it, but you know, with the Order, it's never just one thing."

A furrow appeared on Eryx's brow, a mixture of anxiety and concern. "I can't help but worry. Now that I'm a target, I fear for the safety of those I care about. And I still have no idea about Richard. After the attack… I'm lost."

Alex's embrace tightened, his voice soft yet steadfast. "Eryx, you're not alone in this. We'll handle the Order, no matter what. And as for Richard, he mentioned he'd visit you, but it never happened. Don't let it weigh on you."

Eryx's eyes searched Alex's, a mix of curiosity and vulnerability shining through. "What do you mean? Did something happen?"

Alex's gaze held a hint of a story untold, a momentary pause before he responded. "It's a conversation to have when you two cross paths again."

A small, genuine smile graced Eryx's lips. "I hope we do. He became a true friend to me."

Alex's lips brushed against Eryx's forehead, his warmth and comfort a steady presence. "I'm sure he thinks the same about you. And remember, no matter what twists this journey takes, we're in it together. Your worries, your fears – we'll face them as a team."

Alex sensed Eryx's grip tightening around him, a silent embrace that sought comfort in their closeness. "Come on, let's get some rest," Alex suggested softly.

Eryx nodded in agreement, his silent affirmation a testament to the unspoken understanding that existed between them. With a final exchange of affectionate touches, they settled into the embrace of sleep, finding solace in each other's presence.

In the morning, London's bustling daytime traffic turned the streets into a chaotic blend of frustration. Alex tightly gripped the steering wheel, his knuckles pale from holding back his irritation. Honking horns and the constant drone of engines created an overwhelming noise, a relentless symphony that echoed the city's exasperation. The roads felt choked, packed with a seemingly endless stream of vehicles that added to the intricate dance of congestion.

Alex let out impatient sighs, his breath mingling with the heavy exhaust fumes that filled the air. He shifted in his seat, searching for a more comfortable posture, his initial patience slowly wearing thin. Time seemed to crawl, each passing minute feeling sluggish and endless, while the glare of the sun bouncing off car windshields intensified the feeling of being trapped.

"I told you taking the tube would have been smarter. Now we're going to be late," Eryx playfully remarked, a glimmer of mischief in his eyes. Lily couldn't hold back her laughter, thoroughly entertained by the friendly banter unfolding before her.

"We won't be late. I've got everything under control," Alex shot back, his voice holding a touch of annoyance. Yet, a faint twitch at the corner of his lips betrayed his attempt to keep up a stern facade.

Eryx affectionately patted Alex's hand, his touch gentle. "Those veins popping on your neck seem to disagree," he quipped, a smirk playing on his lips. Lily's laughter bubbled over at the ongoing exchange, finding their interaction utterly amusing.

"The king of the underworld deserves better treatment than

this," Alex grumbled, his tone a mix of jest and seriousness.

Leaning in closer, Eryx's eyes sparkled with mischief. "But right now, you're not in the underworld, are you?" he teased, a warm and affectionate smile aimed at Alex. It was a smile that Alex knew was just for him, and it sent a rush of warmth through him.

A slow grin spread across Alex's face, his irritation melting away in the face of Eryx's playful charm. "I could unleash some flames on both of you, you know?" he threatened in a teasing manner, though the affection in his gaze was impossible to miss.

Eryx's response was swift, his voice dropping suggestively. "Save it for later." He winked at Alex, feeling his own cheeks flush with the audacity of his words. Yet, he couldn't deny the surge of excitement that coursed between them.

Still recovering from her fit of laughter, Lily joined in, her tone mischievous. "Alright, you two, let's keep the fiery exchanges for when we're not en route to an appointment." Her grin conveyed her enjoyment of the dynamic between them.

They reached their destination, and the house on Downing Street stood proudly before them. It was a place of grandness and strong architecture, radiating authority, history, and a commanding presence. But what truly set the house apart wasn't just its physical appearance – it was the intricate and powerful network of magical protections woven around it.

As they neared the house, a shiver ran down Alex's spine. The magical wards were palpable, a tingling sensation that pricked at his skin like a swarm of tiny invisible needles. These mystical defenses were masterfully crafted, resonating with an ancient and unyielding energy. Stepping over the threshold, Alex felt an unseen barrier pushing against him, as if it were testing his intentions and determination.

The house's exterior blended timeless beauty with an air of mystery. The weathered bricks told tales of centuries gone by, while the gargoyles on the roofline stared down with eerie expressions, seeming to observe every move with an otherworldly intensity. Ivy crept up the walls, its leaves occasionally rustling like the hushed whispers of long-held secrets.

Tall, narrow windows adorned the house, each pane holding a trace of the crackling energy contained within. Faint glimmers danced across the glass, a testament to the protective magic shielding the occupants.

Alex knocked at the door while Lily and Eryx stayed behind him. After a moment of waiting, a man wearing an extremely formal suit answered the door. A man he recognised. "Ganymede. You're still working for the bastard?"

"Hades, yes I still do. Couldn't really leave if I wanted to." Ganymede said.

Ever since they met, Alex noticed how devoted Ganymede was to Zeus. Ganymede's loyalty and hard work for Zeus impressed Alex, and he respected Ganymede's commitment. Ganymede's care and dedication showed in everything he did for Zeus, and Alex liked how Ganymede handled his tasks so skilfully.

Alex could see that Ganymede had special feelings for Zeus. Whenever Ganymede looked at Zeus, there was a softness in his gaze. Ganymede's actions went beyond what was expected of a servant; he genuinely cared. The situation got more complicated with Hera being around.

"Speaking of him, is he here? We scheduled an appointment

for today," Alex asked.

"Yes, he is here. Please, come in and feel welcome," Ganymede replied, and Alex sensed the wards embracing their presence.

As Alex stepped into the house, a feeling of dread grew stronger. The air felt heavy with history and the memories of powerful beings who had been here before. Each step seemed to carry echoes of past conversations, choices, and even clashes that had occurred within these walls.

The house's interior matched its imposing exterior. Tapestries depicted mythical scenes, their threads moving as if by magic. Sconces with blue flames dimly lit the corridors, playing tricks on the eyes.

Ganymede led them to Winston's office, a blend of timeless grandeur and modern function that felt both authoritative and intimidating.

Inside, an intricately carved door led to a massive ebony desk, meticulously organized with parchments and a quill. It faced a window overlooking manicured gardens. Tapestries and paintings adorned the walls, telling stories with vibrant colors and lifelike enchantments. Bookshelves held old tomes, some floating when consulted.

Crystal chandeliers hung from the ceiling. Behind the desk, an ornate armchair acted as Zeus's throne. Despite grandeur, the room felt purposeful, reflecting Zeus's responsibilities— a place for decisions and discussions about fate, bridging mortal and immortal worlds.

They waited on couches, tension growing until the door opened, revealing Zeus and Hera. Zeus had silver-gray hair and a well-fitted suit. Hera looked regal with her focused gaze on Alex.

Struggling to hold back a growing growl, Alex stood up and offered a tense greeting. "Zeus, or are we going with Winston?"

"Either name will suffice, though within these walls, Winston it is," Winston responded, his attention shifting to his wife.

"In this era, I go by Eleanor Thorne," Hera, or Eleanor, announced with her usual commanding tone.

Winston's gaze then turned to Lily and Eryx, his scrutiny intense yet controlled. He couldn't help but notice the discomfort that seemed to ripple across Eryx under his brother's gaze. "Persephone, your timeless beauty remains as strong as ever," Winston complimented, earning a cold glare from Eleanor that could rival any icy storm. He directed his attention to Eryx, extending his hand in a friendly gesture. "And this must be Apollo's vessel, Eryx."

Winston's tone held a mix of curiosity and an attempt at casualness, but his eyes revealed a deeper undercurrent—a longing that he struggled to conceal.

Eryx's cheeks turned red from the unexpected attention, causing Alex to growl and give Winston a sharp glare. "Let's cut to the chase, Winston. Why did you call us? Hermes said it was urgent."

Winston moved away from Eryx, taking position behind his desk. After a contemplative pause, he spoke gravely. "Hephaestus is missing as well as the Staff of Umbra."

Alex froze."What do you mean missing?" Alex asked indignantly.

"Last I heard from him was a couple of months ago and when we found out that the staff was missing I immediately tried reaching out to him." Winston said. "When I arrived at his forge, everything was in chaos as if it was ransacked."

Alex thought about it for a moment. There were only a couple of gods who knew where the staff was hidden. Four of them being in the same room right now as well as Hephaestus.

From what Alex can remember, the Staff of Umbra was more than a mere artifact—it was a repository of raw, untamed magic, a force that could shape worlds or unravel them. The staff's power, rumored to be greater than the collective might of the gods, was a double-edged sword, capable of immense creation and catastrophic destruction.

In the hands of the wrong people, the staff could unleash unimaginable chaos. Its magic, unbound by the laws that governed mortals and deities alike, could tear apart reality itself. It could rend the fabric of existence, opening rifts between dimensions, and allowing eldritch horrors to pour into the world. The boundaries between realms would crumble, leading to a cataclysmic merging of planes, each with its unique rules and inhabitants.

Alex's anger flared at the insinuation. "So, you want us to clean up your mess, is that it?"

"In essence, yes," Winston responded calmly, his demeanor unflinching in the face of Alex's fury.

A tempestuous storm churned within Alex. "No. Do you even recall the last time we extended our help to you?" His words reverberated through the room. Eryx stood, attempting to temper the escalating tension.

"I remember, Alex. My intentions never revolved around harming you. You're my brother," Winston retorted, his tone laced with a hint of remorse.

"Fuck you! Your reckless choices led to Kronos capturing you, and Apollo had to sacrifice himself to salvage your godforsaken skin!"

Enveloped by rage, Alex's focus remained fixed on Winston, until a pair of warm arms encircled him from behind, grounding him in the present moment.

Following a charged pause, Winston's voice resounded once more. "This time, it will be different."

"How? Are you going to let another god be sacrificed?" Alex's tone dripped with skepticism.

"No. This time, we stand alongside allies. Individuals who will stand shoulder to shoulder with us." Winston shifted his gaze between Eryx and Alex. "We're not alone in this battle, if it escalates. You need to trust me, brother."

Alex exhaled heavily, his anger abating slightly. He embraced Eryx, his words laced with reluctance. "Fine, but rebuilding trust isn't a swift process. You'll have to earn it." He turned his attention to Eleanor. "Same goes for you."

Easing the tension, Lily recounted their findings from New York, kickstarting a discussion about the resurgence of Celestial Steel and stolen souls. Alex had given her the details of what's been going on beforehand.

"Celestial steel? Weren't they wiped out?" Eleanor asked.

"We believed so, but apparently not," Lily answered, her voice a voice of reason.

"If celestial steel is back, that means they have Hephaestus. We need to find and free him from The Order before it's too late."

Everyone nodded determinedly. "Time to go," Alex's tone was resolute yet tinged with annoyance. The room buzzed with emotions they hadn't fully dealt with, mirroring the upcoming chaos they were heading into.

24

Eryx

ONCE THEY LEFT WINSTON'S HOUSE, Eryx felt a rush of relief wash over him, as if a heavy weight had been lifted from his shoulders. The atmosphere inside had been stifling, suffocating even, and the unsettling unease that had settled within him since encountering Winston had begun to dissipate. It was almost like a strange connection had tied them together, something beyond the ordinary, almost like a familial bond.

Outside, the afternoon sun cast warm, dappled patterns on the pavement, and the gentle breeze carried with it the faint scent of blooming flowers. Birds chirped merrily in the trees, their songs a stark contrast to the eerie tension inside Winston's home.

Lily's voice broke into Eryx's thoughts, surprising him. "You're not related in the usual way, Eryx," she said softly, her eyes filled with understanding. "Sorry for the intrusion, but my gift lets me sense thoughts, and yours were quite strong."

Eryx's cheeks flushed with embarrassment, his private

thoughts exposed and laid bare. He nodded, his curiosity piqued despite his discomfort. "It's okay, Lily. I should know these things."

Alex, his protective instincts flaring, couldn't hide his irritation. "Lily, Eryx doesn't need to know all of this."

Lily's gaze remained steady, her eyes reflecting compassionate determination. "Hiding the truth won't be helpful, Alex."

Eryx appreciated Lily's honesty, though he couldn't shake the vulnerability that had come with having his innermost thoughts exposed. He turned to Alex with a reassuring smile, hoping to ease his friend's concerns. "Alex, it's fine. I want to understand."

The trio continued down the sunlit sidewalk, their footsteps echoing softly against the pavement. Eryx's inner turmoil had shifted from the oppressive unease he had felt inside Winston's house to a newfound curiosity mixed with a hint of trepidation.

He thought about Lily's gift, wondering how it worked and what it meant for him. Was there truly a connection between him and Winston that transcended the ordinary bonds of family?

It was a concept he had never considered, and the implications were both intriguing and unsettling.

Lily sensed his thoughts and spoke, her voice gentle as she explained her gift. "My ability allows me to sense thoughts, emotions, and connections between people. It's not always easy to control, and sometimes, I pick up on things unintentionally."

Eryx nodded, grateful for the clarity.

As they walked, Eryx's unease continued to ebb, replaced

by a growing sense of acceptance and understanding.

Alex, while still protective, seemed to relent a little. "I just don't want you to get too involved in all of this, Eryx. It's a world filled with complications and dangers."

Eryx met Alex's gaze, his own eyes reflecting determination. "Alex, I'm already involved. I can't ignore what's happening around us, and I won't shy away from the truth."

Lily nodded in approval, her gift allowing her to sense the sincerity in Eryx's words. "He's right, Alex. Eryx has a role to play in this, whether we like it or not."

"Okay. Fine. Don't tell me that I didn't warn you." Alex said and continued on walking.

Outside Winston's house, on a calm afternoon, Eryx found himself engrossed in a conversation that unraveled the intricate ties between gods and mortals. Lily, her voice patient and soothing, was the one to break down the complexities.

"Apollo's divine soul is still connected to Zeus, or Winston," she explained, her eyes softening as she gauged Eryx's reaction. "Their bond is deep, as Apollo is Winston's son with Leto. That's why you might sense a connection in your own soul. But remember, even though the connection exists, its nature is different, especially considering your human origin."

Eryx absorbed the information, his expression shifting from curiosity to contemplation. The weight of his newfound knowledge settled upon him like a cloak of responsibility. "It's a bit overwhelming, but I'm starting to understand."

But understanding wasn't universally embraced. Alex, his hostility palpable, couldn't contain his anger. "You don't owe that guy anything, Eryx. After everything he's done."

Eryx, unwavering, met Alex's heated gaze with a firm one

of his own. "Alex, it's not for you to decide. I can form my own opinions and judgments, alright?"

Alex's anger was evident in the clenching of his fists, the tension in his shoulders. His voice, however, remained strained. "I just don't want to see you hurt, Eryx."

Lily, ever the mediator, sought to steer the conversation toward a productive path. Her gaze shifted between the two men as she asked, "What's our next move?"

Eryx leaned back, the tension slowly easing from his body as he contemplated their options. He realized that understanding the divine complexities was one thing, but navigating the path forward was another challenge altogether. "I wouldn't mind grabbing a bite. How about we head to a local pub?"

The tension in the air dissolved as Alex and Lily shared a knowing chuckle at Eryx's suggestion. "Sure thing," Alex agreed, his voice lighter. "There's a Wetherspoons nearby."

As they made their way to the pub, Eryx couldn't help but reflect on the conversation. The complexities of his newfound connection with Apollo, and by extension, Zeus, weighed heavily on his mind. He couldn't deny the allure of knowing more about his own heritage, but he also understood the potential dangers and consequences that might arise from these newfound ties.

Alex's hostility, while protective in nature, was also a reminder of the challenges ahead. Eryx appreciated his friend's concern, but he was determined to forge his own path and make his own choices, even in the face of uncertainty.

The Wetherspoons pub buzzed with activity as Eryx took in the surroundings. The place was a blend of old and new, with classic woodwork and vintage decor contrasting with the modern crowd. He couldn't help but notice the diverse patrons, many of whom emanated an otherworldly presence.

"There's a lot of supernaturals here," Eryx observed, his eyes scanning the room. Beside him, Alex nodded in agreement.

"London has better laws when it comes to supernaturals. Discrimination is taken seriously," Alex explained, and Eryx nodded in understanding. The supernatural undercurrents of the city were undeniable.

They settled into a cozy spot at the back of the pub, with Alex seated beside Eryx and Lily opposite them. A waitress promptly handed them menus and then left them to peruse their choices.

"So, Celestial Steel. That's what we found in the morgue, right?" Eryx inquired once they had all glanced over the menu.

"Yes," Alex replied, his voice tense with the weight of their discoveries.

"What makes it so dangerous?" Eryx probed, his curiosity piqued.

"It's an artifact that, when forged into a weapon, can kill gods and their souls," Lily answered, her gaze unwavering.

Eryx's brows furrowed. "Kill gods? Aren't gods supposed to be immortal?"

Lily offered him a gentle smile, her eyes holding a world of wisdom. "That includes you now, Eryx. And yes, we are immortal, but we can still be killed. If our souls are extinguished, that's the end for us. There's no coming back."

Eryx's surprise mingled with a hint of unease. "I had no idea."

"Alex, didn't you tell him everything?" Lily turned her gaze to Alex, a trace of irritation in her voice.

Alex bristled slightly, his defensive response swift. "He had a lot to process already, Lily."

Their waitress returned, breaking the tension, to take their orders. Alex ordered a beer and pasta, while Lily and Eryx opted for the same choice.

Once the waitress departed, Alex took the initiative to steer the conversation. "Where do you think The Order might be keeping Hephaestus?"

Lily's eyes flickered with contemplation. "It's hard to say. They're nomadic, never staying in one place for long."

Eryx leaned forward, his curiosity unabated. "What's Hephaestus's role in all of this?"

"Hephaestus knew the location of the Staff of Umbra, and he's the only one who can forge celestial steel into weapons," Alex explained.

Eryx processed the information, his mind racing. "And the staff?"

"It's another artifact, and its power is beyond even that of the gods themselves," Lily added, her words laden with significance.

As their food arrived, a quiet moment passed, and they began to eat. Eryx was lost in thought, his appetite momentarily forgotten. The gravity of their mission weighed on him, and the revelation about Celestial Steel added an extra layer of complexity.

"Can we head to the Royal Albert Hall later? There's a concert happening," Eryx suggested, eager to shift the focus.

Alex's expression softened, and he nodded. "Sure. It would be nice to unwind for a while."

Their conversation drifted toward lighter topics, providing a temporary respite from the weight of their responsibilities.

Yet, Eryx couldn't shake the sense that their journey had only just begun. In this bustling Wetherspoons pub, amidst supernaturals and secrets, he had become entangled in a world far more complex and perilous than he could have ever imagined.

* * *

"Sweetheart, are you ready?" Alex's voice echoed through the luxurious penthouse of the Hotel Savoy. Eryx stood before the mirror, wrestling with his clothes, trying to make them cooperate.

"Just a sec! Dealing with this stubborn shirt," Eryx replied, his fingers deftly adjusting the fabric as he attempted to make it behave.

Alex strolled closer, a playful glint in his eyes. "What's the struggle? Looks like you're attempting a gymnastic routine in there."

Eryx playfully glared at him and swatted his arm. "How about lending a hand instead of cracking jokes? This shirt used to fit perfectly, but now it's playing games."

"Maybe we should ditch the concert and stay in," Alex pondered with a suggestive smile as he lent a hand with Eryx's clothes, his touch light and teasing.

Eryx chuckled, shaking his head. "I'm not missing out on the Royal Albert Hall just because you're tempted to keep me in bed. Nice try."

A mischievous grin curled on Alex's lips. "Well, you do have a fine-looking ass. Can't blame me for trying."

Eryx's cheeks turned warm, a mix of embarrassment and affection filling him. "Do you think I've gained weight?"

Alex's touch traced over Eryx's body, assessing the fit of the clothes. Eryx's skin tingled under his fingers. "It's not about weight. Your body's adjusting to the changes from your god soul. Perfectly normal, given you've got a god inside you."

With a blend of adjustments, teasing, and tender moments, they finally got ready. They exchanged mirrored looks and smiles. "We're looking pretty damn good," Eryx commented, a smirk on his lips. Laughter passed between them, lightening the mood.

"Guys! We're gonna be late! If you're doing anything other than getting ready, I swear I'm heading out without you!" Lily's voice drifted from the living room, a mix of exasperation and amusement.

Eryx leaned in for a quick, affectionate kiss on Alex's lips. Their lips met, lingering briefly in a sweet connection. "Let's not keep Lily waiting. Ready to shine at the concert hall?"

Alex returned the kiss, his lips lingering briefly before he pulled away with a playful smile. "Absolutely. Let's do this."

As they made their way to the concert, Eryx couldn't help but feel a sense of gratitude for the man beside him. He knew that he was navigating uncharted waters, but having Alex by his side made every challenge easier to bear. They shared a connection that transcended the ordinary, a love that grew stronger with each passing day.

Their playful banter and affectionate moments were a testament to the depth of their relationship. It wasn't just about the physical attraction; it was about the emotional connection they shared. Eryx felt understood and cherished in a way he had never experienced before.

Walking into the Royal Albert Hall's impressive entrance, Eryx's eyes widened in awe. The modern elegance around him was breathtaking. Excitement hummed in the air, matching the contemporary atmosphere. The interior spread out before him, a perfect blend of classic and cutting-edge design.

Metal accents and LED lights traced captivating patterns along the hall's architecture. The polished chrome against matte surfaces created a stunning contrast, honoring the venue's history while embracing a futuristic feel. Eryx looked up at the dazzling LED dome, shifting with vibrant colors.

Under his feet, a thoughtfully designed pattern guided him to the heart of the hall – the stage. It was where musical legends had performed, emotions transformed into digital melodies, and stories told through modern keystrokes.

Chic chandeliers hung from above, artfully blending tradition and technology. Their light guided him along the corridors, inviting him to enjoy the modern elegance.

In the avant-garde seating, the audience settled into comfortable yet stylish chairs. Excitement gleamed in their eyes, a shared appreciation for contemporary art and culture binding them.

Eryx felt a mix of respect and excitement as he became part of this modern wonder. The Royal Albert Hall wasn't just a venue; it celebrated human creativity. He could almost hear the harmonies, applause, and stories echoing through its walls.

Gazing around the majestic Royal Albert Hall, Eryx couldn't help but be awestruck. The grandeur of the venue took his breath away, and he leaned closer to Alex, whispering, "This place is incredible. Thanks for bringing me here, Alex."

Alex's fingers interlocked with Eryx's, and in that simple

touch, they shared emotions that words couldn't express. "I'd do anything for you," Alex murmured, his eyes brimming with unwavering devotion.

Lily, their playful friend, couldn't resist teasing them. "Okay, lovebirds, our front-row seats are waiting. Let's not keep the performance waiting."

Chuckling together, they made their way to their seats, anticipation filling the air like a sweet melody.

The concert began, and the music washed over them, enveloping them in its beauty. Eryx found himself swept away by the enchanting melodies and the crowd's enthusiastic reactions. The atmosphere in the grand hall was electric, alive with the shared emotions of the audience.

Amidst the music's splendor, Eryx felt a familiar presence in his soul, a gentle yet unmistakable voice that whispered in his thoughts. *Eryx?*

Keeping his emotions hidden, Eryx replied mentally. *Apollo?*

Apollo's urgency became apparent, his voice carrying a weight that sent a shiver down Eryx's spine. *Something feels off, Eryx. We can't let our guard down. The energy isn't right here.*

Eryx shifted his focus from the performance to Apollo's warning. *What's wrong, Apollo? What's happening?*

Apollo's sigh echoed in his mind, transcending mortal limits. *The vibrations here are distorted. Please, be cautious and stay alert.*

Eryx's heart raced, his senses heightened by the cryptic warning. *We'll be careful*, he promised.

As the concert concluded, the electric energy of the performance still crackled in the air as the crowd dispersed, leaving behind a sense of anticipation.

Eryx pulled Alex and Lily aside, a hushed urgency in his voice. "Guys, we've got to talk."

Their expressions turned serious, and they huddled closer, ready to listen. Eryx recounted his encounter with Apollo, his words setting the stage for a tense exchange.

"I'm not picking up anything strange," Alex said, his voice tinged with concern, "but we can't just shrug off Apollo's warning."

Lily's eyelids fluttered shut briefly as she tapped into her intuitive senses. "It feels like something is blocking my senses."

Alex's demeanor shifted, his gaze vigilant. "Stay sharp, people. Lily, cover our rear. Eryx, you're with me."

Their plan was set, and they moved cautiously through the bustling hall, their every step laden with uncertainty. Eryx's heart pounded as he wondered what unseen threat lurked in the shadows, just beyond their reach.

As they navigated the maze of corridors, Eryx couldn't shake the feeling that the music, which had moments ago been a source of wonder, was now a mere backdrop to something darker and more ominous. The warning from Apollo hung over them like a storm cloud, and they remained on high alert.

The trio reached a quieter area, away from the boisterous crowd. Eryx spoke with a voice filled with conviction. "We need to stay together and watch each other's backs. Whatever Apollo sensed, we can't afford to underestimate it."

Alex nodded in agreement, his eyes scanning their surroundings. "Lily, keep your senses sharp. Eryx, stay close."

As they weaved through the Royal Albert Hall's parking

area, an unspoken sense of danger seemed to pulse in the air. Eryx's heart raced, his instincts on high alert. He couldn't put his finger on it, but something felt profoundly wrong.

Suddenly, Apollo's essence flared within Eryx, a warm surge of power that prompted an involuntary halt. He glanced at Alex and Lily, who instinctively fanned out defensively, their expressions tense.

Eryx, hold it! Apollo's voice sliced through his thoughts, Eryx pausing abruptly as if frozen in time.

A car nearby burst into flames, its fiery explosion sending shockwaves rippling through the night. The acrid smell of smoke filled the air, and the heat from the burning car was palpable. The flames painted the surroundings in a blinding, chaotic brightness.

Eryx's ears rang from the blast, his senses momentarily scrambled. His heart pounded in his chest, a mixture of fear and determination coursing through him.

"Alex!" Eryx's voice sliced through the chaos, laden with worry and urgency.

"Over here!" Alex's voice, tinged with relief and controlled anger, reached Eryx's ears. He spotted his friend emerging from behind a partially shattered pillar, unharmed but clearly shaken.

Eryx nodded, his attention shifting to Lily. Before Alex could respond, Lily's voice cut through the turmoil, her tone a blend of impatience and tension. "Could use a hand here!"

Eryx's heart sank, and his muscles tensed. He turned to face the direction of Lily's voice, his senses honed for any sign of danger. The night seemed to hold its breath, the shadows around them growing more sinister.

"Shadow wraiths," Alex's voice turned grim, his gaze locked

on the looming threat. Eryx exchanged a knowing glance with him, understanding the stakes at hand.

Eryx's eyes widened as his gaze settled upon the oncoming threat. The eerie sight before him seemed like a convergence of darkness itself, a manifestation of nightmares given life. The Shadow Wraiths slithered forth, their forms a grotesque symphony of inky blackness and ethereal gloom.

Tendrils of shadow coiled and writhed, each movement an unsettling dance between the corporeal and the intangible. Their silhouettes seemed to shift, merging and splitting like tendrils of smoke, defying any sense of defined shape. The air around them seemed to waver, distorting the very fabric of reality, as if the darkness held secrets and horrors untold.

Their eyes, if one could even call them that, glowed with an eerie, malevolent light, casting an unholy radiance that sliced through the surrounding obscurity. Their mere presence seemed to devour light, leaving an impression of emptiness and foreboding in their wake.

The wraiths emitted faint, chilling whispers, an unsettling symphony of voices that seemed to come from nowhere and everywhere simultaneously. It was a cacophony of echoes, like the anguished cries of lost souls fused with the sinister murmurs of the abyss.

As Eryx locked eyes with the advancing horde, a shiver raced down his spine. These creatures were a manifestation of fear itself, a living embodiment of darkness that sent a chill through his very soul.

"Eryx, fall back behind me," Alex ordered with a firm edge, his voice tense. Eryx was about to protest when Apollo's essence flared anew, a voice in his mind urging compliance.

"But I can help," Eryx protested, determination in his voice.

"We don't have time for this. We'll neutralize these wraiths first, then zero in on the source," Alex said as Lily's shout spurred them into action. "I need you to go back inside and stay there till I get you, okay?" Alex pivoted, unleashing a torrent of fiery hellfire to counter the advancing shadows.

Just as Eryx was about to retreat, a figure abruptly blocked his path. The man's dark presence seemed to ooze malevolence as he seized Eryx's arm.

"Let go!" Eryx's voice rang out, a blend of fear and anger tingeing his words. "Alex, help!"

A chilling laugh cut through his plea. "Oh dear, they can't hear you right now."

Eryx's heart raced as Apollo's presence surged within him.

Let me take over, Apollo's words held a mix of urgency and assurance.

How? Eryx's thoughts raced.

Focus on our connection, Apollo's instruction was a lifeline, a means to amplify their strength.

Eyes shut tight, Eryx surrendered, his own consciousness receding to give Apollo the reins.

The air hummed with a charged energy, a power unmistakably celestial. Apollo surged forth, his control over Eryx's form absolute. He conjured an ethereal bow and arrow, the otherworldly weapons solidifying in his grasp.

Facing his captor, Apollo's voice resonated with divine authority. *"Shut it, fool!"*

The air crackled with an otherworldly energy, an invisible shield emanating from Apollo. He released the arrow, its trajectory swift and true. The impact was fiery, the assailant's cry echoing through the night.

"This ain't over, Apollo," the man's threat seemed to dissipate as his voice faded into the abyss.

"Eryx!" Alex's shout cut through the tumult, a lifeline amidst the chaos.

Eryx turned to see Alex and Lily approaching, his relief washing over him like a tide. Yet, in that moment, an ominous darkness engulfed him, and the world blurred into shadow. Amid Alex's anguished cry, Eryx succumbed to the void.

In the ethereal realm, Eryx's senses swirled in a disorienting whirlpool of darkness. His consciousness felt like it was adrift, lost in a void without form or light. Fear and confusion gnawed at him as he struggled to find a foothold.

Then, like a beacon of hope, Apollo's presence emerged. It was a radiant warmth, a comforting embrace amidst the darkness. Eryx clung to it desperately, seeking refuge from the abyss.

Hold on, Eryx, Apollo's voice echoed through the void. *I will guide us back.*

Eryx relinquished control willingly, letting Apollo's celestial power take the reins. A surge of divine energy enveloped them, dispelling the shadows that threatened to consume them.

25

Alex

ALEX HELD ERYX CAREFULLY, his heart racing with worry. Eryx felt limp and cold in his arms, like a fragile porcelain doll teetering on the edge of breaking. His breathing was slow and shallow, each exhale a testament to his distress. Alex's fingers tightened around Eryx's hand, a lifeline in this moment of uncertainty.

Beside him, Lily's voice broke through his anxiety, practical and composed. "Alex, we have to go before the media arrives. We need to get Eryx out of here."

Alex nodded, his gaze still fixed on Eryx's pale face. He followed Lily's instructions, gently placing Eryx in the back seat of the car and settling beside him. The engine roared to life, and they sped away, the road blurred by Alex's racing thoughts.

They arrived at the hotel, and together, they carried Eryx to the penthouse. Lily fetched potions meant to aid Eryx's recovery. With gentle care, they helped Eryx drink the potions, watching as he swallowed them in his weakened state. Then, they tucked him under the covers, his form appearing even frailer against the soft sheets.

Lily broke the heavy silence, her voice carrying a note of concern. "Did you see anything?"

Alex sighed heavily, guilt weighing on his shoulders. "No, I didn't. I should've been more vigilant."

Lily's reassuring words washed over him. "This wasn't your fault. You couldn't have predicted this."

As their conversation shifted to speculation about the attack, Alex couldn't help but feel frustration welling up within him. "Was it random, or did they track us?"

Lily admitted uncertainty. "It's hard to say."

Reluctantly, Alex realized they needed to inform Winston, their leader. He grimaced at the thought of leaving Eryx's side. "We should tell Winston."

Lily offered a solution, her presence a calming force in the room. "I'll do it. You stay with Eryx."

Alex nodded, his gaze still fixed on Eryx's fragile form. He couldn't help but feel a surge of determination and self-doubt warring within him. In moments like these, he questioned his ability to protect the one he cared about most.

Eryx's breathing remained slow and shallow, a testament to the draining ordeal he had endured. As Alex watched over him, he couldn't help but feel a surge of frustration and guilt. It wasn't just about physical safety; it was about the responsibility he felt for Eryx's well-being.

Lily's competent presence reassured him, and her words of comfort carried a weight that eased his anxiety. They were a team, and he had to trust in their abilities to navigate the unknown.

Eryx's recovery, though slow, showed promise. The color returned to his cheeks gradually, and he seemed less frail than when they had first brought him here. The potions worked their magic, rejuvenating his depleted strength.

Understanding dawned on Alex when Lily mentioned the silencing ward. He couldn't imagine how Eryx must have felt, unable to call for help in his moment of need. It added another layer of vulnerability to an already dire situation.

Their conversation continued, shifting to the attack itself. The unknown assailants, their motives, and their connection to Eryx remained a mystery. Alex couldn't shake the feeling that they were just beginning to uncover a much larger threat.

As Lily prepared to inform Winston, Alex watched her with a mixture of gratitude and concern. She was strong, and her determination to protect Eryx mirrored his own. They were a team bound by loyalty and shared experiences, and in times of crisis, that bond became their greatest strength.

Alex's thoughts returned to Eryx, his stubborn determination to keep him safe burning even brighter. He knew that the challenges they faced were far from over. But in that moment, as Eryx's breathing steadied and his color returned, Alex found a glimmer of hope amidst the uncertainty.

Late at night, a knock sounded, and Lily entered cautiously, her steps hesitant as she delivered the unexpected news—Winston's visit. Alex's reaction was a mix of concern and frustration, his brow furrowing as he processed the information. "You couldn't have told me earlier?" His voice held an edge, a hint of annoyance at the sudden intrusion.

Lily, always the voice of reason, reminded him of the importance of Winston's insights, despite Alex's reservations. Her words were a reminder of the bigger picture, the world beyond their immediate concerns.

Winston's entrance brought with it an air of tension. His

voice, neutral and composed, cut through the room's unease. "I'm here to assess Eryx. Not to argue." He spoke with a clarity that left no room for doubt.

Reluctantly, Alex acquiesced, though not without a stern warning. He needed to protect Eryx at all costs, and Winston needed to understand the gravity of that responsibility.

Winston approached the bedside, his gaze unwavering as it settled on Eryx's motionless figure. But then, something unexpected happened. Guilt and sadness flitted across Winston's face, a vulnerability that Alex hadn't anticipated from the usually stoic deity. It was a glimpse into a side of Winston he had never seen before, a complexity that added layers to his character.

Winston's focus shifted to Eryx's wrist, his touch accompanied by sparks of divine energy that danced like lightning. Ethereal marks, glowing faintly, were left on Eryx's skin. Alex's worry deepened, his anxiety palpable through clenched fists and a furrowed brow. He desperately sought to understand the meaning behind these mysterious marks.

An edge of uncertainty tinged Alex's voice as he questioned Winston's actions. "What exactly are you doing?" His words hung heavy in the tense atmosphere.

Winston's reply was composed and explanatory. "I'm conducting an examination. These glowing marks are traces of dark magic—a lingering effect from someone who came into contact with Eryx. If not addressed, they could have tainted his very being. My purpose is to cleanse him of this malevolent influence."

Alex's mind raced, grappling with this revelation. Dark magic, someone harming Eryx—it stirred his protective instincts. He needed to comprehend the full extent of the threat they faced and how to combat it.

A resolute determination filled Alex's voice as he turned to Winston for guidance. "What steps should we take now? How can we keep Eryx safe?" His eyes bore into Winston's, seeking answers and reassurance.

Winston's gaze held a mix of assurance and caution as he replied. "For now, we wait. When Eryx awakens, I will return. It's vital we uncover the truth behind his condition, as there might be more at play than meets the eye."

As their conversation ended, Winston's attention returned to the faint glowing marks on Eryx's wrist. Without words, he extended his hands, channeling a divine energy that radiated like starlight. The marks responded, enveloped in a shimmering cascade of light that gradually faded, leaving no trace.

The room's atmosphere remained heavy with unanswered questions and looming threats. The tension between Alex and Winston, while momentarily set aside, still lingered beneath the surface. Lily observed the proceedings silently, her role as a mediator and supporter evident in her watchful gaze.

The only sounds were the quiet hum of the city beyond the windows and the subtle rhythm of Eryx's breathing. The room held its secrets close, and as Alex contemplated the dark magic that had touched Eryx's life, he couldn't help but feel a rising storm of emotions within him—fear, anger, and an unwavering determination to protect the one he cared for.

As Winston's visit concluded, the room returned to its silent vigil, waiting for the moment Eryx would awaken and shed light on the truth that lay hidden in the depths of his slumber.

Eryx's eyelids fluttered open a little while later and Alex's heart skipped a beat at the sight. He'd been worried sick since last night. "Alex?" Eryx's voice was hoarse, barely a whisper.

"I'm right here," Alex replied gently, his concern evident. He offered Eryx a steaming mug of tea that Lily had prepared earlier, placing it within easy reach.

Taking the mug, Eryx's tired eyes found solace in Alex's presence. With his help, Eryx managed to shift into a more comfortable position. "How are you feeling?" Alex inquired, his eyes searching Eryx's for any sign of distress.

Eryx managed a tired smile, and that warmed Alex's heart a little. "Like I've been through a rock concert," Eryx replied, a hint of humor despite his obvious exhaustion.

Alex chuckled softly, relieved that Eryx could still find humor in this situation. "I can imagine. Do you want to talk about what happened?"

Eryx closed his eyes briefly, contemplating. Just as Alex thought he might have drifted back to sleep, Eryx began to speak, his words a lifeline that Alex clung to. "Sorry, I was asking Apollo if I should tell you what happened."

Alex leaned in, curiosity piqued. "And what did he say?"

Eryx's response carried a sense of permission. "He said it's okay for me to share."

Before Eryx could continue, Alex sensed the approach of two more individuals. His heart sank, realizing that Winston had arrived. As Eryx questioned their presence, Alex replied, "Winston is here."

Eryx looked puzzled. "Why?"

"He came last night," Alex explained, his tone tinged with acceptance and uncertainty. "Lily informed him about what happened and asked him to assess your condition."

Confusion etched Eryx's voice. "Condition? What condition?"

Before Alex could elaborate, Lily entered the room, followed closely by Winston. The interruption tested Alex's patience, but he held his tongue as Winston approached Eryx's bedside. Though Winston's presence made him uneasy, Alex understood their need for his insight.

Winston began to speak, explaining the influence of dark magic on Eryx and how he had intervened to prevent its corruption. Eryx's gratitude was palpable, and Alex found himself surprised at how Winston's words seemed to humanize the usually distant deity.

Eryx's gaze shifted between Winston and Alex, a grateful smile on his lips. "Thank you. I don't fully understand why you did it, but I appreciate your help."

Winston's response carried a weight that left Alex momentarily speechless. "I did it because you carry my son's god soul within you, and I needed to mend the harm I inadvertently caused along with Alex."

Alex's thoughts raced with a mixture of gratitude, confusion, and concern. He'd always been the protector, the one who shielded Eryx from harm, but now he had to accept that there were forces beyond his control. The bond between them was stronger than ever, and he couldn't help but wonder what other trials lay ahead in their intertwined destinies.

Alex's shock simmered beneath the surface, a tangle of emotions stirred by Winston's revelation. Trust was hard to rebuild, but at least Eryx's life had been safeguarded. The penthouse was bathed in the warm hues of evening, a sense of unease hanging in the air.

Winston's apology for the intrusion led to the inevitable request for Eryx's story. Eryx took a deep breath, his gaze shifting to Alex with a mix of reassurance and determination, before recounting the events of the previous night. His voice was steady but carried the weight of an unsettling truth.

Alex's eyes remained fixed on Eryx, his expression unreadable. He listened intently, his thoughts racing as the pieces of the puzzle fell into place.

As Eryx's words settled, a heavy silence hung in the air. Alex's gaze shifted to Winston, his inquiry direct. "Did you have any idea this could happen?"

Winston's response was measured, his voice carrying the weight of responsibility. "I had suspicions, but it wasn't confirmed until now."

Lily, her presence in the room previously unobtrusive, broke the silence. Her surprise was evident in the widening of her eyes and the slight parting of her lips. "I never thought something like this was possible."

Winston nodded in acknowledgment, his eyes locking onto Eryx. "It is possible, though it exacts a toll on the vessel. Swapping bodies like that is draining, which likely explains your magical exhaustion, Eryx."

Winston's smile towards Eryx carried a strange sense of shared understanding, a connection forged through the revelation of the supernatural. The room held a charged tension, fragile yet potent, as the pieces of Eryx's harrowing experience began to align, revealing a clearer picture of the truth.

Eryx's face bore the scars of his ordeal, and his emotions were laid bare as he recounted the events of that fateful night. He felt a mix of vulnerability and relief as he finally shared his story with those he trusted. His inner turmoil, hidden behind a façade of strength, was now exposed to the world.

Alex's thoughts raced, a storm of uncertainty and concern.

He couldn't help but feel a surge of anger towards Winston for withholding such critical information. Yet, beneath the anger, there was a glimmer of understanding, a recognition that they were all in uncharted territory.

26

Eryx

AS THEIR TIME IN LONDON DREW TO A CLOSE, the memories of their journey remained etched in Eryx's mind, despite a few bumps along the way. The experience had brought him and Alex closer, forging a connection he treasured above all else.

Winston's departure, shortly after lunch, was accompanied by his promise to stay in touch about the Hephaestus and Staff of Umbra situation. Anticipation mingled with relief as they left behind a place that had stirred both wonder and worry.

On their way to London Heathrow, Alex's persistent concern became a constant refrain. Eryx found it endearing, even if it occasionally felt like overkill. Although he was genuinely feeling better, Alex's vigilance sometimes bordered on adorable annoyance. Lily, with her mischievous nature, only fueled the fire, encouraging Alex and amplifying his worries. The two of them were a pair of troublemakers, and Eryx couldn't help but shake his head at their antics.

Upon arriving at LaGuardia Airport, Lucas and Gabe

awaited them.

Gabe took the driver's seat while Lucas occupied the front passenger seat. Eryx settled in the back next to Lily and Alex. As they settled into the car, Alex broached the topic of their absence and the progress on the case.

Lucas began, "Gabe and I managed to breach Chronokeep's system. We didn't find anything significant."

Gabe interjected, "Tracking him down was incredibly elusive. It's as if his digital trail is intentionally obscured."

Alex inquired further, "In what way?"

"It's like he's hidden right in plain view," Gabe explained. "We couldn't dig up much about him beyond basic info like his age and birthplace."

Alex showed his approval, "And what's the latest from Emma, Olivia, and Marcus?"

Gabe continued, "Olivia's deep inside the company, gathering intel on Mr. Janssen. We're waiting for her updates. Meanwhile, Emma and Marcus are meeting with Mr. Shill later today. They told us they'll contact us once they have new information."

"Excellent job, everyone," Alex commended. "Let's convene for a meeting today. Lily, would you like to join us during the meeting, or do you have to go back to Washington?" Alex asked Lily.

"I still have a couple of days here. Themis said the next meeting won't be for a while," Lily replied, and Alex nodded.

"Also, sir. The four wolves have given us permission to talk to them. Shall I call their Alpha to see if they could come today?" Gabe asked.

"Go ahead, we need the information they have regarding their disappearance," Alex ordered.

Eryx, feeling a bit hesitant, finally spoke up, "Um, what about me? Will I be going with you guys?"

Alex turned his attention to Eryx, a warm smile on his lips. "Actually, I spoke to your friends earlier. They mentioned that you three needed some quality time. I thought it might be good for you."

Eryx's face lit up with surprise and gratitude. "You really did that?"

"For you, absolutely," Alex replied, his hand reaching over to give Eryx's a reassuring squeeze. Eryx felt a rush of warmth at the gesture, struck once again by Alex's genuine care and thoughtfulness.

Gabe and Lucas dropped them off at Alex's house. Before their hands could even touch the handle, it swung open. Alex's face lit up with a joyful smile as he saw who was on the other side. A man stood there, bearing an uncanny resemblance to Alex himself, albeit much younger. His hair cascaded in beautiful curls around his face, enhancing his striking features. In that moment, Eryx knew that this was one of Alex's children.

"Father!" The man exclaimed, embracing Alex and Lily with a fervor that radiated genuine affection. Eryx couldn't help but feel a warmth at the sight. "And Mother! I've missed you so much!"

"Zagreus! My dear, I've missed you too," Lily responded, her voice tinged with a hint of longing.

As the embraces loosened, Zagreus turned his attention to Eryx, his eyes sparkling with curiosity. Walking toward him, Zagreus enveloped Eryx in a welcoming hug. "And you must be Eryx," he said, breaking the embrace and offering a warm smile. "It's truly wonderful to finally meet you."

Eryx returned the smile, genuinely touched by the reception. "Likewise," he replied, his voice sincere.

Alex took charge, steering the group inside the house. Cerberus, the three-headed guardian, leaped onto Eryx, showering him with enthusiastic licks. Laughter filled the air as no one rushed to his rescue, relishing in his amusing predicament.

"Son, what brings you here?" Lily inquired, her curiosity piqued.

"Just returning Cerberus and Mr. Whiskers, Mother. Father entrusted them to my care while you were away," Zagreus explained. "By the way, how was your trip? Hermes mentioned something about meeting Zeus in London."

Eryx couldn't help but interject, "How did Hermes even know about that?"

Zagreus simply shrugged, a hint of amusement dancing in his eyes. "Hermes has a knack for being in the know when it comes to godly matters. Besides, he's the messenger of the gods."

Lily recounted their London adventures, her words capturing Zagreus's full attention. With unwavering focus, he absorbed every detail.

"I'll see what I can do, but I can't promise anything at the moment," Zagreus said softly.

"Thank you, my son," Alex expressed his gratitude, a touch of pride evident in his eyes.

Zagreus's duty beckoned, and he shared his intent to check on the underworld and attend to matters involving Melanoe and Macaria. With heartfelt farewells and embraces, he left them through a portal.

Turning to Alex, Eryx chimed in, "You guys have to go to

your headquarters now, right?"

Alex nodded, a blend of concern and resolve on his face. "Yes, sweetheart. We have to resolve this case swiftly. Don't worry, Ari and Dion will be joining you soon."

Eryx's reluctance was evident, his attachment to the comfort of home surfacing. "Alright, just be careful out there." He pressed a kiss to Alex's lips and shared an embrace with both Alex and Lily.

Shortly after Alex and Lily departed, a knock echoed through the house, causing Eryx's smile to grow wider. He missed his friends dearly, and seeing Ari at the door was like a comforting hug. As Ari stepped aside, Dion's smug expression came into view, nearly sending Eryx into a fit of joy. Suppressing his excitement, he settled for hugging these dear people, conveying his warmth through the embrace.

Guiding them inside, they moved to the kitchen where Eryx had prepared mugs of hot tea. Dion and Ari settled in, Ari's raised eyebrow showing his observation. "So, you're really settled in here, huh? Should I call a moving company?" Ari teased.

Eryx shrugged, a mix of confusion and amusement in his eyes. "Honestly, I've lost track of what's going on."

As they sipped their tea, Ari's curious gaze delved deeper. "So, what do you know then?"

Eryx leaned back in his chair, reflecting on his feelings for Alex. "Well, I know that I'm starting to care for Alex much more than I expected. It's happening faster than I thought."

Ari's words cut through his contemplation, her insights hitting Eryx with a sense of realization. "Actually, I think there's more to it. The resonance between Apollo's god soul and your emotions might be speeding things up," Ari pointed out, shedding light on the mysterious pull he felt.

Apollo's name hung in the air, causing Eryx's heart to tighten. Dion's concerned glance didn't go unnoticed, prompting Eryx to reassure him. "Yeah… I'm okay. But did Alex tell you about what happened in London before we left?"

Curiosity piqued, Ari and Dion listened as Eryx recounted his encounter with Apollo, the shadow wraiths, and the revelation about the god's soul residing within him. The room fell silent as his friends absorbed the gravity of the situation.

Ari's voice broke the silence, tinged with awe. "You met Father?"

Simultaneously, Dion's voice emerged, laced with disbelief. "The Staff of Umbra?"

Eryx nodded, feeling a sense of vulnerability. "Yes, both."

A flurry of questions followed, unraveling the mysteries surrounding his recent experiences. As their conversation unfolded, Dion and Ari shared their unique perspectives on the situation, piecing together a larger puzzle.

Eryx raised an eyebrow at Dion's confession, a playful smirk forming. "So, Father? Are you two siblings now too? Lily said that I am technically related to both of you thanks to Apollo."

Dion chuckled, rubbing his neck sheepishly. "Yeah, Ari, Apollo, and I are siblings. So, technically, you're part of the family. I am sorry that we never mentioned it."

Eryx embraced Dion, his affection genuine. "Don't worry about it. Actually, having a brother and a sister sounds great."

"Why did Father hide this from us?" Ari's concern filled the room.

"Maybe he had his reasons," Eryx mused, his thoughts delving into the complexities of their father's actions.

Eryx's question shifted to their awareness of Winston's presence in London. "You guys knew he was there?"

Dion nodded. "Once we found out Father and Hera were in London, we've been keeping tabs on each other. But this move was definitely unexpected."

Eryx leaned in, sharing his own theory. "You know what I think? He's afraid. I believe he still carries guilt from what happened during the war."

Dion's reaction showed his knowledge of the situation. "You're well-versed in this, huh?"

Eryx sighed. "It's hard not to be. Alex was moments away from punching Winston in the face, and I had to step in."

"That idiot," Dion muttered. Ari refocused the conversation on the immediate concerns.

As the conversation flowed, the Staff of Umbra, and Hephaestus's potential capture dominated the discussion. Eryx confirmed that Winston and Hera had suspected the staff's use, a development that Dion identified as a significant problem.

Dion's thoughtful expression deepened. "And Hephaestus, possibly taken?"

Eryx nodded. "Yes, it seems he's the only one who can forge weapons from celestial steel."

Ari and Dion exchanged meaningful glances, their unspoken understanding guiding their next steps. "In that case, we need to train you. It's time for you to gain control over your powers," Ari declared, her determination palpable.

Dion took Eryx's hand, leading him through the house with a purpose. "Where are we going?" Eryx asked, his curiosity sparked.

Dion's grin was infectious. "Alex has a huge backyard. Why not use it for training?"

Eryx's incredulity matched his thoughts. "We're starting now?"

Dion's enthusiasm was unwavering. "Why not? The sooner we begin, the better."

Ari chimed in, sealing the decision. "Alright, it's time. Cerberus and Mr. Whiskers, come!" Eryx commanded the ever-loyal dog, and his cat.

Gathered in Alex's spacious backyard, Eryx, Ari, Dion, Mr. Whiskers, and Cerberus stood beneath the bright sun. The garden around them was vibrant with colorful flowers and swaying trees. Cerberus, sniffed the air in curiosity, while Mr. Whiskers, the cat, perched on a nearby fence post, observing with a keen gaze.

Ari began to explain the training. "Eryx, we're going to start with something simple – feeling vibrations around you. Everything, from the ground to the air, emits vibrations, and you can learn to sense and control them."

Eryx looked intrigued but a bit uncertain. "Vibrations?"

Dion chimed in to simplify. "Think of it like the energy all around us. Because of Apollo, you can tune into his energy and use his magical affinity for light and music."

With a nod from Ari, Eryx closed his eyes and took a deep breath. He concentrated on his senses, feeling the solid ground under his shoes and the gentle caress of the breeze on his skin. It was almost as if he could hear a soft hum in the air, a subtle background melody.

"Now, let the energy flow through you," Ari instructed gently. "Imagine it's like delicate threads intertwining with your being."

Eryx took another breath, envisioning the energy as shimmering threads of light weaving through his body. He felt a sense of connection, as if he were a part of the very fabric of the world around him.

Dion added more guidance. "Now, try to manipulate this energy. Picture it as if you're creating ripples, much like dropping a stone in water."

Eryx imagined ripples radiating outward from his core, like a stone creating gentle waves in a tranquil pond. To his amazement, he sensed a slight shift in the environment – as if his thoughts were leaving subtle imprints on the energy around him.

Ari's excitement was palpable. "You're doing wonderfully, Eryx. Keep going. Experiment with different patterns."

With determination, Eryx persevered. He visualized diverse shapes and forms, experimenting with changing the energy's flow. Gradually, he felt himself gaining better control, his mind and energy intertwining with newfound ease.

Dion's enthusiasm filled the air. "You're getting the hang of it! You're channeling the energy that's present all around us."

As Eryx opened his eyes, his newfound connection to the vibrations around him filled his senses with heightened awareness. The garden seemed to come alive in a different way – the colors were more vibrant, and the air hummed with unseen energy. He could see shimmering threads of energy intertwining with every living thing, creating a delicate tapestry of light.

He focused on Ari, Dion, Mr. Whiskers, and Cerberus, noticing that each emitted a unique pattern of energy. Ari's energy danced like flames, vibrant and passionate. Dion's energy flowed smoothly, like a calm river. Mr. Whiskers's energy sparkled playfully, like sunlight on water. Cerberus's energy was a complex interweaving of threads, representing his three-headed nature.

Eryx's heart swelled with wonder as he realized he could perceive these hidden aspects of the world. He experimented, sending gentle ripples of energy towards Cerberus, who responded with a joyful bark, clearly sensing the connection.

Ari observed with a delighted smile. "You're not just sensing the vibrations, Eryx. You're starting to see the essence of of your surroundings."

Dion nodded in agreement. "Your magic give you a whole new way of experiencing the world."

Eryx's gaze shifted to nearby flowers. As he extended his senses, he saw the life force within them, pulsating with vitality. It was as if he glimpsed the very soul of nature itself.

"This is incredible," Eryx breathed in awe, his heart racing with the beauty of what he was discovering.

Ari's voice was filled with encouragement. "Remember, Eryx, you're connected to the divine. Your magic are a gift that can bring balance and healing."

Dion chimed in, his words carrying a sense of responsibility. "As you learn to use these abilities, always keep in mind the impact they can have."

Eryx nodded, his determination evident. "I'll make sure to use them wisely."

As the sun dipped lower in the sky, casting a warm glow over the garden, Eryx felt a sense of gratitude for his friends and the journey that lay ahead

27

Alex

"GABE, ARE THE WOLVES IN THE BUILDING ALREADY?" Alex asked Gabe as they entered the Shadowguards Headquarters.

Alex wondered how the wolves were fairing since they got their souls back. He could still feel the wrongness of their souls when Leo tracked them back. It was almost as if they were being controlled, like a puppet.

He knew for a fact that Morvain was leading the Order. He had his suspicions, but it wasn't confirmed until they took Hephaestus.

"Yes, sir. They are in the interrogation room," Gabe said, and Alex nodded.

Upon entering the interrogation room, Alex saw only Lucas there, while the wolves were on the other side of the one-way glass.

"Lily, do you want to come in with me?" Alex asked Lily.

Lily shook her head. "No, the wolves don't know who I am. Take Gabe with you. I'll keep watch here with Lucas." Alex nodded in understanding.

"Gabe, let's do this," Alex said, and they entered the other room. As they walked in, the four wolves looked up, and they appeared to be in better condition than before.Alex wasn't taken aback; shifters possessed an astonishingly rapid healing ability that outpaced that of other supernatural beings. Shifter's unparalleled healing prowess could mend injuries with remarkable speed and efficiency. Wounds that would hobble or incapacitate others were mere setbacks for shifters, quickly stitching themselves back together. This exceptional ability bestowed upon them the advantage of swiftly recovering from harm, a trait that set them apart from their supernatural counterparts.

One of the wolves stood up - Alex guessed he was the Alpha Mate - as a form of greeting. "You must be Director Knight." Alex nodded. "I'm Henry Hansen, the Alpha Mate of Jared." He turned to introduce the rest. "And these are my pack mates: Rio, Dan, and Layla."

"It's good to finally meet all of you, though we wished it were under better circumstances," Alex said, extending his hand for Henry to shake. "Have a seat. This won't take long."

"I just want to thank all of you for giving us our souls back," Henry said.

"You should be thanking Leo Rodriguez; he was the one who tracked your souls and got them back inside your bodies," Alex clarified.

Henry nodded. "But we still want to show our appreciation to your team nonetheless. My mate wanted to join your cause in protecting the city."

Wolf packs typically adhered to a stance of neutrality in matters beyond their own territories. The idea of a wolf wanting to actively engage in safeguarding the city was uncommon, and it intrigued Alex. It was a departure from the usual dynamics he had encountered between different supernatural factions.

"We'll contact Alpha Hansen to further communicate with him if he's willing," Alex said, pausing for a moment. "How are you all doing? I want to know if you feel anything different."

"Jared told us the stories about it. From what we could tell, we don't feel anything different. We actually feel a little better than before we got taken," Henry said, and all his pack mates nodded in agreement.

Alex nodded. "That's good to hear, though we would still like to monitor your progress for a couple more weeks just to make sure."

"Of course. We know that getting a soul stolen wasn't a normal everyday occurrence."

"Good. Now, I want to know what happened before your souls were stolen," Alex inquired.

"We were on a pack run when I smelled something wrong in the forest. I followed the scent, and it led to a clearing," Layla, the brown-haired woman, answered.

"The three of us followed her through the woods, but we were too late," Rio interjected.

"Once we got to the clearing, we saw a man wielding a staff. It was almost as if he knew we were there that night," Dan continued.

"He was just standing there, smiling. The staff was glowing, and we didn't know what kind of magic he was using," Henry said. "We howled for the rest of the pack since the man was in our territory, but nobody came. It was like our calls were muted."

Alex's thoughts raced. The fact that they couldn't call for

their pack mates made him suspect it was the same person who attacked Eryx in London.

"What does this man and staff look like?" Alex asked urgently.

"We couldn't recall. You see, us shifters have a memory when it comes to recalling faces, but this one we just couldn't remember. As for the staff, it appeared to be made out of wood with a crystal orb resting on top, suspended within a void of obsidian. It didn't feel right to us. Too powerful," Henry explained.

Fuck.

The Order having the staff didn't bode well. The Staff of Umbra possessed a unique and discerning nature when it came to choosing its wielder. Not just anyone could harness its potent magic; only a select few magical beings were attuned to the staff's energies and possessed the necessary qualities to wield its power.

This suggested that Morvain had managed to find someone who could wield it, and they needed to find this person as soon as possible.

"What else can you tell us?" Gabe spoke up, pulling Alex from his racing thoughts.

"The last thing we remember was the man using the staff to steal our souls. We couldn't remember anything more than that," Henry said.

Alex nodded. "Thank you for coming and sharing your account of events. It really helped us piece everything together." He stood and shook Henry's hand once more before turning to Gabe. "Escort them out to the lobby and give them Dr. Sloane's contact information." Gabe nodded and guided the wolves out.

As he walked to the opposite room, Lily immediately stood up and walked towards him.

"Do we think that the man was in possession of the Staff?" Lily asked.

"I believe so. We need to find that man quickly," he answered, turning to Lucas. "Lucas, do we have any updates on the rest of the team?"

But before Lucas could answer, Emma burst into the room looking worse for wear.

"I need your help. Marcus… It's bad," Emma said urgently.

They all rushed to the medical bay where Emma had taken Marcus.

"What happened, Emma?" Alex growled, his concern evident.

"The meeting with Mr. Shill happened. They went to a restaurant and then to the park. Somehow Mr. Shill knew what we were up to and cast a spell on Marcus. He fought back, but Mr. Shill was surprisingly strong for a human. I tried to help, but most of my enchantments weren't working until someone else showed up."

"What did the man who helped look like?" Alex was already forming a suspicion.

"He looked like Marcus, just a bit taller and more muscular. I'm sorry, sir. I should have done more," Emma replied, her voice filled with regret.

Hermes.

"It wasn't your fault, Emma," Alex reassured her, placing a comforting hand on her shoulder.

The thought of a human overpowering his team members was deeply unsettling.

They reached the medical bay shortly after, where Dr.

Sloane was already waiting for them.

"Doctor, how is he?" Alex inquired urgently.

Dr. Sloane sighed wearily. "He's stable for now. I need the two of you to come inside. I can't have all of you in there at once."

Alex nodded, understanding the necessity. He turned to Lucas and Emma. "Lucas, Emma, please wait outside with the rest of the team."

Once inside the medical bay, Alex's eyes landed on Marcus's unconscious form, connected to various monitors and equipment. The room was filled with an air of tension and worry, each machine's beep a reminder of Marcus's precarious state.

"Let me cut to the chase – we've run tests, and there's nothing glaringly wrong. He's just… drained," Dr. Sloane stated.

Alex's frustration was evident in his voice. "Could it be magic-related?"

Dr. Sloane nodded. "It's possible, but his magical readings are normal. We're stumped."

As Alex was about to press for more details, a portal materialized in front of them, originating from the Aether. Hermes emerged, his aura carrying a sense of urgency.

Hermes wasted no time. "You won't find anything through your tests. The one who did this carried dark magic within their soul, and it's latched onto Marcus."

Alex's anger was palpable. "Is this connected to the person we encountered in London?"

Hermes shook his head. "I don't know. But it is possible."

"Emma told us that the person who did this was a human. But we were told that it can only be transferred through touch and by a magic user, no less," Alex protested.

Hermes corrected him. "That used to be true. The Order has figured out a way to transfer dark magic using humans. Since humans lack inherent magic, they can carry dark magic temporarily without detection."

Lily's inquiry followed naturally. "So how do they pass it to magic users?"

"Dark magic can't survive in a human host for long. A ritual is performed, allowing the bearer to cast a spell that transfers the dark magic essence to a magic user."

Alex's voice was laced with indignation. "So, this was a targeted attack?"

Hermes nodded, sadness in his eyes. "Yes. I know you didn't want this, but I've taken care of the human responsible."

The gravity of the situation sunk in for Alex. "This changes everything."

Hermes's empathetic smile held a tinge of sadness. "I know. But we'll tackle this, together."

"So, what's the plan now? The only one who can destroy dark magic is Winston," Lily stated, her frustration evident.

Hermes contemplated for a moment before speaking carefully. "There might be a way, though I'm not sure if you'll be on board with it."

Alex's curiosity piqued. "What is it?"

Hermes leaned in slightly, his voice measured. "Eryx. He managed to locate the celestial steel on the bodies, didn't he?" Alex confirmed it with a nod, a sense of unease growing in his gut. "If he can find celestial steel, it's possible he can locate dark magic as well, and potentially even neutralize it."

Lily's skepticism was palpable. "But how? He couldn't protect himself from it back in London."

Hermes addressed her concern. "He was vulnerable because his magical defenses were down. He wasn't taught how to erect his own magical barriers. Uncle, I implore you, consider asking Eryx to help my son."

Alex's frustration transformed into protectiveness. "What if something goes wrong in the process?"

Hermes held his gaze, his emotions barely contained. "You promised to keep my son safe from harm, and I trust that promise still holds. Please, uncle, I'm begging you."

A sigh escaped Alex as his anger subsided. "I'll talk to him, but I can't guarantee anything."

Hermes nodded, gratitude in his eyes. "Thank you. That's all I can hope for."

Lily's practicality took over. "Are you planning to stay here for a while?"

Hermes affirmed her question with a nod. "I believe it's time for us to get to know each other better."

Leaving Hermes with his son in the room, Alex and Lily exited, the weight of their decision hanging heavily over them.

* * *

As he approached his house, the warm glow of light spilled through the windows, indicating that Eryx was still awake. The prospect brought a smile to his face. He longed to ask Eryx to move in with him, but apprehension held him back; he worried it might be too soon.

The front door creaked open, revealing the inviting aroma of a delicious meal being prepared. Alex followed his nose, leading him straight to the kitchen. There, he found Eryx dancing around and lost in his own world with earphones in place. Alex couldn't resist, wrapping his arms around Eryx, and they both shared a chuckle at the unexpected embrace.

"Hey, sweetheart," Alex whispered, his lips brushing against Eryx's shoulder in a tender kiss. Eryx took Alex's hand and held it against him, their connection grounding them. Alex playfully pinched Eryx's behind. "So, what's on the menu?"

"Fettuccine, and for dessert, some good ol' flan," Eryx replied, his creations promising a delightful feast. "How was your day?"

Alex's shoulders sagged at the memory. "Rough. But let's save that conversation for when we're on the couch, comfortably eating. You can fill me in on your day too. Sound like a deal?"

"Deal," Eryx agreed, shooing Alex toward a seat. "Now go sit down; dinner will be ready soon."

Alex couldn't help but tease. "What if I'd rather eat you than the food?"

Eryx smacked him lightly with a spatula, the playful reprimand a mix of affection and amusement. "Maybe, if you're good, we'll see about that later." He leaned in for a kiss, leaving Alex with a smile and a sense of anticipation.

Well, it was better than nothing, Alex thought as he settled into a seat, eagerly looking forward to the delicious meal.

After finishing their meal and tidying up, they settled back onto the couch, Eryx resting his head on Alex's shoulder. In the warm cocoon of their shared space, Eryx's gentle question hung in the air. "Are you going to tell me about what's been stressing you out?"

Alex knew there was no avoiding it. With a sigh, he decided to open up completely, recounting the weighty events of the day. "Hermes actually asked me to take you to Marcus. He's hoping that you can try to take out the dark essence inside Marcus and destroy it."

Eryx's response was a subtle nibble on his lower lip, a gesture Alex found utterly endearing. "I'll give it a shot, but I'm going to need your help to bolster my magical defenses."

Alex leaned down and planted a soft kiss on Eryx's forehead. "You'll have my full support. Now, how about you? What did you and Ari end up doing today?"

Eryx launched into a recount of his day, and it was clear that his time with Dion and Ari had been eventful. Training sessions and magic lessons had filled the hours since morning. "Dion and Ari helped me fine-tune my magic skills, especially after learning about what happened in London."

Alex raised an eyebrow, curious. "Sounds like quite the day. But why are you still standing? I would have thought you'd be falling asleep by now."

A playful glint danced in Eryx's eyes. "Dion explained that Apollo can manipulate sound vibrations, so we focused on that aspect." Eryx stood up, a mischievous smile playing on his lips. "Watch this," he said, excitement tingling in his voice.

Alex couldn't help but smile, his heart swelling with affection. He was witnessing something intimate, a facet of Eryx's identity that was unfolding before his very eyes. As the last notes of the melody faded into the air, Eryx turned to Alex, a mixture of excitement and uncertainty in his eyes.

"What did you think?" Eryx asked, his voice tinged with a blend of eagerness and vulnerability.

Alex looked at Eryx with curiosity. Eryx's hands moved smoothly in the air, shaping something unseen. And then, the air responded. Vibrations spread out, like ripples, making the room hum in a strange way.

The sound changed into a melody, filling the room with a magical feeling. Alex smiled, impressed by Eryx's new skills.

Eryx's hands moved gracefully, creating vibrations that matched the air around them. It was like he was making patterns out of thin air, like an invisible design. It felt like Eryx was using the very essence of sound.

The room filled with a gentle hum as Eryx moved his hands. The sound was soothing, creating a peaceful feeling. Alex watched Eryx closely, totally fascinated.

Eryx's expression changed as he focused even more. He twisted his wrist, and the hum turned into a lively tune. It was like Eryx was leading an orchestra with invisible instruments, making layers of music with his fingers.

The air was alive with Eryx's music. The melodies went up and down, creating a beautiful dance. It was amazing to see Eryx's progress under Dion and Ari's guidance.

Alex couldn't contain his enthusiasm. He stood up and walked over to Eryx, pulling him into a warm embrace. "That was incredible," he whispered, his voice filled with genuine awe. "You've come so far, and I'm so proud of you."

Eryx's face lit up with a radiant smile, his insecurities dissipating in the warmth of Alex's praise. "Thanks, Alex. I couldn't have done it without you, Dion, and Ari."

Alex chuckled, his fingers gently tracing Eryx's cheek. "You've got a natural talent, Eryx. And I have a feeling you're only scratching the surface."

Eryx pulled back and leaned in, their lips meeting in a tender kiss. As they pulled apart, Eryx's eyes sparkled with determination. "I can't wait to keep learning and growing."

Alex chuckled, touched Eryx's face, and said, "You're a natural, Eryx. And you're just getting started."

Alex's heart surged with a potent mixture of affection and desire as he gazed into Eryx's eyes. Their kiss deepened, their hands eagerly exploring each other's heated and eager forms. In the midst of this intense connection, time seemed to slow, extending the electric charge that coursed between them. Eventually, they pulled away, their foreheads touching, their breaths mingling as they tried to steady themselves.

Alex's voice, tinged with an earnest plea, flowed from his lips. "Move in with me. Please. I want you here with me."

Eryx looked at Alex with a mix of emotions, clearly moved by his words. He nodded, a silent agreement, and said, "Sure, Alex. I need you too. Just… promise not to hurt me."

"I promise," Alex said earnestly. Without delay, he kissed Eryx passionately, carrying him in his arms towards the bedroom. The bond between them grew stronger with each step, leading them with desire.

Entering the bedroom, excitement and longing filled the air. Alex gently placed Eryx on the bed, their eyes locked in understanding. Their need and deep feelings guided them without needing words.

Eryx's lips drew Alex in, and he couldn't resist. They kissed passionately, sending shivers down Alex's spine. He explored Eryx's body with his hands, igniting sparks of pleasure.

Clothes came off quickly, revealing their heated bodies. Skin against skin, they explored each other's shapes, a dance of intimacy and longing. Fingertips traced fire on their skin, and their shared moans echoed their desire.

In a mix of passion and tenderness, Alex kissed Eryx again, their bodies moving together, echoing their heartbeats. Time felt fuzzy as their connection grew stronger, the barriers between them disappearing.

28

Eryx

ERYX FOUND HIMSELF walking down the corridors of the Shadowguards headquarters, his hand intertwined with Alex's. A sense of anticipation and uncertainty gnawed at him. He questioned his decision to take on the task that lay ahead. He was aware that his newfound magic were still raw and untamed, but here he was, venturing into the unknown to attempt the healing of Alex's teammate.

Apollo's presence surged within him, a comforting presence that both reassured and steadied him. Grateful for the god's guidance, Eryx pressed forward with newfound determination, though his steps were laced with a hint of trepidation.

I'll be right here with you, Apollo's voice resonated within Eryx's thoughts, a soothing reminder of his presence.

Eryx dared to voice the doubts that echoed in his mind. *Can we truly heal people? Can I do this?*

Apollo's essence responded, a blend of reassurance and wisdom. *Yes, Eryx. I can use Light magic and it is a rare gift, one that only those with a pure soul can wield. Its essence holds the power to counteract the darkness that plagues our world. It can mend what has been torn asunder, and it can cleanse what has been tainted.*

Eryx's steps faltered for a moment, his thoughts racing as he absorbed Apollo's words. A sense of awe washed over him, realizing the profound nature of his task. He found himself without words, a profound gratitude swelling within him.

Thank you, Eryx told Apollo, his thoughts carrying his gratitude to the god whose power he now channeled.

Apollo's response was a gentle hum, a testament to their shared connection and the mutual trust they had forged. As they continued their journey down the corridor, Eryx held fast to Alex's hand, feeling a mixture of determination, responsibility, and hope.

They reached the entrance of the medical bay, the door opening to reveal Alex's team gathered in the waiting area. As Alex and Eryx stepped inside, the team rose to their feet, an air of determination surrounding them.

"Why are you all still here?" Alex's voice held a tinge of confusion, his eyebrows furrowing.

Gabe, standing amongst the group, answered, "We couldn't leave Marcus alone, sir. We wanted to show him we care."

Alex exchanged a puzzled glance with Eryx, piecing together the situation. "Hermes didn't leave Marcus?"

Gabe shook his head, his expression grave. "No, sir. We stayed because we didn't want him to wake up and think we'd abandoned him."

Eryx observed the team's tired and somber faces, realizing the extent of their dedication. He understood the bond that existed between them all, a camaraderie that went beyond mere colleagues.

Placing a gentle hand on Gabe's shoulder, Alex addressed his team with a mixture of gratitude and concern. "Thank you, everyone. Your dedication is truly appreciated. But you all look like you need some rest. Marcus wouldn't want you worn out on his behalf."

A silent agreement passed amongst the team members, their weariness evident. Gabe spoke for them, his tone hopeful. "Keep us updated, please."

"I promise," Alex assured them, his voice carrying the weight of his words. "Now go home and get some rest. We'll take care of Marcus."

The team exchanged nods and glances, their solidarity unbroken. They filed out of the medical bay, leaving Alex and Eryx in their own space.

Alex turned his attention to Eryx, his gaze softening. "Are you absolutely sure you want to do this?"

Eryx's conviction shone in his eyes, his resolve unwavering. "Yes, Alex. If there's a chance to help someone and save their life, I'll do whatever it takes."

Alex's touch was gentle yet fervent as he cradled Eryx's face in his hands. His words held a depth of admiration. "You're incredible, you know that?" Before Eryx could reply, Alex claimed his lips in a fervent kiss, their connection pulsating with shared emotion. "Now, let's head inside."

Inside Marcus's room they found Hermes sitting next to the bed. This was the first time Eryx meeting the godly messenger and he immediately felt calm. Hermes saw them once he took his gaze off Marcus and his eyes grew wide and darted off to hug Eryx.

Alex's hand was on his shoulders showing him support.

Hermes pulled back and Eryx could see the tears in his eyes. "Ah I am sorry, Eryx. I didn't mean to do that. I just didn't think Alex would be able to convince you to come."

Eryx just smiled at Hermes. "Of course, I would. I consider Marcus as a friend and he needs help."

"Shall we see if we can help Marcus?" Alex said.

They all nodded and positioned themselves on either side of Marcus's bed. His grip on Alex's hand tightened, a blend of determination and nervousness coursing through him. The room was bathed in a gentle, soothing light, casting a calming ambiance around them. Eryx closed his eyes briefly, focusing on his connection with Apollo, seeking the guidance he needed.

Apollo's presence filled Eryx's mind, a comforting reassurance that uplifted his spirits. With a deep breath, Eryx felt a surge of energy radiate from within, his inner light responding to his call. This wasn't their first experience with his light magic, but this situation held a weight of urgency and responsibility.

Trust in your light, Eryx, Apollo's voice resonated in his thoughts, a guiding presence. Your inner radiance holds the power to combat the darkness in Marcus. Believe in its purity.

Eryx nodded mentally, his focus sharpening on the task ahead. He felt the warmth of his inner light, a beacon of hope and healing within him. As he directed his thoughts toward Marcus, his hands began to emit a soft, golden glow.

Start by channeling your inner light, Apollo's guidance flowed naturally. *Imagine it as a force of healing and cleansing. Let your energy flow through your hands.*

Eryx embraced Apollo's instruction, envisioning his inner light as a gentle stream flowing through his palms. He could sense Apollo's wisdom guiding him, a steady stream of encouragement that bolstered his confidence.

Now, extend your light towards Marcus, Apollo's voice urged him on. *Visualize it as a radiant energy, reaching out to dissolve the darkness that's affecting him.*

Eryx's hands hovered above Marcus's prone form, his palms bathed in a soft, golden radiance. He concentrated on his inner light, allowing it to extend like a warm embrace, enveloping Marcus in its healing energy. With Apollo's guidance, Eryx felt a surge of determination, a belief in their ability to make a difference.

The darkness may resist, Apollo's voice conveyed understanding. *But remember, your light is a force of positivity and vitality. Darkness can't withstand its brilliance.*

Eryx nodded inwardly, his resolve unwavering. He intensified the flow of his inner light, focusing on the area of Marcus's chest where the darkness had taken hold. He imagined his light as a potent cleansing energy, working its way through Marcus's being, pushing back against the dark essence.

Let your light unravel the darkness, Apollo's guidance remained steadfast. *Picture it dissolving the tendrils of darkness, one by one, until only light remains.*

Eryx deepened his connection with Apollo, his inner light growing stronger as they worked together. He visualized the light as shimmering tendrils, gently intertwining with the dark essence and dispersing it. Their combined energy filled the room with palpable intensity, a clash of opposing forces.

Your light is your weapon, Eryx, Apollo's encouragement resonated in his thoughts. *Direct it with intention, purpose, and the knowledge that you have the power to heal.*

Eryx pressed on, his focus solely on his inner light. He channeled its energy with unwavering determination, picturing it as a brilliant surge that reached every corner of Marcus's being. He sensed the darkness resisting, but he persisted, his faith in the potency of his light unwavering.

Release one final surge of light, Eryx, Apollo's voice remained unwavering. *Let your inner radiance pierce through the darkness, banishing it entirely.*

With Apollo's words echoing in his thoughts, Eryx summoned the last reserves of his energy. A burst of brilliant light erupted from his palms, filling the room with its brilliance. The darkness within Marcus trembled, its grip weakening under the sheer intensity of the light.

As the radiance subsided, Eryx's hands lowered, his breath ragged from the effort. Apollo's presence gently faded, their connection ebbing away. Eryx opened his eyes, meeting Alex's gaze with a mixture of exhaustion and hesitation.

They waited in anticipation, a quiet hush enveloping the room as they watched Marcus's prone form. The air seemed charged with a sense of hope, and as if in response to Eryx's efforts, Marcus's eyelids began to flutter.

Eryx's heart skipped a beat, a surge of relief flooding through him. He exchanged a glance with Alex, their shared concern giving way to cautious optimism. Slowly, Marcus's eyes opened, revealing a glimmer of awareness within.

"Marcus?" Alex's voice was a mixture of hope and concern as he leaned closer.

Marcus blinked, his gaze slowly focusing on the faces before him. He seemed disoriented for a moment, but then a faint smile graced his lips. "Hey," he rasped weakly.

Eryx felt a rush of gratitude and accomplishment as he

witnessed Marcus's response. The darkness that had gripped him was gone, replaced by a renewed sense of vitality.

"We were worried about you," Alex admitted, his voice laden with genuine concern.

Marcus's smile grew slightly, and he attempted to sit up.

"Careful, you're not fully healed up yet," Hermes interjected after a prolonged silence, his voice carrying a mixture of concern and care.

Marcus looked at Hermes, confusion etched across his face. "I remember you," Marcus rasped, his voice holding a note of recognition.

Hermes exchanged glances with Alex and Eryx before returning his gaze to Marcus. "You do?"

Marcus gave him a curt nod, his gaze steady. "My mom used to show me pictures of you. And tell me stories about your adventures together." Eryx could discern the depth of emotion in the young man's expression.

Hermes smiled at him sadly, his memories painted vividly across his eyes. "She was indeed a formidable woman."

"You're my dad, aren't you?" Marcus asked, his voice carrying a mixture of curiosity and realization.

Hermes paused, his gaze meeting Marcus's. "How did you know?"

"Well, my mom wasn't really subtle, and it was incredible how smitten she sounded while talking about you," Marcus replied, his voice tinged with a hint of wistfulness.

Hermes was quiet for a moment, a complex blend of emotions crossing his features. Eryx observed as tears welled up in the god's eyes. "I am sorry, sorry that I couldn't be there with you," Hermes finally admitted, his voice carrying a heavy weight of regret.

Eryx watched as Marcus gently placed a hand on top of his father's, an unspoken connection forming between them. Hermes's vulnerability touched his heart as he continued, "I had to do it to protect you, and I wanted you to grow up and experience life like what you're having now."

"It is okay, I understood what you did. Mom used to tell me that if I ever met you, not to let my anger get in the way and to hear you out," Marcus said, their shared emotions tangible in the air. Their tears fell as they spoke, a testament to the depth of their feelings.

"Thank you," Hermes whispered, the weight of his past choices and their consequences evident in his voice. Marcus closed his eyes, exhaustion evident in his features as sleep claimed him, the emotions of the conversation having taken their toll.

"Hermes, we'll leave you with him. Please make sure to call us if anything changes," Alex said, his voice filled with both gratitude and concern for their teammate.

Hermes turned to Eryx, his gratitude palpable as he embraced him. "Thank you. Both of you."

Eryx smiled warmly. "It was the least we could do. We're just glad that everything seems to be okay now."

With their goodbyes exchanged, they left the room, leaving Hermes to keep watch over his sleeping son. The weight of the moment hung in the air, a mixture of emotions lingering long after they departed.

Eryx and Alex found themselves settled in a corner booth of Alex's favorite modern diner. The warm glow of the pendant lights above cast a cozy ambiance, offering a stark contrast to the recent upheavals that had taken place in their lives. Eryx was still getting accustomed to the idea of cohabitating with Alex, but the easy camaraderie between them felt like a promise of good things to come.

As they savored their meals and shared stories, a sudden beep emitted from Alex's SHD, briefly interrupting their lighthearted atmosphere. Eryx's curiosity was instantly piqued by the concerned furrow on Alex's forehead as he checked the device.

"What's up?" Eryx inquired, his interest immediately engaged.

Alex exhaled a sigh, his focus intent on the screen of his SHD. "Got a report from Olivia about Sven Janssen."

Eryx leaned forward, eager for details. "And what did she find?"

Alex's voice carried a note of frustration as he shared the information. "Unfortunately, not much. Sven seems to be running things from the shadows, but we're short on specifics. However, she did manage to snag a sketch of him from an employee who caught a glimpse."

Eryx's anticipation grew as he waited for more. "Can I see the sketch?"

Alex swiveled his SHD to face Eryx, revealing the drawn image of Sven Janssen. Recognition washed over Eryx as he immediately identified the man in the sketch, a mixture of surprise and unease filling him.

Concern etched Alex's features as he probed, "You all right?"

Taking a moment to process, Eryx weighed his words before responding. "Yeah… I know this guy."

Alex's eyebrows knitted further, his tone tinged with worry. "You do? Where from?"

Eryx hesitated, the significance of his revelation sinking in. "He's the one who attacked me in London."

A muttered curse from Alex underscored the gravity of the situation. Eryx nodded in agreement, his realization that their path just got more complex settling heavily within him.

29

Alex

THE NEXT MORNING brought an unexpected jolt of sensation as Eryx's mouth wrapped around his cock, the sensation electrifying. Beneath the sheets, Eryx's head bobbed rhythmically, sending waves of pleasure coursing through him.

"That's it baby, suck it." Alex moaned

Eryx's enthusiastic movements sent a rush of heat through Alex's body, intensifying the already arousing sensations. With a hand gently guiding Eryx's head, Alex encouraged him to explore deeper depths of pleasure.

Encountering the urgent desire in Eryx's eyes, Alex withdrew his cock from his lover's mouth, observing the enticing sight of Eryx's flushed, plump lips glistening with a sheen of moisture. The intimate connection they shared ignited a fervent heat between them, making every sensation heightened and profound.

"Please, baby. I need you in my mouth." Eryx begged.

Without a moment's hesitation, Alex responded to Eryx's plea, granting him exactly what he desired. The sensation of Eryx's mouth on him was exquisite, sending sparks of pleasure coursing through every nerve in his body. As their intimate connection deepened, Alex could feel his own urgency building, a sure sign that he was rapidly approaching the edge of release.

"Baby, Im coming!" Alex moaned.

"Come for me! Come down my throat!" Eryx's needy moan vibrated against him as he expertly took him in once more, his mouth encompassing Alex with a captivating combination of pressure and warmth. In the throes of heightened pleasure, Alex surrendered to the electrifying sensations building within him. With a final, intense surge of pleasure, he reached his peak, his release pulsating through him as Eryx skillfully guided him to completion.

Alex felt Eryx shift beside him in bed, followed by a tender kiss. Soon, they both emerged from the cozy sheets and shared a shower together. The warm water cascading over their bodies seemed to wash away the remnants of sleep.

As Alex stood in front of the bathroom mirror, expertly gliding the razor over his face, he overheard Eryx engaged in a phone conversation.

"Yeah… Okay… What time do you want me there? Yeah, sure, I'll see you soon," Eryx's voice resonated from the bedroom.

With his shaving completed, Alex stepped out and walked over to Eryx, who was perched on the edge of the bed, vigorously towel-drying his lustrous blonde hair. It had grown longer in the past few weeks, and although Eryx seemed somewhat disenchanted with the length, Alex secretly adored how it framed his features.

Taking a seat next to him, Alex inquired, "So, who was on

the phone?"

Eryx let out a sigh, his expression somewhat troubled. "It was my manager. We haven't been in touch since the attack. He wants me to come in today for a discussion."

Alex contemplated the situation. "Maybe Ari or Dion gave him some insights into what happened?"

Eryx shrugged slightly. "I can't say for sure. But regardless, I have a gnawing feeling about this meeting. Still, I have to go."

Understanding the necessity, Alex suggested, "If possible, take Cerberus or ask Ari to accompany you. Safety comes first."

A hint of regret shadowed Eryx's eyes. "I'd love to, but pets aren't allowed in the building, and Ari's probably tied up today."

Alex sighed, a mix of concern and frustration. "Eryx…"

"I know, I know," Eryx responded, his voice tinged with an equal mixture of understanding and exasperation. "It's not the safest choice, but I feel trapped. What else can I do?"

Part of Alex wanted to insist on accompanying Eryx, but he knew his own duties demanded his presence at the office. "Just promise me that you'll call me if anything seems off or if you need me."

Eryx's lips curved into a soft smile. "You've got it. I promise."

Leaning in, Alex sealed their conversation with a lingering kiss, a silent exchange of emotions that words couldn't encapsulate. The minutes passed quickly, and they both finished getting ready for the day, preparing to face their day.

As soon as Alex got into the headquarters, His initial concern was checking up on Marcus. Entering Marcus's room, he found the young man already seated and meticulously adjusting his uniform. Hermes was there, assisting his son – a sight that seemed almost surreal, considering their rocky history.

"Should you be up and about already?" Alex inquired as he stepped in, his gaze moving between father and son.

Marcus's head snapped up so swiftly that Alex wondered if he'd accidentally startled him. "Sir! I was informed that I'm fully healed and cleared for discharge," Marcus replied, his tone a mixture of eagerness and respect.

Raising an eyebrow, Alex turned his attention to Hermes. "Is this accurate, Hermes?" He was impressed by the extent to which Hermes appeared invested in being a responsible parent – a side of the god that he hadn't expected to see.

Hermes met his gaze evenly. "Indeed, Dr. Sloane confirmed his recovery and actually remarked that he's in better shape now than before the incident."

Alex's lips curved into a genuine smile. "Well, if the doctor's given the green light, I'm glad to hear it."

Marcus seemed momentarily taken aback, his shyness revealing itself as he spoke. "I never got the chance to properly thank both you and Eryx for saving my life."

"As long as you're safe and well, that's all the gratitude we need," Alex assured him, his hand finding its place on Marcus's shoulder in a comforting gesture.

Hermes's voice entered the conversation again, inquiring, "Is there something specific I can do to assist, Alex?"

A sense of responsibility lingered in Alex's expression. "Actually, yes. I want you to keep a close watch on Eryx today. He'll be in the city, and I want him under surveillance."

Although he trusted Eryx's instincts and capabilities, the memory of the attack in London still weighed heavily on him.

Hermes's brow furrowed with concern. "What's happening?"

"The individual they were trailing is the same person who targeted Eryx. I'm almost certain he's aware of Hephaestus's location and has the Staff of Umbra in his possession," Alex revealed, prompting Hermes's nod of understanding.

"Does the rest of the team know about this?" Marcus inquired, displaying a keen interest in their ongoing operations.

"Not yet. Once we finish up here, you can join me in the meeting room where we'll discuss everything in more detail," Alex explained, appreciating Marcus's engagement.

The trio shared a purposeful look, each of them aware of the gravity of the situation at hand.

Alex called for an urgent meeting as soon as he and Marcus left the medical bay. The two entered the meeting room to find everyone already assembled, looking refreshed and ready for action. Seeing the camaraderie among his team, Alex couldn't help but smile – these people were his second family.

As he stepped to the front of the room, all eyes turned to him. He addressed his team with gratitude and purpose. "Team, thanks to your unwavering dedication, we've managed to uncover Sven Janssen's appearance. Eryx has confirmed that he's the same man who attacked him in London."

Questions and speculations started flowing, reflecting the urgency of their situation. Olivia's voice cut through, asking the question that was likely on everyone's minds. "Do we suspect he's connected to the Order?"

"Yes, it's highly likely that Sven Janssen is tied to the organization," Alex affirmed. "Furthermore, he possesses a dangerous staff that's more powerful than the gods themselves."

Gabe, ever the practical one, pressed for a plan of action. "So, what's our move?"

Before Alex could lay out their strategy, a shrill alarm pierced the air, signaling a high-risk incident that could potentially lead to casualties. A wave of urgency swept through him – they had no time to waste.

Gabe swiftly accessed his SHD, a device designed to detect magical anomalies. "Sir, the source of the distress call is coming from Central Park."

"Everyone, gear up and let's move!" Alex barked, the urgency galvanizing the team into swift action. They scrambled to don their equipment, the atmosphere in the room charged with purpose and determination. The clock was ticking, and their skills were needed to respond to the threat in Central Park.

As they hurriedly prepared for whatever awaited them, Alex's mind was focused on their mission – to protect and defend against the unknown danger that had just emerged.

30

Eryx

"RICHARD? WHERE HAVE YOU BEEN?"
Eryx was in a Starbucks near his record label when he saw Richard walk in. Of all the Starbucks in New York, Richard had chosen this one. He was wearing a hoodie and a pair of black sunglasses, but Eryx could still tell it was him.

Richard saw him and walked over. "Eryx! How have you been?"

"I asked you first," Eryx said as the barista asked him for his order. "I'll have a pumpkin spice latte, please."

"I've been around. Look, can we sit down first before you bombard me with questions?" Richard said.

Knowing how famous Richard was, it was a miracle that no one was swarming him at that very moment. Even through his disguise, it wasn't that difficult to tell it was him.

Eryx bought another latte for Richard just because he could, and sat down where Richard was sitting.

"Speak," Eryx said as he sat down and gave Richard his latte.

Richard sighed. "What did Alex tell you?"

Eryx raised an eyebrow at Richard. "He didn't tell me much. Other than you were supposed to visit me and you never did."

"Well, I was going to, but I had to go back and report to my mother," Richard said cryptically. Eryx didn't know what to think of it.

"What did you have to report to her?" Eryx asked, his skepticism showing but he didn't care.

"My mother… She… She had to know everything that's going on around me, and she decided to keep me in her house for a couple of days."

Eryx thought about Richard's explanation. "I don't think that's the case, but I'm going to let it go for now because you've become a person that I care about and I don't want to lose that."

"Thank you," Richard said as he took a sip of his latte. "So, what's your agenda for the day?"

"I'm actually heading to my record label today. Sam wanted to see me. Though, I have a bad feeling about it."

"A bad feeling?" Richard asked. "Maybe I should come with you."

"You're welcome to come with, but yeah. My gut is telling me to be cautious." Eryx took a sip of his own latte and looked at his watch. "Anyway, we better go if you want to come with me."

They finished their drinks quickly and headed to Eryx's meeting.

Eryx and Richard entered Eternal Records, engaged in conversation when they accidentally bumped into someone. Eryx looked up to identify the person.

"Landon?! What are you doing here?" Eryx exclaimed, genuine surprise in his voice.

"Eryx! Hey!" Landon responded, his expression mirroring his surprised tone.

"What brings you here?" Eryx asked, curiosity piqued. "Oh, by the way, this is Richard Lane." Eryx introduced the two. They shook hands, but their gaze held longer than expected.

The palpable sexual tension between them was undeniable.

Landon hesitated and then admitted, "Well... I actually own the label."

Eryx's eyes widened in astonishment. He glanced at Richard, who raised an amused eyebrow at Landon's revelation. Landon's humility shone through, as he was never one to flaunt his achievements.

"You never mentioned that when we were dating." Eryx teased, a playful grin forming.

Landon chuckled, scratching the back of his neck. "You didn't ask! And I'm not one to brag about it."

Eryx nodded, understanding Landon's modesty. He had always admired that trait in him.

As they caught up, Eryx learned that Landon kept a close watch on his various business ventures, including Eternal Records. Landon spoke with visible joy about his endeavors, radiating pride in building something meaningful.

Their conversation shifted to Eryx's current situation, where he explained he had been called in for a meeting with his manager that morning.

"Ah, I see. Well, if you want, I can wait for you here. Afterward, we can all catch up over food as friends, of course," Landon suggested with a warm smile.

Eryx found comfort in Landon's presence and appreciated the offer. Their history was complex, but they had managed to forge a new friendship.

"Sure, that sounds great," Eryx agreed, returning the smile. "It's been a while since we caught up. Richard, are you okay with waiting here with Landon?"

"Absolutely, no problem," Richard replied, and Eryx could have sworn he blushed.

With a final hug, Eryx left to attend his meeting, a mix of emotions swirling within him. The unexpected reunion with Landon brought him joy, and he looked forward to reconnecting with an old friend after the business matters were sorted.

Entering the room, Eryx expected to see his manager's familiar warm smile. However, upon stepping in, his senses were immediately on high alert.

Seated at the desk was Sam Mitchell, but something felt off. His smile seemed forced, lacking the warmth Eryx was used to. Suppressing his unease, Eryx spoke cautiously, "Sam, is everything all right?"

Sam responded with a deep chuckle that sent shivers down Eryx's spine. "Oh, everything's perfectly fine, Eryx. Please, take a seat."

Eryx hesitated before moving to a chair and sitting down. He studied his manager, an increasing sense of disquiet creeping over him.

"You know, Eryx, I've always admired your talent," Sam said, his voice resembling Sam's yet tainted with something unsettling. "Your music holds a unique power."

Eryx's heart raced as suspicion grew within him. This didn't seem like the real Sam. There was an unnatural quality to the man's demeanor and words.

The imposter leaned forward, locking eyes with Eryx. "Ah, you possess a remarkable ability."

Eryx's pulse quickened. "Who are you?" he demanded.

The imposter's grin widened, revealing unnaturally sharp teeth. "Just someone who deeply appreciates your talent."

Before Eryx could react, the imposter's form shifted.

In moments, Sam's appearance morphed into someone familiar yet twisted—the man who had attacked him in London.

"Sven Janssen. What have you done to Sam?" Eryx's voice held a fierce growl.

Sven's grin widened, a cruel glint in his eyes. "Sam's fate? Let's just say he's no longer among the living."

Eryx froze, anger surging through him. "You killed him just to take his form?"

Sven's laughter held a chilling edge. "Ah, the power to manipulate lives and forms is exhilarating."

Eryx's mind raced, suspicions confirmed. The true nature of the situation was becoming clearer.

The imposter leaned in, his voice tinged with twisted glee. "Everything connected to you is a fair game to us."

Desperation gripped Eryx, and he instinctively reached out for Apollo's presence. However, the god remained silent, a barrier between them.

"Don't waste your energy trying to reach Apollo. Your connection is severed," Sven sneered.

Eryx's heart sank as he realized his magical abilities were useless. Panic churned within him as he struggled against the imposter's hold.

"The truth is, I'm more than a shapeshifter. I'm a mimic," Sven taunted. "I can copy any ability of those whose blood I consume."

Eryx's eyes widened in horror.

"You're not the only one with surprises," Sven hissed. Suddenly, a staff materialized in Sven's hand—the Staff of Umbra. The dark artifact emitted an ominous glow, sending shivers down Eryx's spine.

Eryx fought against the mimic's grip, but his efforts were futile against Sven's strength.

However, just as Sven was about to use the staff against him, a sound echoed from behind the door. The door burst open, and Eryx recognized familiar voices—Landon, Richard, and Hermes—calling out his name.

Sven momentarily released his grip, startled by the intrusion. Eryx took advantage of the opportunity, breaking free and putting distance between them.

But Eryx's escape was brief. Sven's sinister smile displayed a twisted satisfaction as he unleashed a dark wave of magic that engulfed Eryx. Despite his struggle, Eryx felt his strength waning, consciousness slipping away.

The last thing Eryx saw before succumbing to darkness was Sven's triumphant expression. Eryx was ensnared by the mimic's grasp, powerless to resist as the world around him dissolved into nothingness.

31

Alex

THEY REACHED CENTRAL PARK JUST IN THE NICK OF TIME to witness the chaotic scene. People were running in fear as the HIB struggled to keep things under control. Detective Collins was on the sidelines, aiding in the evacuation. Alex marched straight over to the detective, his team right behind him.

"Detective, what's going on?" Alex's voice cut through the noise of panicked cries.

"We've got reports of shadowy creatures attacking people," Detective Collins answered urgently.

Upon hearing the description, Alex's senses went into high gear.

"Get everyone out of here quickly. These creatures won't stop until they get what they want," Alex commanded, and the detective nodded, passing on the order to his fellow officers.

"Marcus, are you good to help with evacuations?" Alex turned to Marcus, who nodded with determination. "Go, but be careful."

Marcus rushed off to assist the HIB in getting people to

safety. Alex then focused on his team, quickly assigning tasks. "Gabe, set up a protective barrier around the park's edge. Lucas, back him up and watch his back. Emma, make sure the evacuated folks are safe. Olivia and Lily, come with me."

Navigating through the park, they found themselves engulfed in a dense, ominous fog. Lily's powers were brought forth to create a protective shield against potential threats lurking within. The atmosphere was charged with tension, and the air seemed to thicken with anticipation.

As they pressed on into the fog, their gaze fell upon an unexpected figure at the heart of it all. Ares stood confidently amidst the shadows.

"Brother, what an unexpected pleasure," Ares greeted them with a self-satisfied smirk.

"Ares. I thought I ended you during the last war," Alex retorted, his stance firm and ready for battle.

Ares chuckled, exuding an air of arrogance. "You should know better than to think I can be so easily eradicated."

Alex's gaze remained locked onto Ares, his senses alert and ready. He could feel the readiness of Lily and Olivia, waiting for his command.

"Why are you here?" Alex's voice carried a mixture of caution and suspicion.

Ares grinned knowingly, shifting his attention to Lily. "What a shame, Persephone, that you chose him over me. We could have ruled together."

Lily's response was swift and vehement. "Fuck you!"

Ignoring Lily's retort, Ares pressed on, his words sending a chill down their spines. "Speaking of hell, do you happen to know where Eryx might be?"

The mention of Eryx's name cast a heavy shadow, and a

sense of foreboding settled over the group. Alex's eyes bore into Ares, anger and concern simmering beneath the surface. "What have you done with Eryx?"

Ares turned away, his tone dripping with cryptic intentions. "Let's just say he's en route to Hephaestus."

The mention of Hephaestus struck a nerve. Before anyone could react, Ares signaled to the Shadow Wraiths, who lunged forward in a coordinated assault.

Drawing his bident, a formidable weapon bestowed upon him by Nyx as a ruler of the Underworld, Alex prepared himself to fend off the onslaught. The Shadow Wraiths encircled them from all sides, an unyielding surge of darkness striving to engulf them. The battle had been unleashed, and the fate of Central Park hung precariously in the balance.

Fueled by anger, Alex let out a burst of fiery energy, scorching the Shadow Wraiths until they vanished. But these dark creatures wouldn't give up easily; they kept coming back, as if they couldn't be stopped. Alex felt frustrated, especially knowing that Eryx was in danger. He tapped into his special underworld powers to neutralize the threat.

Lily, using her earth magic, made shields from the ground to protect people. She commanded roots to hold the Wraiths in place, keeping them from causing more harm. Olivia's flames joined the fight, burning away the Wraiths with intense heat. Her fire felt like a strong warrior, pushing back the darkness.

With every swing of his bident, Alex's weapon glowed with a mix of bright and dark energy. It was like gold and black sparks colliding and lighting up the fog. Their powers blended together, making a powerful mix of magic that filled the air with energy.

As they fought, the ground shook, and the park cracked open, releasing dark smoky tendrils. These dark wisps combined with Alex's flames, creating a unique power. The battle turned into a dance of light and shadow, a mix of their strengths.

Their combined might made the Shadow Wraiths weaken.

"Olivia, if you're running low, fall back," Alex's command was clear, tinged with genuine concern for his teammate's well-being.

"I can still fight. Don't worry about me," Olivia's voice resonated with determination, her resolve undeterred amidst the chaos.

From the shadows, Ares taunted them, prompting Alex's furious gaze to dart around, seeking him out. "Ares, you coward! Show yourself and face me!" Alex's challenge reverberated, his anger a tempestuous force.

Finally, Ares emerged, adorned in the armor of wars long past. His strides exuded unwavering confidence as he closed the distance.

"Backing down? Far from it, dear brother," Ares' voice carried a mocking edge.

"Cowardice suits you, letting your underlings do your bidding," Alex retorted, launching a bident strike at Ares. However, Ares moved with uncanny agility, evading Alex's assault with a maddening grin.

"I wanted to assess your mettle, determine if you're still a worthy opponent. And it seems your power has waned," Ares' smirk was a blend of mockery and unsettling confidence.

Ares materialized his weapon, the formidable Doru, in an instant, clashing against Alex's bident in a shower of sparks. A realization hit Alex like a bolt of lightning; Ares had grown more potent since their last encounter.

"You're one of the reason I turned my back on the gods. You betrayed not only me, but our own blood," Alex's voice trembled with bitterness as he parried Ares' ferocious attacks.

Ares' smug demeanor remained unbroken, his words a cryptic dance. "They offered me something irresistible, something you'll never comprehend."

Amidst their weapon clash, Alex wrestled with his brother's newfound might. Fatigue gnawed at him; wielding the bident in this realm sapped his strength. Yet he pressed on, his pursuit of answers relentless. "What offer? Tell me!" Alex's demand was fueled by urgency.

Ares' chilling laughter cut through the chaos. "That's my secret to hold, and your burden to never uncover."

A surge of hellfire surged through Alex's veins.

In a blaze of power, he rose, his eyes aflame with a mixture of underworld magic and raw determination. His bident crackled with a fusion of golden radiance and shadowy aura. With a mighty cry, he lunged forward, unleashing a torrent of hellfire-infused strikes against Ares.

The battlefield transformed into a dance of blazing flames and encroaching shadows, a cataclysmic clash that transcended mere mortal battles. Alex's attacks were a visual symphony, each strike an explosion of fire and darkness.

Ares was forced onto the defensive, his confidence waning as he grappled with the newfound might that Alex wielded. The ground shook with the force of their battle, trees swaying and shadows quivering. Every move, every strike was a testament to his unyielding strength.

In a heartbeat, Ares vanished, momentarily leaving Alex vulnerable. A searing pain radiated across Alex's back as Ares struck him. Alex stumbled, his grip on the bident faltering. Blood stained his clothes, a grim testament to the brutality of the battle.

As his vision blurred, Lily's urgent cry pierced the turmoil. "Alex!" She sprinted towards him, her concern palpable.

But Ares was faster, intercepting Lily's path. Overwhelmed by dread, Alex watched as Ares raised his spear, his intentions unmistakably malevolent. Alex closed his eyes, a final thought echoing through his mind

I'm sorry, Eryx. I've let you down.

In a blaze of brilliance, a blinding light erupted from above, its intensity so overwhelming that Alex was forced to shut his eyes tight. The atmosphere quivered with its raw power, and a commanding voice resonated, a voice that reverberated with the fusion of Apollo's authority and Eryx's unyielding determination. It was a voice etched into Alex's soul — a voice he would never forget.

"Release him, asshole!" The voice thundered forth, a potent mixture of Apollo's commanding presence and Eryx's fierce will. The words bore into Alex's very being, stirring something deep within his heart before there was nothing at all.

32

Eryx

ERYX'S EYE FLUTTERED OPEN, revealing a cold and dark environment that sent a chill down his spine. He tried to move his hand, only to realize that he was tightly cuffed to the wall. As he surveyed his surroundings, he noticed guards patrolling the area, adding to the feeling of entrapment

Desperation compelled him to continue struggling against his restraints, but it was clear his efforts were in vain. The cuffs held firm, rendering him powerless. He instinctively reached within himself, seeking Apollo's familiar presence, but his connection to his magic seemed severed. Nothing responded, and he realized escape was unlikely.

"Don't bother trying. Those cuffs nullify your magic," a deep, gravelly voice broke the silence beside him.

Startled, Eryx turned toward the voice. What he saw was astonishing—a man bearing marks of significant trials. Half of his face bore burns, yet his striking brown eyes held a mixture of painful experiences and resilience. Despite their dire circumstances, the man stood unashamedly naked, revealing a physique that spoke of strength and hardship.

"Well, I kind of figured that out. What are you here for?" Eryx's curiosity overcame his anxiety, and he found his voice.

"The bastard came into my forge, and we fought. As you can see, I lost," the man replied with a bitter chuckle.

A moment of realization dawned upon Eryx, though it seemed almost unbelievable. "Forge? Wait… Hephaestus?" he cautiously ventured.

"Yeah, that's me. Depends on who's asking," Hephaestus replied, a teasing glint in his eye that defied their dire situation.

Despite sharing Eryx's captivity, Hephaestus remained remarkably composed, finding humor amidst the predicament.

"I'm Eryx, by the way," he introduced himself to Hephaestus, nodding in acknowledgment.

"What did the bastard want with you?" Hephaestus asked, curiosity mixed with irritation.

"Alex told me they want me because I am Apollo's vessel," Eryx responded, weariness evident in his tone.

"No kidding? And Alex? You mean Hades? How is he?" Hephaestus's voice held a note of hope, a rare glimmer in their dire situation.

"Yeah, and he's doing alright. Hopefully, he wouldn't keep me locked up at home if we ever get out of here," Eryx added wryly. "What did he do to you?"

A palpable silence settled, and Eryx worried he had touched a painful nerve. He was about to apologize when Hephaestus finally spoke, his words carrying a weight Eryx could only begin to fathom.

"Once he locked me up here, the only thing he did was take my blood," Hephaestus said with a somber tone.

"Damn," Eryx muttered, empathy surging through him. "Did you know what he was?"

"No. I never really asked. He usually knocked me out before I could even do that," Hephaestus replied, hinting at the cruelty he endured.

Eryx's heart went out to the man who had suffered so brutally. Determination surged within him, solidifying his vow to free them from this hellish confinement.

"He said he was a mimic," Eryx shared, his voice edged with anger and frustration.

"Damn. That's why he's so damn powerful. Mimics are rare and damn hard to kill," Hephaestus commented, revealing a grim understanding of their adversary's strength.

Just as Eryx was about to reply, the sound of approaching footsteps caught both their attention. The thud of boots grew louder, and Eryx's heart raced as he realized they were no longer alone. The door to his cell creaked open, revealing none other than Sven.

"Well, what do we have here? I see you guys got acquainted while I was gone?" Sven's voice dripped with smug amusement, his smile exuding a sickening sense of satisfaction.

"Fuck you," Eryx managed to grit out.

"Sorry, not my type," Sven retorted, his tone dripping with taunting derision. He roughly grasped Eryx's face, his grip turning into a vicious slap against Eryx's cheek.

"What do you want?" Eryx's voice, though strained.

"Oh, nothing much, really," Sven replied casually. He released one of Eryx's hands from the cuffs, clasping it in his own. From his suit, Sven produced a gleaming knife, a chilling sight that sent shivers down Eryx's spine. "Just a little bit of your blood."

Eryx's eyes widened in terror, and he struggled against the cuffs, trying to wrench his hand free. But Sven's grip was unyielding. The cold touch of the blade met his skin, and a searing pain sliced through his hand as Sven cut into it. A guttural scream escaped Eryx's lips as his blood welled up, painting his hand a deep crimson.

With a gruesome twist, Sven brought Eryx's bleeding hand toward his own mouth, and horror cascaded over Eryx as he realized Sven's abhorrent intention. Sven's actions were an affront to every sense of decency, a nightmarish violation that stripped Eryx of his agency.

"You're disgusting," Eryx spat out, his voice shaking with a mixture of revulsion and fury.

In response, Sven's fist connected with Eryx's stomach, the impact knocking the wind out of him. A final, patronizing pat on the cheek punctuated the assault, leaving Eryx seething with rage and helplessness.

As Sven left the cell, locking the door behind him, Eryx slumped against the wall and passed out.

He awoke once more, this time to the deafening sound of an explosion reverberating through the walls. Groggily, he turned his gaze to Hephaestus, finding the god knocked out, his usually imposing figure now helpless. Panic surged through him as he realized the direness of their situation.

Before he could attempt to wake Hephaestus, the cell door was abruptly flung open, crashing against the stone wall. The sight that greeted him was both unexpected and relieving— it was Hermes. Eryx's heart leaped at the sight of the god, a glimmer of hope breaking through the darkness that had enveloped them.

"Eryx?" Hermes' voice held concern and urgency.

"Hermes? How did you get in? Sven?" Eryx's words tumbled out in rapid succession, his relief palpable.

"Well, did you know that your friend Landon is a Hesperian? And Sven is gone; the only ones here were the guards that we took out," Hermes explained, his tone a blend of casual explanation and triumph.

"Hesperian? What do you mean?" Eryx furrowed his brows in confusion, struggling to make sense of the sudden revelation.

"Long story short, he's a three-headed dragon," Hermes stated matter-of-factly, as if dropping the information casually. "Also, I brought your other friend along."

"You brought Richard here?" Eryx was stunned.

"Well, yeah, a demigod can always be helpful in times like this," Hermes said.

"Where is he?" Eryx asked.

"He's outside waiting with Landon keeping an eye out," Hermes answered.

Eryx was left stunned by this revelation, his mind grappling to process the truth behind Landon's and Richard's identity. The revelation opened a chasm of disbelief, shaking his perception of reality to its core.

As the magnitude of the situation began to sink in, Eryx worked to regain his focus. Hermes skillfully removed his cuffs, freeing Eryx from their oppressive grip. With newfound mobility, Eryx managed to free one of his wrists from the remaining cuff.

He glanced back at Hephaestus, his ally in the face of adversity, still unconscious. The weight of their shared experiences solidified the bond between them.

Hermes directed his attention to Hephaestus, his brows

furrowing with concern. "Hephaestus?"

A raspy reply emerged from Hephaestus, "H… Hermes?"

"Damn, I think the mimic drained a lot out of him after it took mine," Eryx explained, his voice heavy with anxiety. The well-being of Hephaestus was paramount, and his current condition was a cause for worry.

Hermes's expression darkened, his frustration evident. "A mimic?" he cursed, mirroring Eryx's anger at their adversary's audacity. It was clear that Hephaestus needed to regain consciousness.

With coordinated effort, they managed to release Hephaestus from the cuffs, giving him space to gradually awaken. The toll of his encounter with the mimic was apparent, the effects lingering even after the threat was gone.

"Shit. A mimic?" Hermes repeated, disbelief and concern in his tone. The mimic had wielded formidable power, leaving them all vulnerable in its wake.

"We need to get out of here," Eryx asserted, his voice carrying a mixture of exhaustion and determination. Hermes nodded in agreement, acknowledging the urgency of their situation. They carefully helped Hephaestus to his feet, providing support as he struggled to regain his equilibrium.

Guiding Hephaestus, they made their way out of the cell that had held them captive. Stepping into the open was a breath of fresh air, a stark contrast to the oppressive atmosphere they had endured. Eryx's gaze was drawn to a nearby window, and he was taken aback by the surreal sight before them—an endless stretch of water, an unnatural phenomenon that defied explanation.

"Where are we?" Eryx's voice held a mixture of aston- ishment and bewilderment. He turned to Hermes, seeking understanding.

Hermes's expression turned grave as he spoke, his words carrying a weight that matched the gravity of their situation. "We are in the Abyss. It is a part of the hells that even gods fear to enter, as it can corrupt them."

They trudged forward, supporting Hephaestus between them, their steps heavy with exhaustion but bolstered by the renewed determination to escape. As they emerged into the open, an unexpected sight greeted them—a three-headed dragon, the very creature they had known as Landon and Richard beside him.

To Eryx's amazement, the dragon was engaged in an unusual activity, each head leisurely licking one of the others as if grooming itself like a cat.

"Is… Is he bathing himself?" Eryx questioned in bewilderment, unable to reconcile the imposing dragon before him with the image of a feline-like creature.

Hermes's amused response came, "Yeah, think of him as a giant house cat. That's how the stories were told of him."

"Stories?" Eryx inquired, curiosity piqued.

"There can only be one Hesperian Dragon, and Landon is it," Hermes explained, respect evident in his tone as he patted the massive creature.

Taking a moment, Eryx approached the dragon, his hand tentatively resting on its colossal body. "Hey Landon. Thank you—all of you—for coming for me," he expressed, gratitude swelling within him.

Landon offered a gentle lick, an oddly endearing gesture that momentarily reminded Eryx of Cerberus and Mr. Whiskers.

"It is nothing," Richard replied.

Eryx glared at his friend. "We're not done here, mister. A demigod?"

"Ah… yeah…" Richard rubbed the back of his neck.

After a while, the dragon extended one of its necks, a clear invitation for them to mount him and depart the Abyss.

"Is this safe?" Eryx couldn't help but voice his anxiety.

"Of course it is. I think," Hermes teased, a mischievous glint in his eye.

Before long, they were airborne, the sensation of flight both exhilarating and nerve-wracking. As they soared through the surreal landscape of the Abyss, Eryx turned to Hermes with a question that had been nagging at him.

"How's Alex?" Eryx inquired, concern lacing his voice.

A moment of silence followed before Hermes replied, his tone heavy. "Last I heard, he was fighting Shadow Wraiths in Central Park."

A sinking feeling settled in Eryx's chest. "Damn," he muttered inwardly, knowing the gravity of the situation. He tried to reach out to Apollo, a comforting presence that had been restored to him.

Apollo? Eryx's mental call was met with a reassuring response.

I'm here, Apollo's voice echoed within him.

Are you ready to kick some ass? Eryx asked with a mixture of determination and anticipation.

I thought you'd never ask, Apollo's reply carried a hint of amusement. *It's about time you accept your destiny.*

Eryx closed his eyes, embracing the truth of who he had become. With that acceptance, his soul blazed with newfound strength, allowing Apollo to take over and wield his power in the impending battle.

33

Eryx

THEY SURGED FROM THE ABYSS with shared urgency, emerging into a scene that set Eryx's emotions ablaze. Amidst the chaos and violence, his heart clenched at the sight of Alex facing an imminent threat from an adversary wielding a menacing spear. The surge of anger and protectiveness within him was fierce; no one would harm Alex while he drew breath.

Landon effortlessly shifted back into his human form. As they advanced toward the unfolding confrontation, Eryx extended his hand, calling forth the newfound power resonating within him as he was guided by Apollo's presence. In his grip materialized a bow and arrow, a symbol of the weapon he had wielded during the London battle.

The arrow shot forth with unwavering determination, finding its mark with precision, a barrier between the assailant and Alex.

"Release him, asshole!" Eryx's voice rang out, his fury echoing across the tumultuous scene.

The man's attention snapped to Eryx, his features registering a mix of surprise and irritation. Hermes's voice interjected, pinpointing the identity of the looming threat. "Fucking Ares. I should have known."

Beside him, Landon emitted a low, rumbling growl, his instincts on high alert. The air crackled with tension, Eryx's anger intensifying as he comprehended the weight of Ares's identity.

"Do you want me to shift again, Hermes?" Landon offered, his voice a deep rumble, reflecting his readiness to defend.

"No, stay human," Hermes instructed, caution woven into his tone. "We don't want to reveal your true form. Take care of Hephaestus, and I'll assist with the Shadow Wraiths. Richard, help us." Richard nodded, and they started blasting the shadow wraiths.

As Eryx met Ares's intense glare, he couldn't help but notice a change within himself. Once upon a time, just the thought of facing a god like Ares would have left him quaking in his boots. But now, something was different; a newfound confidence and strength surged within him, bolstered by the presence of Apollo within his very being. This wasn't the same Eryx who had started his journey—he was a vessel for the divine, a force to be reckoned with.

"Come on, Ares. Let's play," Apollo's voice flowed through Eryx's lips, an echo of power that resonated with a courage he hadn't known before.

Ares's growl reverberated through the air as he charged toward Eryx. Yet, it was as if Eryx's body instinctively knew how to react, evading Ares's attacks with a grace that surprised even him.

"Is that all you can do?" Eryx taunted, his words a mixture of challenge and defiance.

Ares's response was swift and fierce. He unleashed the full force of his might, wielding his spear with precision and intensity. Eryx found himself moving with a fluidity that transcended his mortal limitations, each dodge and evasion executed with an almost preternatural skill. His voice remained steady, his words laced with taunting confidence, even as Ares's strikes grew more powerful.

"You should have died that day!" Ares's voice boomed, his rage fueling his attacks. The power behind Ares's spear was undeniable, but Eryx's newfound abilities allowed him to match the god's intensity, if not surpass it.

Seizing the opportunity, Eryx maneuvered behind Ares, his bow and arrow in hand. The arrow found its mark, striking true.

"Are you just going to lie there and die?" Eryx's words dripped with a mixture of challenge and triumph.

Ares clenched his stomach, a growl of pain escaping him. Despite his wounds, the god's defiance remained unbroken.

"I will get you next time, Apollo," Ares spat, his words laced with a promise that echoed through the air. In a swirl of black mist, Ares disappeared, his shadow wraiths vanishing with him, leaving behind an eerie stillness.

Apollo relinquished control of Eryx's body. An immediate rush of his own consciousness flowed back, and he didn't waste a moment. Rushing to Alex's side, he cradled his head gently on his lap.

"Alex? Stay with me," he pleaded, his voice tremulous with worry. His gaze darted around, the encroaching crowd of onlookers only intensifying his anxiety. "Why isn't he healing?" Eryx's voice cracked as he voiced his concern, tears already streaming down his face.

"The spear has slowed down his healing," came the somber reply, and Eryx turned to find Hermes kneeling beside them, his presence a comforting reassurance.

Desperation and fear gripped Eryx's heart. He looked around at the expectant faces surrounding him, waiting for a solution to materialize. The silence was heavy, pregnant with anticipation, as he hung onto Hermes's every word.

"Are you willing to do whatever it takes to save him?" Hermes's question was both a challenge and a lifeline, searching for Eryx's resolve.

Eryx's response was unwavering and immediate. "Yes. I will do anything."

With those words, a path forward was laid out. Hermes rose to his feet and offered his assistance, helping Eryx lift Alex from the ground. The urgency of the situation was palpable, the gravity of the decision they were about to make weighing heavily on them all.

Hermes opened a portal to the underworld, his actions purposeful and determined. He turned to Lily, their leader, seeking her support. "Persephone, we need you just in case things get rough," he instructed, and Lily nodded in acknowledgment.

Addressing her team, Lily's orders rang out with clarity. "All of you, make sure everybody is alright. Marcus, help these gentlemen carry Hephaestus to the medical bay." The team dispersed efficiently, each member falling into their roles with practiced precision. Eryx exchanged a glance with Landon and Richard, a silent acknowledgment passing between them.

With no time to spare, Hermes's command echoed, urging them into action. "Come on, we're running out of time."

Guiding Eryx, they moved with purpose, entering the portal that led to the underworld. The realm of shadows awaited them, a place fraught with both danger and potential salvation. As they stepped through the portal, Eryx's heart pounded with a mixture of trepidation and hope, every step forward a testament to his unwavering commitment to save Alex, no matter the cost.

Stepping into the shadowed realm of the underworld, they were met by a figure draped in a somber black robe—a figure both frail and yet radiating a potent sense of power.

"Charon, we seek your aid. Hades has been struck by Ares's spear, and his wounds are not healing as they should," Hermes's voice was edged with urgency, the weight of their predicament palpable.

Charon's gaze shifted from Hermes to Eryx, his eyes seemingly piercing through the fabric of their beings. "This aid will come at a cost," his words carried a haunting cadence, a reminder of the inevitable balance between life and the afterlife.

Eryx's voice quivered with desperation as he interjected, "I'll pay anything. Please, save him." A comforting touch from Lily conveyed her shared concern, her silent support a beacon in the darkness.

Lily took a step forward, her voice resolute amidst the turmoil. "Charon, reveal the price we must pay."

"My Queen," Charon acknowledged her with a nod, his voice carrying a weight that echoed through the cavernous space. "To rescue the king, a tether of souls must be woven. His soul has been wounded, its care compromised."

Lily's gaze held a mixture of resolve and apprehension. "Could I be the one to forge this connection?"

Charon's response held a note of regret. "Unfortunately, my queen, only a soul of the purest essence can enact such a binding."

Eryx's heart quickened with hope, his voice trembling with a mixture of anticipation and hope. "Could I be that soul?"

Charon's response was affirmative, resonating with a depth of understanding. "Yes, your soul shines as one of the purest. But be aware, this path comes with its own set of risks. Once the binding is established, it cannot be undone."

Eryx's resolve was unwavering, his decision swift and unhesitating. "Yes."

Charon's skeletal hand gestured for Eryx to join him, urgency underlying his every movement. "Time is of the essence. The king's essence wanes, his god soul slipping away."

A shared glance between Lily and Eryx spoke volumes, their silent agreement unspoken yet profound. Addressing Hermes and Landon, Charon conveyed the somber reality. "Regrettably, only Eryx can accompany the king on this journey. The binding demands it."

Lily's voice held a touch of vulnerability as she gave her final instruction. "Once all is done, bring him back to the palace." Charon nodded in understanding.

Amidst the ethereal realm of the underworld, Eryx stood alongside Charon, a sense of gravity weighing heavily upon him. The air was laden with a mixture of anticipation and trepidation, as Eryx prepared to undertake a ritual of unparalleled consequence—one that could bridge the chasm between life and death.

Charon guided Eryx through the intricate steps of the ritual. His voice, a haunting whisper, instructed Eryx as they got off the boat after a while of traveling. They walked along the shores of the Styx.

As they reached a point where the boundaries between realms seemed to blur, Charon halted, turning to face Eryx. The air around them hummed with an intensity that sent shivers down Eryx's spine.

"Eryx," Charon's voice reverberated like a lament, "the path you tread is one of sacrifice and bravery. To bind your soul with another is to forge a bond that defies the very fabric of existence."

Eryx nodded, his determination unwavering. His thoughts were consumed by Alex, by the love and connection they shared. This was a choice he had made willingly, knowing that it held the potential to alter the course of their lives forever.

"Place your hand upon the waters of the Styx," Charon instructed, his voice carrying an air of solemnity. Eryx complied, extending his hand until his fingertips brushed the surface of the river—a touch that felt both chilling and electrifying.

"The Styx, a river that divides realms, shall witness this binding," Charon intoned, his words carrying a weight that seemed to resonate with the very currents of the river.

Eryx's heart raced as Charon continued, "Your intentions must be pure, your will unwavering. The connection you seek to create shall be fueled by the depth of your emotions, by the very essence of your being."

With a deep breath, Eryx closed his eyes, summoning memories of his time with Alex—moments of laughter, shared dreams, and unspoken understanding. He let their memories surge within him, a blazing fire that illuminated his very soul.

Charon's voice echoed around him, intertwining with the subtle symphony of the underworld. "Now, extend your feelings beyond yourself. Seek the presence of the one you wish to bind with."

As Eryx reached out with his heart, he could sense Alex's soul, a distant beacon amidst the vast expanse of existence. Their connection pulsed, a rhythm that resonated with the beating of two hearts that had found solace in one another.

With a voice that trembled with emotion, Eryx whispered, "Alex, if you can hear me, if you can feel me, know that I do this because I can't live without you."

As if in response, he felt a warm current surround him, a sensation that transcended the physical realm. It was as if Alex's presence was there with him, an affirmation of their bond.

"Let your intentions merge," Charon's voice was a steady guide, grounding Eryx amidst the swirling emotions. "Imagine a thread of light, a thread that weaves your souls together."

Eryx visualized that thread, a shimmering strand of light that bridged the gap between them. The bond was formed not just of love, but of shared experiences, of trials faced together, and of the unspoken promises they had made.

With Charon's guidance, Eryx continued the ritual, each step a testament to his commitment. As the ritual reached its culmination, he felt a surge of energy, a fusion of his essence with that of Alex's. The boundaries of their souls seemed to blur, and for a moment, he felt a profound sense of unity—their souls woven together in a tapestry of emotion and destiny.

Charon's voice resonated around them, "The binding is

done. Your souls are intertwined, two parts of a greater whole."

Eryx opened his eyes, the weight of what he had undertaken settling upon him. He could feel Alex's presence, a steady presence that assured him they were now connected in a way that transcended the mortal coil.

As the ritual concluded, Charon's gaze held a mixture of solemnity and understanding. "The path you have chosen is one of sacrifice that defies the boundaries of existence. But remember, the binding you have forged is unbreakable."

With a nod, Eryx understood the gravity of his choice. He had willingly given a piece of his soul to be intertwined with Alex's, an act that bound them together in a way that would endure through eternity. As they stood at the crossroads of the living and the afterlife, Eryx's heart was filled with both hope and the weight of the responsibility he had assumed— a responsibility born out of love and a bond that could withstand even the barriers between life and death.

34

Alex

ALEX FOUND HIMSELF in a state of suspended consciousness, drifting through the boundaries between realms. Moments passed like fleeting dreams until slowly, a sensation of warmth and familiarity began to seep into his senses.

As his awareness sharpened, he could feel the softness of a bed beneath him, the gentle play of shadows on the walls, and the distinct scent of the underworld—a unique blend of earthiness and a hint of something ethereal. He tried to open his eyes, his vision blurred at first, but gradually the room came into focus.

He was in his own chamber in the Underworld, the place he called home as the king of this realm. The room was adorned with rich, dark hues that echoed the essence of his dominion. He blinked several times, trying to comprehend the transition from the chaos of battle to the calm embrace of his own abode.

Alex's fingers grazed the luxurious fabric of the bedspread as he pushed himself into a sitting position. His head throbbed dully, a lingering reminder of the spear that had struck him in the heat of battle. The memory of the confrontation with Ares, the binding ritual, and Eryx's selfless act flooded back to him, mingling with the sensations of pain and determination.

A soft exhale escaped his lips as he recalled Eryx's sacrifice. The memory of the ritual—their souls intertwining in a tapestry of profound connection—filled him with a sense of awe and gratitude. He knew that Eryx had risked everything to save him, to forge a bond that defied the boundaries of life and death.

He turned to the side, and his heart skipped a beat. There, sleeping soundly beside him, was Eryx. His chest rose and fell with each steady breath, and Alex could feel the reassuring warmth of Eryx's presence as if it radiated from him.

Alex's smile grew as he watched Eryx, a mixture of emotions swirling within him. He marveled at the depth of Eryx's care, at the lengths he had gone to save him. The sight of Eryx by his side filled him with a warmth that transcended the boundaries of the room.

Alex's movements were gentle so as not to wake Eryx. He settled himself beside Eryx, entwining their fingers together. The bond between them felt tangible—a thread of connection that defied the realms and the challenges they had faced.

As he lay there, the weight of his responsibilities as the ruler of the Underworld and the intensity of his emotions intertwined. He knew that their journey was far from over, that the challenges they faced were bound to continue. But for now, in the quietude of that chamber, he found solace in the presence of the man who had become his rock.

After a while, Eryx stirred beside him, and Alex couldn't

help but chuckle. Eryx seemed to ignore him initially, but then he turned, his eyes softening as he looked at Alex. Without warning, Eryx leaned in and planted a passionate kiss on his lips. "Alex! Are you okay?" he asked with genuine concern.

Alex laughed, his heart swelling at Eryx's affectionate display. "Never felt better, sweetheart." He gazed at Eryx, his eyes tender. "I should be asking you that. After what you did, I… I don't even know what to say."

Eryx's response was filled with sincerity, his words touching Alex's heart deeply. "If you're asking me if I have any regrets about what I did, then no. I would do it again a thousand times over because you're worth it." Eryx's smile was sweet and filled with affection.

Alex's response was to capture Eryx's lips once more, savoring the connection they shared. He considered himself incredibly fortunate to have this incredible man back in his life. He broke the kiss, his gaze fixed on Eryx. "Enough about me, tell me what happened to you."

Eryx sighed and began recounting his harrowing journey, his words evoking a surge of anger and concern within Alex. As Eryx spoke of the dangers he faced in the Abyss, Alex felt a mixture of emotions welling up within him. He could sense the tranquility radiating from Eryx's soul, a stark contrast to the turbulence of his own feelings. It was almost like Eryx's presence was a soothing balm to his soul.

"Calm down, big guy. I'm here now, and we can worry about the Order another time," Eryx's words were soothing, grounding Alex in the present moment.

Alex embraced Eryx, holding him tightly as if he could protect him from any harm. "I'll never let you out of my sight ever again," he teased, attempting to lighten the mood.

Eryx chuckled and returned the hug, their connection tangible and reassuring. "Speaking of, I've been thinking," Eryx said as they finally pulled away from the hug.

Alex raised an eyebrow, feigning curiosity. "Uh oh, that's never good."

Eryx playfully smacked him on the thigh. "I want to join your team," he declared.

Alex was taken aback, unsure if Eryx was joking or being sincere. He couldn't help but ask, "Are you joking?" When Eryx remained silent, his expression earnest, Alex realized the truth. "You're being serious, aren't you?"

"Yes, doofus, I am being serious," Eryx affirmed, his eyes locking onto Alex's.

"Baby, you're not trained. Just because you have Apollo guiding you doesn't mean you're strong enough to fight the monsters that we face," Alex voiced his concerns.

Eryx's determination was unwavering as he responded, "I know that. That's why I'm hoping you'll help me train. Please, Alex, I have to do this."

Alex searched Eryx's eyes, looking for the reasons behind this decision. "Why? What made you want to do this?"

Eryx took a deep breath, his gaze steady. "Those bastards killed, Sam and I am not just going to stand here and do nothing about it."

A sigh escaped Alex's lips as he weighed Eryx's request. "What about your music? You've already built a career out of that, haven't you?"

Eryx's smile remained bright despite the seriousness of the conversation. Alex's thumbs brushed Eryx's cheeks gently. "I know I have, but I'm willing to put that on the back burner for now in order to make this world a little safer," Eryx reassured him. His eyes held a mixture of determination and sincerity. "I'll still play, my music will always be a part of me. Don't worry, okay?"

Alex leaned in, capturing Eryx's lips in a tender kiss. As their lips parted, he met Eryx's eyes. "Fine, but you'll have to train, okay?"

Eryx's smile grew even more radiant, his happiness shining through their shared connection. "Thank you!" His gratitude resonated within Alex's soul.

With a playful chuckle, Alex gave in to Eryx's determination. "You always get what you want, don't you?"

Eryx's laughter filled the room, a joyful sound that warmed Alex's heart. "Only when it matters the most."

As they lay together, their fingers entwined and their souls bound by an unbreakable connection, Alex couldn't help but think that Eryx's presence had brought a newfound purpose and meaning to his life.

Afterword

Thank you for embarking on this journey through my novel. It's my sincerest hope that you've found enjoyment in the pages of "The Echos of Destiny." Your support means the world to me, and I'm immensely grateful for every moment you've spent with Eryx and Alex.

If you've found this story to be a captivating experience, I kindly invite you to share your thoughts through a review. Your feedback matters greatly and helps pave the way for future adventures.

Rest assured, Eryx and Alex's story is far from over. Book Two awaits, promising more twists, challenges, and heartfelt moments. Until we meet again within the pages of their next chapter, thank you for your support and enthusiasm.

Warmest regards,

Ken Sanchez

About the Author

Hey there, I'm Ken Sanchez, your new M/M fantasy/Romance author! I'm all about crafting mesmerizing worlds where love and magic collide. With a heart that beats for LGBTQ+ romance and an imagination that knows no limits, I'm thrilled to invite you to explore the realms I've conjured. Picture a dreamer who spins tales, fusing passion with ink to create M/M fantasy stories that resonate. Enchanted by the possibilities of love and the allure of magic, I've poured my heart into every word I write.

Follow me on Instagram at: @itskiliansanchez

Also by Ken Sanchez

No Matter What

In the vibrant heart of London, amidst iconic landmarks and hidden gems, two lives collide in a tale of unbreakable bonds and unwavering love. When David's memories are stolen by a violent attack after a promising date, his best friend Ryan steps up to mend the shattered pieces. As they navigate the city's playful quirkiness and emotional depths, David and Ryan's friendship blossoms into something unexpected. Guided by a series of heartfelt letters, signed with the promise 'No Matter What,' they embark on a journey of self-discovery, tracing their shared past and forging a future full of hope and passion. Amidst the backdrop of playful banter, stolen glances, and the rich tapestry of London, they unveil the truth about their connection and embrace a love that transcends memory.

'No Matter What' is a heartwarming and witty novel that captures the magic of friendship, the power of resilience, and the joy of finding love where you least expect it."